ARGENTINA, AUSTRALIA AND CANADA

ARGENTINA, AUSTRALIA and CANADA

Studies in Comparative Development 1870–1965

Edited by
D. C. M. Platt
and
Guido di Tella

St. Martin's Press New York

Printed in Hong Kong
Published in the United Kingdom by The Macmillan Press Ltd.
First published in the United States of America in 1985

ISBN 0–312–04868–8

Library of Congress Cataloging in Publication Data
Main entry under title:
Argentina, Australia, and Canada.
Includes index.
1. Argentina—Economic conditions—Addresses, essays, lectures. 2. Australia—Economic conditions—Addresses, essays, lectures. 3. Canada—Economic conditions—Addresses, essays, lectures. I. Platt, D. C. M. (Desmond Christopher St. Martin), 1934–
II. Di Tella, Guido.
HC175.A834 1985 338.9 84–17884
ISBN 0–312–04868–8

Contents

List of Tables

44avo congreso internacional de americanistas
44th international congress of americanists

Preface

The chapters in this volume, subject to some abbreviation and editing, are those papers delivered to a symposium organized for the 44th International Congress of Americanists, at the University of Manchester, England, in September 1982. The papers from two of the Argentine contributors, Guido di Tella himself and Roberto Cortés Conde, which, most unfortunately, could not be delivered in person because of the contemporaneous conflict in the South Atlantic, are now incorporated. We are grateful to the organizers of the Congress for the successful administration of the symposium, and to the Congress itself for the financial support that it has given so generously towards the cost of publishing this volume.

D. C. M. Platt
Guido di Tella

Notes on the Contributors

Peter Alhadeff, St. Antony's College, Oxford, economist and economic historian; papers on economic policy in 1930s Argentina now in the course of publication.

Christopher Armstrong, York University, Toronto, author of *The Politics of Federalism, Ontario's Relations with the Federal Government, 1867–1942* (1981).

Warwick Armstrong, McGill University, articles on the theme of dominion capitalism in Argentina, Australia, and Canada.

Roberto Cortés Conde, Torcuato di Tella Institute, Buenos Aires, author of articles and books on the economic and social history of Latin America, notably *El Progreso Argentino, 1880–1914* (1979).

Carlos F. Díaz Alejandro, Yale University, economist and economic historian, author of articles and books on Latin American economic history and development, and international trade and payments.

Ian M. Drummond, Trinity College, University of Toronto, publications include *Imperial Economic Policy 1917–1939* (1974) and (with R. S. Bothwell and J. English) *Canada since 1945* (1981).

John Fogarty, University of Melbourne, articles on the comparative development of Argentina and Australia.

Charles Jones, University of Warwick, author of *The North–South Dialogue: a Brief History* (1983) and of essays on the history of British business enterprise overseas.

H. V. Nelles, York University, Toronto, author of *The Politics of Development, Forests, Mines and Hydro-Electric Power in Ontario, 1849–1941* (1974).

J. C. M. Ogelsby, University of Western Ontario: books include *Gringos from the Far North: Essays in Canadian–Latin American Relations, 1866–1968.*

D. C. M. Platt, St. Antony's College, Oxford, economic historian; books and articles on foreign trade and finance in Latin America.

Carl E. Solberg, University of Washington, Seattle; articles and books, the most recent of which is *Oil and Nationalism in Argentina: a History* (1979).

Guido di Tella, St. Antony's College, Oxford, and the Catholic University, Buenos Aires; recent books include (with C. P. Kindleberger, eds) *Economics in the Long View* (1982).

Michael J. Twomey, University of Michigan, Dearborn, economist: articles on current and historical economic problems of Latin America and India.

Introduction

To select three countries, and then to open up a discussion, implies that some common traits are presupposed and that useful comparisons can be made. At the very least, we assume that the experience of one of those countries can supply a better understanding of some aspects, whether historical, economic, or political, of another. Contrasts are as useful as direct comparisons. In the case of the three countries selected – typical examples of 'regions of recent settlement', in Hilgerdt's phrase – the value of bringing the three together is obvious, and it is perhaps surprising that it has not been done before (although two at a time have indeed been compared).

Ezequiel Gallo, in the introduction to that useful and pioneering book *Argentina y Australia* (Instituto Torcuato di Tella, Buenos Aires, 1979), edited by John Fogarty, Héctor Dieguez, and himself, spelt out very clearly the reasons for a comparative approach. Taking Argentina and Australia together, he explains that both were transformed while placed within an economic universe which, under British control, was relatively homogeneous – and in which both Argentina and Australia were exporters of primary material and importers of manufactured goods. Both enjoyed natural resources which gave them a privileged position relative to the non-European world. Both were semi-populated, inheriting little or nothing of the habits and traditions of a precapitalist era. Both were large and distant.

In all except the very last respect, Canada's experience was exactly parallel. Canada, of course, was always under the shadow of her enormously dynamic neighbour, the United States, and Canada, comparatively speaking, was not far from Western Europe. But Canada was a huge new territory, semi-populated, rich in natural resources, an exporter of primary materials in return for manufactured goods.

As we shall see, key elements in a realistic contrast between the three countries, Argentina, Australia, and Canada, are clearly the political tradition and the origins of the immigrant population, and in these areas the experiences of Canada and Australia, as British

Dominions, are more closely comparable than the history of a country of Southern European origins such as Argentina.

The aim of this book is not simply to draw attention to points of similarity. 'Compare and contrast' is the rubric so often attached to the more interesting of the questions in a standard examination paper, and the reason is plain. Points of comparison are useful and entirely relevant, but we want to encourage deductions, results. And further, as economists and historians retreat respectively into specialisation and antiquarianism, within continents, in countries, inside countries, by periods, by themes, and even by ideologies, it does no harm to look around and perhaps to detect influences more powerful than those immediately within grasp.

One of the more valuable features of the chapters in this volume is their readiness to accept the non-economic aspects of the comparison – differences in politics and in personalities. Nationality is not the determinant so much as the nature of the enterprise. Differences of language and traditions, of custom and acknowledged responsibility, of ambitions and loyalties, all count for much, and their form and shape are revealed and discussed at many points within the papers printed below. But it is by bringing forward these differences that so much becomes clearer. Gallo explains that comparative studies have the supreme virtue of suggesting new lines of investigation. The priorities of the Italian tenant farmer, in his unsociable hut on the Argentine pampas, make more sense (perhaps better sense) than those of the small farmer on the Canadian prairies, in his frame house with a telephone, his local school, co-operative elevator, and circulating library. The climate, of course, makes a difference. But so do long-term expectations such as the length of settlement, the desire or otherwise to return 'home', the identification with a new country and nationality.

But more, what one realises from these chapters is the independent initiative of the settlers, the internal resilience of such societies in countries supposedly so firmly linked with (and controlled by) the metropolis. Argentina, Canada and Australia have experienced an amazing expansion over the last century. They have much in common so far as their economic development is concerned; their social history contains both similarities and outstanding differences; they share little in politics.

The thirteen chapters that make up this volume range from the general to the specific, from economic approaches to historical analyses and cultural interpretations. Of these chapters two discuss possible frameworks for an analysis of the development paths of the so-called 'regions of recent settlement'. While the first, by John Fogarty (an economic historian), is quite sceptical of economic theories of any kind, the second, by Guido di Tella (an economist), attempts to develop a macroeconomic framework applicable to land surplus countries, which incorporates both the 'staple' and the 'frontier' theories.

Fogarty is impressed by the different reactions of all three countries to similar events. He prefers, to a more general approach, renewed research on the specific historical circumstances that prompted the reactions of each society at different times.

Fogarty is particularly critical of the staple theory, which has been so popular with Canadian economists after Innis, and which has taken control of Argentine historiography since the 1960s. Oddly enough, the staple theory has never made much progress in Australia. The Australian approach is strongly reflected in Fogarty's work. He bases his criticism on what he considers to be the exaggerated emphasis placed by the staple theory on demand conditions. Fogarty's opinion is that it is the degree of openness and creativity of the environment which explains, to a great extent, why some countries attained a marked superiority in the production and marketing of some specific staples. What he calls the 'super-staples' are precisely those for which non-economic factors have been important, i.e. beef in Argentina, wool in Australia, wheat in Canada, lamb in New Zealand. In each country the quality of entrepreneurship and the nature of the institutional environment have had distinctly different effects, even allowing for the characteristics of each staple. But equally crucial has been the willingness of Governments to assume different degrees of responsibility and initiative in the promotion of economic development.

The state was instrumental in the determination of immigration policies and land tenure legislation. It was of critical importance in the provision of infrastructure: transportation (railroads and shipping), primary goods, storage and marketing facilities, and even scientific and technological assistance.

Fogarty's conclusion is that rather than demand-conditions, or availability of free lands, it is factors such as entrepreneurship, inventiveness and adaptability at the producer's or at the government level which, in the end, really counted.

In the following paper, di Tella takes the opposite line. He claims that the areas of recent settlement shared some very significant characteristics which were basically economic. Naturally, non-economic elements were also important. But di Tella's attempt to understand the degree to which economic analysis can throw light on development and differences is what separates his chapter from Fogarty's. The emphasis is placed on the peculiar supply conditions prevalent in these countries, i.e. the existence of unlimited supplies of 'waste lands'. Di Tella analyses the concept of a moving frontier, its inextricable links with the technological level reached at the time, and the interplay which takes place between phsyical expansion and innovation. He stresses the peculiarities of frontier expansion, and in particular the cases where significant, though not necessarily discontinuous, technological changes created economic opportunities that could not be taken advantage of immediately, and gave rise to expansion in vigorous disequilibrium. In these instances the 'closing of the frontier' genuinely means something, and describes a state of affairs where one would expect growth to falter if no adequate substitute land were found (an idea also to be found in Cortés Conde below). While the peculiarities of the supply side are emphasized throughout the chapter, changes in demand conditions are also considered; on certain occasions they reinforced the expansionary process, while in others they achieved the opposite. Di Tella's interpretation of the staple theory, as emphasizing the peculiarities of supply, is in contrast with Fogarty's preference for demand. Di Tella tries to identify, as special cases of the more general search for abnormally high profits by Schumpeterian entrepreneurs, Turner's frontier approach (in North's version), Innis' staple approach, and Adam Smith's vent for surplus (as reinterpreted by Williams). In di Tella's view, the search for new, rent-yielding lands is seen as similar to the search for quasi rent-yielding innovations, so that the discovery of new lands is akin to the discovery of new technologies.

These changes in the sources of profit and rents, and consequently in the sources of accumulation, their interaction and their shifts, are crucial for an adequate understanding of the extraordinary development of the areas of recent settlement, as well as of some of the problems encountered. While basically disagreeing in their approach, Fogarty and di Tella reach a point at which they rely on concepts such as entrepreneurship and innovation to explain what each of the authors thinks explainable.

After the two general chapters with which we begin, we move on to more specific. The first of these, by Carl Solberg, deals with the influence on economic efficiency of the different land tenure policies adopted by Canada and Argentina during their formative years, that is from 1880 to the world crisis of the 1930s. Solberg emphasizes that both were land surplus countries; not surprisingly, after their respective governments achieved internal control and peace, both were able to attract a massive inflow of immigrants and capital, and both became world agricultural exporters at the same time, a position they retained until 1930. Important differences can be detected in rural marketing, in transportation, and in educational policies, but the most notable of all lay in their policy towards land. Canada encouraged, successfully, owner-operator farms, while Argentina based her expansion on large estates divided and farmed by tenants, a difference, in turn, which arose out of the very different political alliances ruling each country (and contributed to the development of two very different types of society). Solberg accepts the view that Argentina's rural life was impoverished by the system of temporary tenants moving from one place to another in an almost 'nomadic' way. Community life was therefore weak and co-operatives rare (except in the few areas where small-holdings had developed). On the other hand, the Canadian rural sector was much richer in social life, co-operatives flourished, and farmers enjoyed a superior standard of housing and education.

However, the useful point is that these social differences did not mean necessarily an irrational or an inefficient system of agricultural production. On the contrary, Argentina was able to maintain throughout a higher degree of flexibility; she could switch production more easily from grain to cattle and back. Argentine agriculture was not inferior to that of the prairies; it was more competitive in costs and more adaptable to shifting demands. While wheat yields were certainly higher in Western Canada, the land and debt structure left agriculturalists entirely exposed – an uncomfortable position to be in whcn prices fell. Argentine farmers, throughout, were a formidable competitor, with substantially lower costs of production. Solberg disagrees with those who condemn the pampas' land tenure system as backward and inefficient, and inferior to that of Canada. It was a system that needed reform, but which had a rationale of its own. Solberg's contribution makes one think twice about simplistic generalizations which gloss over the reasons behind different behaviour and the specific causes that give rise to them.

Warwick Armstrong's chapter takes up the theme of the development of the industrial sector. He thinks that similarities were sufficiently strong to warrant an attempt to answer a common question, i.e. why did industrial growth take place at all in these nineteenth-century, European outgrowths? Armstrong claims that Argentina, Australia and Canada were not only obviously distinct from European countries but also quite distinct from the other imperial dependencies of the day. His analysis begins with the conventional staple approach, which he considers sufficiently explanatory for the beginnings of the process and for the forward and backward linkages. But he feels that it has to be enlarged – not so much by the kind of analysis pioneered by the dependency school, with its emphasis on the external relationships between the core and the periphery (quite inadequate for these three countries), but by an investigation of the divisions that run *within* societies rather than between them. Armstrong does not deny the problems of imperial hegemony, or the role of transnational corporations, but he emphasizes the internal social structure of the countries.

What needs to be said, however, is that the 'Europeanized' elite, even if they borrowed techniques, institutions and attitudes from the advanced industrial societies, were able, gradually, to assert themselves and to attain a position of autonomy within their own countries. Once they had done so, they built up their strength, economic, social and political, and kept for themselves an important share of the surplus (or of the quasi-rents) even when a proportion continued to be siphoned-off to the European countries. Such a retained surplus became indeed one of the more important sources for the financing of those backward linkages referred to by the staple theorists. In the case of Argentina and Uruguay, the linkages were sufficiently generalized to avoid the creation of an enclave economy, typical of some other Latin American countries, and the same was true, to an even greater extent, for Canada and Australia. One important derivative was the creation and growth of an industrial sector. And it is here that Armstrong feels that the staple theory has to be expanded, so as to take social factors into consideration. The effectiveness of the response was conditioned by the nature of the society, its structure and its ruling coalitions, and not simply by mere economics and technology.

Díaz Alejandro, in his paper, compares the development of Australia, Argentina and Brazil before the World Crisis. He dismisses the idea that Argentina was at one point richer than Australia and allowed herself subsequently to fall disastrously behind. He presents tables which take the story back to the 1880s, and which depict the evolution of per capita gross domestic product in all three countries. Although he admits these tables to be 'conjectural', the results are most illuminating and they are not to be found elsewhere. They support, in fact, his contention that Australia was 'born rich', and economically superior in per capita terms throughout. Díaz Alejandro argues that this, fundamentally, was the consequence of a much greater mineral endowment, not to be found in Argentina or even in Brazil. He describes Australia as an 'early Kuwait', a fact which the relative similarity of agricultural and pastoral endowments has tended to disguise. Moreover, Australia's important gold and mineral-processing sectors created much greater backward linkages. Not only were they different in themselves, but they relied on quite different economic agents. They generated interest in scientific and agricultural research; they gave rise to a strong labour force which coalesced with dynamic non-rural entrepreneurs and created a different and more diversified ruling alliance, more dependent on innovation and (mineral) discovery. Díaz Alejandro sees in this fact (a consequence of the characteristics of the major staples, so much stressed by staple theorists) one of the significant differences in the growth stories of the two countries, Argentina and Australia.

The other major difference, in this case policy-determined, was the more restricted immigration policy of Australia, hence a scarcity of labour, an incentive for greater labour productivity, and a higher per capita income. The contrast was with Argentina's policy of 'peopling the wilderness', advocated by its founding fathers, Alberdi in particular. The aim was to accelerate the 'Europeanization' of Argentina, with its cultural and social implications. One consequence was to keep wages lower, and allow Argentine landowners to retain a larger proportion of the inter-marginal rent than would otherwise have been the case. But another was to increase drastically the relative size of Argentina's population and to enable her to alter the level which Australia herself was unable to reach, at some risk to her international role.

One can conclude with Díaz Alejandro that Argentina was never as rich as Australia, that the main differences lay in mineral endowments, that Argentina was able to narrow the gap but was never able to close it altogether, and that minerals had different, and more positive, backward-linkages.

Ogelsby's contribution is of a different kind to those of the others (principally economic). It deals with the evasive but very central question of cultural identity. Ogelsby finds that a common characteristic, even if proceeding at a different pace, has been the rather explicit search for a national identity. The search is in itself an indication that the problem existed and, at the same time, that a solution has yet to be found. Ogelsby sees a dichotomy in each of the three countries, one group laying stress on the forgotten values of the past, supposedly essential to the national heritage, and another the links with either Britain or France, or in the case of Argentina, with Europe in general. He underlines the strongly evocative role played in Australia by the 'bush', as something which Australians had in common even when each state still maintained its autonomy. The Argentines had their vision of the *gaucho*. For Australia and Argentina, both men of the bush and the *gaucho* evoke an independent, untamed attitude uncontaminated by material progress, and even anti-establishment. Ogelsby does not find the same for Canada, where the Mounties became something of a national symbol representing law and the authorities as well. Canada has been torn between the so-called 'imperialist', pro-British tradition and the pro-US continentalist tradition, while the pro-French tradition, ironically, took the form of increased nationalism in reaction against both British and American influence.

The bush and *gaucho* ethos, Ogelsby says, were not the product of indigenous societies; the discussion of 'civilization' versus 'barbarism' was carried out among quite sophisticated and cultured people. Those who can loosely be labelled as in favour of 'civilization' were not content with the traditions of the past. They considered them weak, completely superseded and, if followed, at risk of condemning culture to dangerous isolationism; they thought that the country – any of the three – could consider itself a member of the international community of advanced nations of Europe. The 'barbarians', in turn, were afraid that an internationalist attitude would merely mirror (poorly) alien values, and that of small even if weak local traditions could be enriched, and become in any case the necessary springboards for the eventual cultural fulfilment of their communities. Ogelsby concludes that the attempt to find an identity, no matter the strategy, has forced individuals to think about themselves and about their nations. It shows also that the experience is not unique, and that peoples of different countries share the same approach even when denied by their co-nationals. Argentina, Australia and Canada have much in common in their search for an identity, but the identity itself is different in each case. Each is endowed with identifiable characteristics, even if at times these have not been so easily grasped by the participants.

Charles Jones analyses the evolution of banking in Argentina, Australia and Canada during the nineteenth century and up to 1914.

He identifies some of the main elements, more particularly the increased role of the State, and to do this he has to set aside some interpretations which he finds misleading. The first of these attaches importance to the great frequency of bank failures with their disruptive consequences, which in turn create the need for a more stable system (i.e. a more stable oligopoly organized presumably in the public's interest). The appearance of Central Banks is interpreted as the inevitable and welcomed end-result. The second interpretation, which has been more in vogue from the 1960s, sees the evolution of banking as a response to the needs of economic growth and development. The history of banking is a contest between new, risk-taking, banking entrepreneurs, and anachronistic and restrictive regulations, a contest which forces, despite many individual failures, a change in the banking legislation. The third line of interpretation singles out the negative and at times sinister connotations of banking and financial power, at times in collusion and at times in opposition to those governments which have tried to impose some kind of control.

All three interpretations can be found in each of the countries, more so in Australia and Argentina, and less so in Canada. Still, Jones finds that these interpretations, even if voiced at the time and reproduced by later scholars, are quite misleading, particularly because they disguise the basic motive for the evolution of banking legislation and government involvement, i.e. the supply of funds to growing countries under governments permanently short of cash. Tax and income lay at the core of most government action, even if disguised by political reasoning.

To support his view, Jones analyses specific cases in the three countries. For Argentina, he takes the creation of the *Banco de Descuentos* in the 1830s, the *Banco de la Nación* in the 1880s, the rationale of which, despite some developmentalist and at times populist rhetoric, was very much determined by the requirements of public finance. In Australia, two very relevant cases are cited, the Trustees Savings Bank in New South Wales in the 1870s, and, later, the foundation of the Commonwealth Bank in 1911. Both, rather than embodying high principles, owed their existence to the need to obtain a cheap source of funds. In the case of Canada, the situation is different because, even if orthodox apologia, radical ranting and developmentalist agitation were never wholly absent, the fiscal motive has been so evident and for such a long period that already, at the turn of the century, Canadian historians dismissed the mythologies that took so long to dispel in Australia and Argentina. In all three countries fiscal needs prevailed over other considerations, and in this there was no difference among them.

D. C. M. Platt addresses himself to a very specific topic, i.e. the financing of the expansion of the two main cities of Argentina and Canada (Buenos Aires and Montreal) over the period 1880–1914. Some primary data is put forward from the municipal reports and accounts which permit a comparison of the sources and application of funds in both cities; they reveal some interesting similarities, even allowing for the obvious peculiarity of Montreal's bi-ethnicity. Both cities grew far faster than most western cities of the day. Consequently, expansion was expensive and far exceeded what foreign capital – conventionally understood to have been responsible for the financing of its major part – was prepared to supply. Platt emphasizes that it was internal and not external finance that was crucial in these two cases, and he suspects that the same was true for the majority of the cities of the New World.

One of the reasons for this was that, although nowadays a very large proportion of city services is likely to be undertaken by the municipality itself, this was not at all the case before the First World War. On the contrary, the salient feature at the time was the diminutive size of city revenues, in line with the restricted range of functions undertaken by Municipalities. Revenues were drawn in both cities from a somewhat similar range of taxes, property taxes heading the list by a large margin. The drastic rise in real estate values, more than tenfold in Montreal between 1880 and 1914, is the key to this source of income and the reason why expansion was at all possible. Both cities were able to draw on proprietors for contributions to the cost of such public works as increased the value of their properties. Both cities relied on credits as well, being able to raise loans at convenient rates in the international market, Montreal even more so than Buenos Aires. But this should not distract from the fact that the really huge costs of city expansion were met neither by the foreign companies nor by the foreign lenders, but rather by the citizens themselves. This was most obviously true of the financing of building, the largest of all calls on urban finance, and surprisingly forgotten in many analyses of city financing. Rents from the land accruing to the *estancieros* living in Buenos Aires were one of the sources of private financing for the more important houses in the Barrio Norte, while significant savings from wages much higher than those prevailing in Southern Europe, and the profits of business within a large city, allowed for the financing of the not-so-palatial houses and the more modest ones as well. If Buenos Aires and Montreal can be used as a guide, city financing was tackled piecemeal and, to an astonishing extent, from local sources. The pattern is plain elsewhere, and it might be that the foreign factor has been systematically overplayed both by its advocates and by its foes.

Roberto Cortés Conde, in his contribution, focuses on the industrial development of Canada and Argentina in the 1920s as a central feature of their divergent economic paths. This is so despite their original similarity, i.e. a high, land/population ratio which differed from those of other countries of recent development. This initial characteristic called for a first stage in which a *mise en valeur* of the land was required. A decline in the rate of growth was then to be expected, if no other changes in the other sectors of the economy were to occur. It was precisely in the development of industry where the significant changes took place.

Industry was able to grow at 5.8 per cent per annum in Canada from 1911 to 1930, and 3.8 per cent in Argentina. The main reason for the difference lay in Canada's performance during the war years, for which Argentina, even when she outperformed Canada in the 1920s, was unable to compensate. Cortés Conde, after explaining the facts, takes issue with Solberg's argument that Canada benefited from protectionist policies, at a time when Argentina could not because of the pressure exercised by the land-owning classes.

For Cortés Conde tariffs were not central. They were more than compensated for by the greater devaluation of the currency in Argentina. The main explanation was that from the very beginning Canada followed an export-orientated, industrialization strategy, while Argentina, even before the 1930s, favoured import substitution. Canada's connections with the international economy were closer than Argentina's, and they enabled her in the 1920s to receive a much higher inflow of foreign capital. Furthermore, her proximity to the US gave her access to the American market for new industrial goods. The growth of traditional staples slowed down in both countries, but in Canada there were new, substantial staples – forestry and mining – while in Argentina nothing of the kind appeared. Canada's new industries, which used those inputs, were much directed towards the export market. In Argentina, from the very beginning, new industries devoted themselves to the local market; they lost thereby the advantages of economies of scale and exposure to foreign technology and international standards.

It was not tariffs but export-orientated versus inward-looking industrialisation which proved to be the fundamental cause for the divergent paths of the 1920s. Cortés Conde's approach, although not as yet well received by political scientists, is increasingly popular with economists.

Two contributions deal with the Great Depression. Peter Alhadeff compares public financial policy during the 1930s for three countries which were deeply dependent on exports of primary goods, and for which a certain similarity in reactions might have been expected. What he finds is that all three, Argentina, Australia and Canada, were consistent in their efforts to maintain good credit standing; they pursued orthodox monetary and fiscal policies. But what was more clearly noticeable was a shift towards internal sources of financing, with an increase of taxes both in absolute amounts and, more particularly, as a proportion of total revenue; conversely, a reduction was experienced in the role of the tax on exports and imports. A difference between the British Dominions and Argentina was that the former had already developed a better tax structure during the 1920s and depended to a lesser extent on taxes on trade; Argentina had thus to make a more intense switch than Australia and Canada. On the other hand, the British Dominions increased their real expenditure by 50 per cent, while the rise in Argentina was only 10 per cent. Accordingly the former incurred budgetary deficits of about 5 per cent of GNP, while Argentina balanced her budget after incurring deficits of up to 7 per cent in 1930.

Alhadeff compares the evolution of unemployment in the three countries. Taking figures that are not easy either to compare or to rely upon, he finds that Argentina performed far better, unemployment never exceeding 6 per cent of the active population, while in Australia and Canada it reached about a quarter of the labour force. Alhadeff suggests that one of the reasons might have been the greater importance of the agricultural sector in Argentina. Argentina's agriculture, in physical volume, was not affected throughout the period; Australia, and particularly Canada, had a much more important industrial sector and one that already relied on exports to the US market. Consequently, they were far more vulnerable to cyclical industrial movements – an idea very much in line with Córtes Condes'. The way in which each economy evolved explains also the difficulty experienced by the British dominions in balancing the budget, as the greater fall in the level of economic activity reduced income, and the obligation to pay both unemployment benefit and assistance to producers increased. The orthodox financial policies of the three countries were adhered to more strictly by Argentina, and Argentina actually performed better in terms of employment and growth. Alhadeff's analysis gives no support to the idea that Government deficits, intentional or not, were beneficial during the depression.

However, there are other structural reasons, such as the importance of the agricultural sector *vis-à-vis* the industrial sector, and the role of non-traditional exports, which may explain, more than anything else, the different impact of the crisis on these countries. It is not impossible that these were so overwhelming that adequate or inadequate fiscal or monetary policies were not the crucial factor, after all.

The second of the two studies on the depression is by Michael Twomey. He assesses the economic performance of the policies pursued by the three Governments. Twomey identifies some parallels in their economic structure which were evident before the crisis, as well as the similarity in their initial reactions to the depression. Increased tariffs and devaluations implied, effectively, a departure from the gold standard. Tax structures lessened their reliance on tariffs and increased preoccupation with internal sources, and no country espoused countercyclical policies, at least avowedly.

The decline in GDP was less in Australia by about 9 per cent, while Argentina's fell by 14 per cent and Canada's, the worst, by 30 per cent.

Twomey analyses supply and demand, and observes that differences in the behaviour of supply are usually underplayed. It is here that an important difference should be identified, as Canada had the more elastic supply curve, while Argentina's and Australia's were more inelastic. Twomey's econometric estimates are interesting. In the context of the depression the more inelastic the better, as a reduction in demand reduced production to a lesser extent, quite in line with the actual performance of the three countries. In turn, demand can be gauged by three proximate determinants – exports, investment and government expenditures. While the first two were affected negatively, the autonomous variable which provided the largest net stimulus in each country, over the decade, was government expenditure. Government deficits increased significantly in the British Dominions, while Argentina reduced its own (thereby aggravating, in Twomey's view, the decline in income – a point where he disagrees with Alhadeff). Twomey finds that 70 per cent of devaluations were translated into relative price changes (which was their avowed aim), and that only 30 per cent were lost in general price increases, a relatively modest spillage. Twomey points out that despite the fact that none of these countries engaged in explicit countercyclical policies, the increases in the deficits in Australia and Canada had precisely that effect. However, he is sceptical about the general utility of such policies given present-day vacillations among economists, and his message is that past policies must be viewed with restraint.

The last two papers deal with institutional arrangements, with the British Dominions, in trade, and in state intervention (electricity supply). The first of these, by Ian Drummond, analyses the development of marketing boards in Canada and Australia during the inter-war period. He puts forward three main questions: the reasons which lay behind the differences between the two dominions, the implications for the international economy, and finally, the conundrum that developments which were so widespread in the Empire were so uncommon elsewhere.

Marketing boards are an all-encompassing concept; they were applied to organizations which were merely promotional or which actually marketed or controlled primary goods, mainly agricultural. Some boards exercised one or two of these functions, and at times even all three. Producers participated in different ways, but the boards had always to rely to some degree on Government intervention; they substituted substantially for the producers' co-operatives so important in countries like Denmark. The empire marketing boards were active both in internal markets and, even more so, internationally. Not uncommonly they tended to contrive a two-price system, the higher applied to the local market, and a lower abroad. The United Kingdom, the principal destination of the exports of these Dominions, tended to think of the Boards as devices through which the flow of products could be regulated so as to raise prices for Empire producers, at the expense of non-Empire countries. Although the mechanics varied, the main aim was to maximize the income to producers, by restricting output and by permitting a myriad of medium-sized producers to behave as oligopolists.

Australasian marketing boards began with the First World War, and they were the most active in developing and extending their use. In Canada, marketing boards were more difficult to get started, partly because – not uncharacteristically – there were quite a few constitutional problems. However, as time went by and particularly after the depression, provincial marketing boards mushroomed, to be joined later by a system of nation-wide boards (intended not so much as producers' organizations as instruments of government). These 'arcane bodies' had a substantial effect on world markets; they made life more difficult for other countries, particularly for the primary producers of South America, and increased manipulative practices in international trade. Even if some countries were not enchanted by the idea, they were compelled to follow suit and to create centralized marketing bodies of their own if they were not to be left at a disadvantage.

The popularity of these arrangements within the Commonwealth, and their rarity elsewhere, is worth considering. To some extent producers' organizations were thought of as a way of extending democracy, and admittedly the idea that they could be financed at the expense of the foreigner had a certain charm. The development of the boards and of manipulative trade practices encouraged barter and bulk purchases, and, as it turned out, the experience was to become of critical importance during the Second World War.

The last contribution, by Christopher Armstrong and H. V. Nelles, deals with the role of the State in the provision of electricity for Canada and Australia. The period covered is more than 80 years, up to 1965. Comparison indicates close similarities. In both countries private companies were gradually replaced by public enterprise, predominant by the 1960s. Cities like Melbourne, Sydney and Winnipeg had pioneered public ownership, while, a decade later, in Victoria and Ontario, it had spread to the State. All the same, the transfer was on a scale far smaller than developments after the Second World War.

Contrary to widespread opinion, socialist ideology played little part in either Australia or Canada, although isolated instances can be found. The trend was promoted by parties both of the right and the left. The main reason was the belief that public ownership of electrical power was a key to rapid economic growth. An abundance of cheap electricity was supposed to create the minimum conditions for the development of a strong economy. The idea even acquired a nationalistic tinge, as it did in the case of francophone Quebec. Private enterprise, supposedly, was unable to keep pace with demand, and what private enterprise would or could not do, the State had to undertake without hesitation. The advance of public ownership was not unconnected with technological change. The technology known at the beginning of the century favoured the existence of a large number of small units with relatively short transmission lines. When the government moved in, it was at the level of the municipality not the province or the state (and even less the nation). Later, the optimal size of the units increased considerably and investment became more indivisible. Moreover, the transmission of electricity, instead of being confined to relatively short distances, became feasible over distances unheard-of a few years before; inevitably lines crossed county and state boundaries, and brought federal authority into question. Even countries with a strong bias against public ownership made an exception for electricity. The huge new units, supplying electricity over several hundred miles, made sense of state control, and capital costs had become so large that only the State could raise money at a sufficiently low rate. It was technology more than anything else, and the pace of its evolution, that lay behind increased public ownership of electricity. While private enterprise continued to be possible, public ownership seemed to reconcile conflicting private and public interests, and became, by 1960, the preferred solution.

This book contains thirteen chapters, and thirteen points of view. All the same, some of its themes are recurrent.

The first, and foremost, is the demand that the argument should extend beyond economics to non-economic phenomena (Fogarty and W. Armstrong). By extension, the historian's preference for the individual case is contrasted with the economist's attempt to find common traits and deliver general interpretations (di Tella, Díaz Alejandro, Twomey), making allowance for dissimilarities only at a second stage. The staple theory is touched upon several times and, with one notable exception (Fogarty), all who mention it seem to think that it can explain much and might even be extended (W. Armstrong). Here an Australian view can be seen as at variance with those of Americans, Canadians and Argentines.

Another theme that recurs on several occasions is the importance of internal factors, both economic and social, by contrast with foreign (Platt, Alhadeff, Ogelsby). And a conclusion common to many is that the policies followed at the time were more rational than might be deduced from the statements of contemporaries, where rhetoric tended to disguise more practical and down-to-earth solutions (Solberg, Jones).

Finally, the addition of Canada to the standard comparison between Australia and Argentina, has enriched all three (Solberg, Cortés Conde). Although we are far from reaching significant statistical inferences, the level of generalisation has obviously improved. The examination of Canada makes it unmistakeably clear that the cultural and historical inheritance of Australia and Canada is not only much deeper but clearly distinguishable from Argentina's, and entirely relevant to the understanding of differences in economic evolution. The blunt fact is that we are talking about different peoples, and it is important that a phenomenon that has been hinted at somewhat evasively in both Australia-Argentine and Canada-Argentine comparisons should come out into the open. In the comparison of Australia and Canada, the mores of the British Empire, in such matters as trade and public ownership, are clearly distinct (Drummond, C. Armstrong).

The thirteen chapters in this book are more than a *tour d'horizon*, even if they fall short of a conclusion. This, perhaps, is not to be expected. But if they achieve at least a better understanding of the common circumstances of Argentina, Australia and Canada, and of their individual peculiarities, the effort will have been more than justified. At least we may be delivered from the strait-jacket of a single vision which ignores or denies the experience to be gained from others.

1 Staples, Super-Staples and the Limits of Staple Theory: the Experiences of Argentina, Australia and Canada Compared

JOHN FOGARTY

I

Over the past thirty years economists have moved away from the earlier notions of strict paths of growth embodied in the likes of the Harrod-Domar model and Rostow's stages. The emphasis in development economics has shifted from the search for a set of factors of production which in combination would more or less produce development, to what Gustav Ranis has described as the growing awareness that the analysis of growth, employment and distribution must be viewed as integrally of one cloth, with the focus on the existence and size of trade-offs amongst those objectives.[1] This has led to the recognition that there is not *one* growth path, but rather alternative ways of achieving a particular growth rate depending on the other priorities held by the society. In searching for these alternative growth paths, Ranis sees opportunities for a fuller 'exploration of the historical laboratory'.[2]

Argentina, Australia and Canada provide a useful historical laboratory for the testing of the staple theory of export-led development, which is the one attempt to provide a theoretical explanation of the development of regions of recent settlement. The central proposition of staple theory has been succinctly stated by Watkins:

> The fundamental assumption of the staple theory is that staple exports are the leading sector of the economy and set the pace for economic growth. The limited – at first possibly non-existent – domestic market, and the factor proportion – an abundance of land relative to labour and capital – create a comparative advantage in resource-intensive exports or staples. Economic development will be a process of diversification around an export trade. The central concept of a staple theory, therefore, is the spread effects of the export sector, that is, the impact of export activity on domestic economy and society.[3]

Or, put another way, it attempts 'to show how the growth experience of a "new" country is concretely shaped by the specific primary products which it successively exports to world markets. It is an attempt to discover in detail how "one thing leads to another" through the requirements and influence of the staple . . .'.[4]

Staple theory is a variant of the export-led growth model which applies specifically to 'new' countries, i.e. regions of recent settlement.[5] These 'new' countries have as their essential characteristic an abundance, or 'surplus', of natural resources relative to endowments of labour and capital. External demand for these natural resources sets in train a transference of labour and capital to effect their exploitation. This is the trade-led 'engine of growth' model which, according to Ragnar Nurkse, 'explained' the development of regions of recent settlement in the nineteenth century. This model, he claimed, was no longer relevant to the developing countries of the post-war era because of the changes in the demand of the centre of the world economy for the primary products of the periphery.[6]

However, as I. B. Kravis pointed out, the demand for the products of the underdeveloped countries as a whole had actually increased in the post-war period, and the problem was to explain why some countries responded and others did not. Kravis suggested that although demand was important, the *crucial* factors accounting for a country's development performances were to be found on the supply side.[7] The essential feature of the staple theory is that it is the character of the staple export industry itself, the different linkages or externalities communicated to the rest of the economy, rather than the mere growth of exports, which is the central determinant of growth in the export-led economy.[8]

In recent years it has become apparent that, in explaining why the development of some economies has been more satisfactory than others, it is necessary to take more seriously Kravis's suggestion that we look more closely at the supply side of the export-led equation. Indeed the main burden of research into exports and national economic growth reported in recent issues of *Explorations in Economic History* is that shifts in *both* the demand and supply conditions were significant in accounting for North American export-led growth, although the shifts in supply function were probably more important.[9] These studies go a long way towards recognising Kravis's essential point.

The analysis of the relationship between international trade and economic development is essentially an exercise in demand/supply analysis. The basic exercise is to identify the 'microeconomic foundations of the historical disturbance' to determine which exports, for example, rose in response to shifts in the conditions of demand or supply and the mechanisms by which this shift brought about change in the economy.[10] As shifts in demand are usually easier to identify through economic indicators (e.g. price data) as exogenous variables, demand has usually assumed paramountcy in the staple theory literature, the conditions of supply being taken as given and subsumed in the technology of the staple industry. As Caves points out, the externalities generated by export-led expansion are by their nature specific to the particular case, and are therefore not susceptible to incorporation in a generalized analysis.[11] In addition, many of the determinants of the supply side are not comfortably handled by economic analysis. Thus such factors as entrepreneurship and inventiveness, although recognized as important, are not easily generalized, and are in danger of being neglected.[12]

It is one of the limitations of theories of economic growth, including staple theory, that they cannot cope adequately with the proximate, or non-economic factors in development.[13] Staple theory has been devised to explain the process of development of the very specific case of the 'new country' characterized by a favourable man/land ratio and an absence of inhibiting traditions.[14] It also applies only to a *specific phase* in the development of these regions; that period during which trade was a relatively large component of total activity and 'led' the growth of gross product.[15] In the three countries considered here, that phase had come to an end by the 1930s. Staple theory suggests that, during this phase, the development of the region was a response to exogenous demand for the region's abundant resources, and that the particular shape of this development was determined by the technology of the staple products and their linkages with other sectors of the economy.

When, however, attention is concentrated on the *actual* experiences of these regions as much is left unexplained as explained by development theory. Concentration on relationships between exports and the national economic aggregates tends to direct attention towards the linkages between the leading sector and the internal economies, while not enough attention has been paid to the leading sector itself.

The most significant thing about the development of the 'Regions of Recent Settlement' is that it was associated with staple industries which not only grew, but within a very short time developed to a high degree of perfection – what might be termed *super staples*. Canadian wheat, Australian wool, New Zealand lamb, and Argentine beef come to mind as examples of *super staples* that led the transformation of their respective economies within a couple of decades. They became the world leaders in the production of these staple products, improvising and adapting imported technologies, but above all standing in the fore as contributors of technological advances.

Perhaps one of the most neglected aspects of development is the association between creativity and development. The mere receipt of factor inputs from overseas created growth, but development depended on these resources being received into an open and creative environment. In addition, these societies developed a flexibility which enabled them to retain their superiority in spite of challenges from other producers, and by producing a superior product they were not only able to respond to demand conditions but in fact created demand in much the same way as did the staple manufactures of the British Industrial Revolution.

Staple theory explains satisfactorily enough the particular pattern of development which followed in the wake of the rise of a successful staple industry. Thus, for instance, the specific network of linkages associated with particular staples accounts for the highly developed transport and commercial infrastructure and the urban concentrations around the ports which characterized all regions of recent settlement. What it does not explain is why these newly-settled regions attained such proficiency in the production and marketing of the staple items. Nor does it explain why these regions excelled in the production of some staples and not in others. Why for instance did Argentines achieve excellence as producers of meat and not as wheat producers, in spite of being in the forefront as wheat exporters? Furthermore, we might ask why the Canadians, without any apparent natural advantages over the Argentines, excelled in wheat production? Resolution of these issues is, I suggest, essential for an understanding of the development process in the nineteenth century regions of recent settlement.

II

One thing that becomes clear from even a cursory glance at the history of the development of various staple industries in the regions of recent settlement is that the reasons for the success or mediocrity of particular industries are to be found within the historical experience of the regions concerned, rather than in global, predisposing forces. World market conditions and the available technology of the late nineteenth and early twentieth century may have predisposed the regions of recent settlement towards the development and/or expansion of export staple wheat production, but these exogenous conditions do not help to explain why some regions, such as the prairie provinces of Canada, became world leaders in the wheat industry, and others, such as the Pampa provinces of Argentina, responded merely by expanding production for export without achieving leadership in either the technological or marketing aspects of the industry. Although the parameters for development, market opportunity, availability of labour, capital and technology, etc. may be set by the shape of the world economy, responses to these opportunities in the various regions were unique to the regions.

One of the consequences of addressing an historical issue through the framework of an economist's development model is that factors which can readily be handled by the economist tend to receive attention while those 'other factors' which Nurkse conceded might well have been the more significant are lost sight of.[16] This poses a dilemma for those who would seek to understand the process of economic development. The very notion of a theory of economic development implies the existence of a set of generalizations about the development process which have universal validity. The problem is that in spite of there being a number of such generalizations which can validly be made, they do not of themselves adequately explain what actually happened. Rather they give us clues as to what *might* have happened. This chapter argues that even within so seemingly homogenous a group as the regions of recent settlement, each region's development experience was unique. It is to individual rather than common experience that we must look for an explanation of the development process.

III

Although in particular cases there is room for argument about the strength of the linkages between staple exports and regional development,[17] successful cases of export-led development can, with benefit of hindsight, be seen to conform to the postulates of the development model. More instructive, however, are those cases which appear to meet the requirements of the model but which were either unsuccessful or whose performance was mediocre. Indeed, within any one region of recent settlement we can find examples of export industries which not only thrived in response to market demand but also displayed great dynamism and provided positive stimulus to development. At the same time other export industries, although successful, are less than dynamic stimulators of the economy. Others still cannot even be regarded as successful. In many of these cases it is the quality of entrepreneurship or the nature of the institutional environment which can be seen as the variable factors accounting for the differing performances.

Some examples will serve to illustrate this point. Until fairly recently, the most universally accepted cliché about the Australian economy was that it rode on the sheep's back, and certainly for most of its history wool was Australia's most important staple export. Although it is undoubtedly true that the growth of the wool industry in Australia was a response to the growing demands of the British textile industry, there was nothing inevitable about this response. In the same year as Spanish merino sheep were brought to New South Wales, a flock was introduced to the River Plate region.[18] English capital was available for sheep breeding in both areas, and both responded to the vicissitudes of the international market for wool (suffering depression in the 1840s, and booming again in the 1860s).[19]

Both Australia and Argentina were supplying the same international market and enjoyed more or less similar endowments of natural resources. Australian wool growing proved to be much more dynamic than Argentine. When we come to the crucial question of why the wool industry in Australia was so dynamic, the answer is surely to be found in features which were specific to Australia. From the beginning, the wool industry in Australia was characterized by entrepreneurship and creative adaptability to the environment of an extremely high order. From the likes of John McArthur, Samuel Marsden and Alexander Riley onwards, the leaders in the industry proved to be men of vision with a capacity to perceive what the market required, and the innovative ability to respond with the production of distinctive types of wool of excellent quality which commanded premiums on world markets. The industry developed its own distinctive system of organization of production, financing and marketing which set the standards for other producing areas. Not only did the Australian industry come to dominate the market, it possessed sufficient internal dynamism to enable it to keep ahead of competition from other producers and from substitutes.

Until Argentina entered its modern phase of export-led growth in the 1880s, the staple exports were wool, hides and tallow, and sheep raising was possibly the most important staple industry. In 1885 Australia and Argentina had nearly the same number of sheep, but whereas the average clip in Australia yielded £6, that in Argentina yielded only £3.5.[20] Twenty years later the ratio of yields per sheep between the two countries was reported to be much the same.[21] This not only reflected differences in wool types but inferior yields of wool per sheep in Argentina: the result of negligent breeding practices.[22]

Both Australia and Argenina were endowed by nature with the resources with which to respond to the increasing demand for wool in Britain and Europe throughout the 19th century. In both countries effective responses were made, resulting in wool production being the most significant staple export. Yet while the Argentine sheep industry conformed to all the requirements of staple theory, there can be no doubt that, on practically every count, the Australian wool industry performed much more impressively. Not only did the Australian breeders apply themselves more successfully to the task of producing high-yielding animals suited to particular regional environment, but they developed management practices and technologies which were later to be adopted by other sheep-producing countries including Argentina. In this respect it is instructive to know that at the present time the dominant breeds of sheep in Argentina's main sheep raising area are the Australian Merino and the Australasian-evolved Corriedale.[23] Australians quickly learned the advantages of careful preparation of the fleece, and developed a marketing system which served the producer well and retained most of the profitable middleman functions within the country.[24] It is probably true to say that the spread effects of the development of the wool industry through linkages to a modern financial and marketing sector were far greater in Australia than in Argentina. Even in that section of the sheep industry, the frozen meat trade, where Argentina might be said to have had comparative advantage both through environment and distance, Australians were the innovators.

Although the Argentine cattle industry displayed little capacity for genuine innovation, it became so creatively adaptive as to warrant the label of Argentina's 'super staple'. The opportunities afforded by the increase in the demand for meat in Europe, particularly Great Britain, in the latter decades of the nineteenth century, were seized eagerly by a small group of *hacendados*, including recently arrived Europeans, who in 1866 had formed the *Sociedad Rural Argentina*.

Three conditions had to be met if Argentines were to take over from North Americans as the principal exporters of cattle to Europe. Firstly, the quality of the livestock had to be improved; secondly, the quality of the pastures had to be upgraded; and thirdly, the most up-to-date methods of animal husbandry had to be practised. These three conditions were accomplished within a remarkably short period of time. In the three decades prior to the outbreak of the First World War, the Argentine Pampa was transformed.

The British shorthorn was the basis of the great improvement of the Argentine herds which, although it began in 1856, reached its transforming momentum in the late 1880s.[25] The introduction of pure-bred stock and the upgrading of the *criollo* cattle by cross breeding were a response to the rising demands first of the cattle exporters, and then of the *frigorífico*; by 1908 over 90 per cent of the cattle in the province of Buenos Aires were improved types.[26]

The rapid and extensive transformation of the Pampean herds from scrawny *criollo* to high-yielding, rapid-maturing, improved breeds required a massive conversion to soft pastures in those fattening areas which developed in the north and western regions of the Pampa. This was achieved mainly by sowing down to alfalfa, the acreage of which increased twelve-fold in the twenty years to 1908.[27] The improvement of the herds also required a revolution in herd management, necessitating investment in wire fencing and the provision of water for the stock.

The rise of the modern Argentine beef industry was accompanied by rapid development of the Pampean economy. The situation of the fattening areas in the west of the province of Buenos Aires made necessary the building of railways which criss-crossed the Pampa in a dense grid. The rapid growth of beef exports was reflected in heavy investment in *frigoríficos* and port facilities, and in the growth of the modern financial and banking facilities which characterized modern export economies.

The rapid conversion of the Pampa to improved pastures for cattle was usually accomplished through tenant-farming agreements by which farmers leased land from pastoralists for two or three crops of cereals, leaving the land sown to alfalfa. This resulted in rapid growth of grain exports at a time when the world market for wheat was expanding. A large part of Argentine grain growing was subsidiary to the cattle industry, but it contributed greatly to the inflow of migrants which, particularly in the decade 1901–10, resulted in Argentina achieving the highest intensity of European migration ever experienced.[28] Thus both directly and indirectly the beef industry proved to be the most dynamic of Argentina's export staples.

There are some interesting similarities between the rise of the modern cattle industry in Argentina and the wool industry in Australia. In both the essential ingredient of success was the response by a relatively small group of dedicated breeders to the demands of the international market. It is true that the rewards for responding appropriately to the requirements of the market were great, but the personal qualities and perceptions of the individuals involved were crucial determinants of the industry's response.

The wheat-growing industry provides a useful vehicle for comparing the experiences of Argentina, Australia and Canada. Wheat growing as a modern export staple has featured prominently in the economic histories of all three countries, where it has been associated with attracting a relatively densely-populated agricultural settlement, massive extension of railway mileage, port installations, and the growth of domestic manufacturing industries. In all three countries, wheat growing for export responded to the same stimulus of increasing demand for wheat in the industrial centre of the world economy through the 1880s to the 1920s, and each was the recipient of large inflows of overseas capital and migration to build the infrastructure necessary to sustain development.

Yet, although wheat-growing was a successful export staple in all three countries, it was in Canada that it assumed the character of a 'super staple'. Although there was a rapid expansion of wheat acreage in Argentina from two million in 1888 to 15.5 million acres in 1911[29] and cereals assumed first place amongst exports, the Argentine wheat-growing industry did not possess the dynamic quality which characterized the expansion of the industry on the Canadian prairie. The Argentine industry developed in two distinct phases. Prior to the mid-1890s, cereal-growing expanded primarily as a consequence of government-encouraged and assisted colonization schemes, designed to settle migrants on small holdings in the northern parts of the Pampas, particularly in the provinces of Santa Fé and Cordoba.[30] These were similar to closer settlement schemes in Australia and Canada in that they were community responses to the perception that, to be held, land needed to be settled. The great expansion in grain growing after 1895, however, developed as an integral part of the modern Argentine beef industry, and owed very little to governmental intervention. This may account for some of the differences between the development of the wheat-growing industry after the 1890s in Argentina, and in Australia and Canada (where the industry continued to develop as parts of government-supported settlement programmes).

It is perhaps no accident that the region where wheat growing developed most 'naturally' in conformity with staple theory, the Argentine Pampa, was also the region where there was least government involvement in the industry. In Australia wheat-growing developed, in most areas, on lands which had been thrown open to settlement by land acts specifically designed to establish a large, small-holding 'yeomanry'. It was not only the demand for wheat in world markets which was responsible for the spread of the wheat industry; it also required the active involvement of colonial governments in the provision of infrastructure in the form of railways and Departments of Agriculture, which performed the all-important functions of adapting and devising new plant types and farming practice suitable to particular areas, and the dissemination of these amongst the settlers. A very strong commitment by governments was an essential prerequisite in Australia for the successful expansion of wheat-growing as a staple industry.[31] The Argentine government, by contrast, was extremely reluctant to provide this kind of essential support.[32]

The wheat boom which transformed the Canadian prairies came later than for Argentina and Australia, but it was quicker and more thorough in is effects. From 4 million acres in 1905 the area under wheat in the Prairie Provinces escalated to 24 million acres in 1930.[33] Wheat exports rose from 2 million bushels in 1891 to 10 million in 1901, and to 46 million in 1911.[34] This rapid expansion in response to rising market demands was dependent on a number of prior developments: the existence of an adequate transport network, the development of dry farming techniques, the introduction of wheat with a shortened growing period, improved handling methods, and the availability of people willing to farm the inhospitable area.[35]

The meeting of this formidable list of conditions was made possible by the willingness of the government to assume a considerable degree of responsibility. The role of the government was crucial to the expansion of Canada's transportation network. The great railway projects of the 1870s and 1880s grew from direct government investment and encouragement to private companies through land grants, subsidies and monopolies which enabled the laying down of the rail network ahead of population.[36] In addition, the government played an active role in attracting farmers and labourers to Canada through extensive advertising in Europe and the US. A network of immigration agents was established to provide prospective immigrants with information on farming conditions and opportunities, as well as cheap rail tickets to the Western provinces.[37]

In addition to its endeavours in attracting settlers to Canada, the government made land available through homestead legislation, assisted settlers with tools, seeds and technical advice, and offered them protection in bad seasons.[38] A feature of Canadian government assistance to prairie agriculture was the provision of technical assistance to settlers in the form of maintaining an extensive network of experimental stations, providing seed testing services, and maintaining effective extensive services. This provision of an extensive institutional and scientific infrastructure contrasted with the situation in Argentina where the necessity for such assistance was recognized but provided only rarely, and then usually in insufficient quantities; so much so that attempts to plug the gaps were occasionally made by private enterprises concerned with improving agricultural productivity such as breweries and railway companies and, of course, the *Sociedad Rural*.[39]

By the mid-1920s the superiority of the Canadian wheat industry was so apparent that it was widely remarked upon in Argentina. *La Nación*, for instance, drew attention to the ample provision of roads in Canada, the extension of its railways, the progress of colonization schemes, and superior productivity.[40] Another newspaper report attributed Canada's superior performance to the work performed by the extensive network of experimental farms distributed from the Pacific Ocean to the Atlantic, forming a vast system which was in intimate contact with the Canadian people.[41]

Remarkable as was the performance of the Canadian wheat growers in comparison with Argentines, it was the Canadian marketing system which put Canada in front of both Argentina and Australia. Australian Departments of Agriculture had more or less matched the Canadians in the development of high-yielding varieties suited to specific areas, and the names of William Farrar and Charles Saunders are equally revered in their respective continents.[42] From the earliest days of the Prairie wheat boom the crop was handled by a public grain-elevator system which not only reduced handling costs but also permitted the classification of grains so that they could be sold under homogeneous classes. A quarter of a century later neither Australia nor Argentina had bulk-handling systems, but this was of more consequence for Argentina where post-harvest rains, damaging the stacks of wheat by rail sidings, were more likely to occur than in Australia. The lack of a modern marketing system was put forward as the main reason for Argentine wheat's reputation for inferior quality due to 'presentation in bad condition, dirty and without uniformity'.[43] Wheat, then, was Canada's 'super staple'. Wheat-growing in that country exhibited performances in productivity, innovation and adaptation, generation of income for producers, provision of infrastructure (physical, institutional and scientific), and marketing and organization, which, in the eyes of Argentine observers at least, were paragons of excellence.

IV

The experiences of Argentina, Australia and Canada in their phases of modern, export-led development suggest that the differences between them are to be found on the supply rather than the demand sides of the equation. This points to one of the basic weaknesses of the staple approach: although it purports to explain how demand for an export staple, through the spread effects of production, determines the shape of a region's economic development, explanation must in the end be sought outside the model. Supply is not merely a response to demand, and the shape and position of the supply curve is often determined by complex variables particular to a given region.

It is valid enough to argue, as does C. Knick Harley, that 'the expansion of the frontier was essentially a movement of the extensive margin of cultivation in response to higher prices at the frontier'.[44] Nonetheless, it would be a mistake to assume that the nature of that response could be predicted solely from the state of the available technology. In the end we have to accommodate the kind of explanation offered by Robert Ankli when discussing the Prairie wheat boom: 'What did happen to make 1896 a watershed was that the Liberals defeated the Conservatives and Clifford Sifton became

Secretary of the Interior.'[45] The staple model does not easily accommodate the vagaries of politics.

Success in the pastoral industries, sheep and cattle raising, seemed to depend on the entrepreneurial and other personal qualities of individuals, rather than the active support of government as in the case of the agricultural staples. The history of successful stock breeding in both Argentina and Australia is dominated by entrepreneurial figures who with their own or borrowed capital created vast empires of stock stations or *estancias*, and who asked very little of governments except to be permitted to pursue their activities with the minimum of restriction.[46] Nevertheless, the institutional arrangements within which the pastoralists operated were often of vital importance.

Although one of the advantages new societies usually enjoyed was more institutional flexibility than in older countries, it was not always easy to achieve the most propitious institutional environment. One of the most important institutional innovations for the Australian pastoral industry was the New South Wales Liens on Wool and Mortgages on Stock Act of 1843, which enabled squatters to offer their stock and future wool clips as security for advances from lending institutions. This could well have been an essential prerequisite for the expansion of the wool industry, but it was not readily accepted by the imperial government and was originally only allowed as an emergency depression measure.[47]

W. T. Easterbrook's observation that in Canada 'bureaucratic influences and outlook have shaped and dominated the nation's economic life; centrally directed, "induced" entrepreneurship established a pattern which remains largely intact . . .' seems particularly relevant.[48] To a large degree the success of the Canadian wheat industry depended on the determination of the central government to settle the prairies. Wheat growing in the Canadian prairie provinces would not have been feasible without the provision of railways, the encouragement and support of settlers, and the very active role played by the government in setting up a network of research stations and extension services and the provision of an extensive grain elevator system. In Australia, too, governments provided the essential transport and technological infrastructure required to make successful, small scale settlement possible. In both these cases there was only limited scope for the exercise of individual enterprise and initiative.

In Argentina where wheat-growing developed 'natually' as an extension of the beef industry there was also little scope for individuals to achieve much in the way of innovation and improvement of plant varieties or farming techniques. Here, however, the government did not commit itself to the provision of scientific and extension services for the agricultural community to anything like the extent of governments in Canada and Australia. Although wheat-growing became an important staple industry in Argentina, it remained at a relatively primitive level of development. This was in no small measure due to the failure of government to perform the entrepreneurial function which the modern wheat-growing industry required.[49]

One of the problems with theories of economic development is that it is most difficult, perhaps impossible, to generalize about some of the elements most crucial to the growth process. Supply-side factors like entrepreneurship, inventiveness and adaptability are difficult to incorporate into customary economic analysis. So much of any particular development experience depends on the attitudes and qualities of the people who were actually involved and the decisions made by these individuals, whether as producers or as members of governments. Thus each development experience was unique, although it undoubtedly shared many features with others. The notion of a production-function existing independently of the human beings who utilize it is erroneous.[50] Yet it seems to be assumed in most models of development.

Staple theory tells us that the development pattern of a 'new' land will be determined by the nature of a region's natural resources and the demand for them, and the technology of the staple production, and up to a point this is a useful generalization. But it does not suggest explanations as to why a particular staple industry develops dynamically in one region and not in another. The cases under consideration illustrate this. It was only on the Pampas that wheat-growing developed as a consequence of the previous staple. Unlike the earlier development of cereal growing in Argentina, the expansion from the mid-1890s did not require the participation of government. In Australia, on the other hand, the transition from pastoral to agricultural occupancy was impelled more by the political and social consequences of the gold rushes than by linkages between the wool and wheat growing industries. In Canada the settlement of the Prairies was part of a national policy which required the State to play a central role in the face of the westward expansion of the United States.[51] It was the difficulty of producing for the world market that required innovative government response in Australia and Canada. The ease with which wheat could be grown on the Pampas enabled the industry to grow without much innovation or assistance from the government.

The study of the development of staple export industries in Argentina, Australia and Canada leads to the recognition that no general, predetermining set of conditions is sufficient to initiate the process of economic development. In these regions of recent settlement one thing is clear. The successful development of 'super' staples, and the associated initiation of economic development, were triggered by local enterprise and intitiative at either the individual or government levels. The investigation of the circumstances in which these developments occur is precisely the sort of thing that Michael Postan claimed economists cannot handle,[52] and it seems that if we want to progress in our understanding of the nature of economic development we should not place too much faith in the power of staple theory or other economic theories to provide enlightenment. Rather we should renew our studies of the historical circumstances in which development occurred in particular societies.

NOTES

1. Gustav Ranis, 'Development Theory at Three-Quarters Century', *Economic Development and Cultural Change*, 25 (Supplement, 1977) 256.
2. Ibid., 259.
3. Melville Watkins, 'A Staple Theory of Economic Growth', *The Canadian Journal of Economics and Political Science*, XXIV (1963) 144. Watkins' footnotes constitute a fair coverage of the staple theory literature as it applies to North America. For a list of the literature on Australia see A. L. Lougheed, 'International Trade Theory and Economic Growth', *Australian Economic History Review*, VIII (1968) 99, note 1. Argentine economic historians have largely ignored staple theory but see Ezequiel Gallo, 'Agrarian Expansion and Industrial Development in Argentina, 1880–1930' in Raymond Carr (ed.), *Latin American Affairs: St. Antony's Papers, No. 22* (Oxford, 1970).
4. Albert O. Hirschman, 'A Generalized Linkage Approach to Development with Special Reference to Staples', ch. 4 in his *Essays in Trespassing: Economics to politics and beyond* (Cambridge, 1981) p. 65.
5. For a discussion on the nature of regions of recent settlement, see John P. Fogarty, 'The Comparative Method and the Nineteenth Century Regions of Recent Settlement', *Historical Studies* (University of Melbourne), 19 (1981) 412–29.
6. R. Nurkse, *Patterns of Trade Development* (Oxford, 1961) p. 23.
7. I. B. Kravis, 'Trade as a Handmaiden of Growth: Similarities between the Nineteenth and Twentieth Centuries', *The Economic Journal*, LXXXX (1970) 859.

8. Richard E. Caves, '"Vent for Surplus" Models of Trade and Growth', in R. E. Caves (ed.), *Trade, Growth and the Balance of Payments: Essays in Honour of Gottfried Haberler* (Chicago, 1966) p. 111. Melville Watkins, op. cit., p. 144.
9. *Explorations in Economic History*, vol. 17, nos 1 and 3 (1980) particularly C. Knick Harley, 'Transportation, the World Wheat Trade, and the Kuznets Cycle, 1850–1913', 218–58. Robert E. Ankli, 'The Growth of the Canadian Economy 1896–1920. Export led and/or Neoclassical Growth', 251–74. Trevor J. O. Dick, 'Canadian Wheat Production and Trade, 1896–1930', 275–302.
10. Richard E. Caves, Douglass C. North and Jacob M. Price, 'Introduction: Exports and Economic Growth', *Explorations in Economic History*, 17 (1980) 3.
11. Richard E. Caves, 'Vent for Surplus', 111.
12. Melville Watkins, op. cit., 148.
13. Gustav F. Papanek, 'Economic Development Theory: the Earnest Search for a Mirage', *Economic Development and Cultural Change*, 25 (Supplement, 1977) 281.
14. Melville Watkins, op. cit., 143.
15. N. G. Butlin, 'Growth in a Trading World: the Australian Economy Heavily Disguised', *Business Archives and History*, IV (1964) 141.
16. Nurkse, op. cit., 18.
17. Jeffrey G. Williamson, 'Greasing the Wheels of Spluttering Export Engines: Midwestern Grain and Growth' *Explorations in Economic History* 17 (1980) 189–217.
18. Herbert Gibson, *The History and Present State of the Sheep-Breeding Industry in the Argentine Republic* (Buenos Aires, 1893) p. 14.
19. Alan Barnard, *The Australian Wool Market 1840–1900* (Melbourne, 1958). John Lynch, *Argentine Dictator: Juan Manuel de Rosas 1829–1852* (Oxford, 1981) pp. 84–7.
20. *The Australasian Insurance and Banking Record 15/2/1887*, p. 75.
21. Francisco Seeber, 'Argentina, Canada, Australasia: Lecciones de progresso comparado, inferioridad relativa de la Argentina', *Anales de la Sociedad Rural Argentina*, 1908, 98.
22. J. F. Guthrie, *A World History of Sheep and Wool* (Melbourne, 1957) p. 174.
23. J. Colin Crossley in Harold Blakemore, Clifford T. Smith (eds), *Latin America: Geographical Perspectives* (London, 1971) p. 425.
24. Alan Barnard, op. cit., ch. 3.
25. Morton D. Winsberg, *Modern Cattle Breeds in Argentina: Origins, Diffusion and Change* (Lawrence, 1968) pp. 9–11.
26. Simon G. Hanson, *Argentine Meat and the British Market* (Stanford, 1938) p. 116.
27. Ibid., pp. 115–16.
28. Blakemore and Smith, op. cit., pp. 417 and 430.
29. James R. Scobie, *Revolution on the Pampas: a Social History of Argentine Wheat, 1860–1910* (Austin, 1964) p. 172.
30. Crossley, op. cit., p. 412.
31. For a fuller discussion of the part played by government in the

development of the Australian wheat-growing industry see J. P. Fogarty, 'The Staple Approach and the Role of the Government in Australian Economic Development: the Wheat Industry', *Business Archives and History*, VI (1966) 34–52.

32. In 1877 for instance the budget for the Argentine Department of Agriculture was only 1/60th of that of the Victorian Department of Agriculture in Australia: James R. Scobie, op. cit., p. 134.
33. R. W. Murchie, *Agricultural Progress on the Prairie Frontier* (Toronto, 1936) pp. 24–6.
34. G. M. Meier, 'Economic Development and the Transfer Mechanism: Canada 1895–1913', *Canadian Journal of Economics and Political Science*, XIX (1953) 4.
35. Caves and Holton, op. cit., pp. 198–9.
36. Ibid., p. 234.
37. William Marr and Michael Percy, 'The Government and the Rate of Canadian Prairie Settlement', *Canadian Journal of Economics*, XI (1978) 760.
38. 'En Canada se sigue con creciente interés el progresso de este páis', *Revista de Economía Argentina*, 18 (1927) 348.
39. E.g. Enrique Klein, 'Trigos de Pedigee de origen Rioplatense', *Anales de la Sociedad Rural Argentina*, Numero Extraordinario, 54 (1920) 57–9. Guillermo E. Leguizamón, 'La inmigración colonizadora en la Canada', *Revista de Economía Argentina*, 20 (1928) 97–100.
40. *La Nación* – 'Nos vamos quendando atrás' (10/2/1927); 'Ejemplos por imitar' (25/2/27).
41. 'La eficiencia en la producción agrícola', *La Prensa* (17/11/1927).
42. For the work of Farrar and Saunders see Edgars Dunsdorfs, *The Australian Wheat Growing Industry, 1788–1948* (Melbourne, 1956) 190–5. Vernon C. Fowke, *Canadian Agricultural Policy: The Historical Pattern* (Toronto, 1946) pp. 233–8.
43. Guillermo E. Leguizamón, 'Los elevadores de granos en la economía agricola', *Revista de Economía Argentina*, 21 (1928).
44. C. Knick Harley, op. cit., 230.
45. Robert E. Ankli, op. cit., 256.
46. An interesting sidelight is provided by the experience of the Australian Mercantile Land and Finance Company, which decided to extend its operations to Argentina in 1910 because of its concern about the legislative programme of the newly-elected Labour government in Australia. See J. D. Bailey, *A Hundred Years of Pastoral Banking: A History of the Australian Mercantile Land and Finance Company* (Oxford 1966) ch. 12.
47. Alan Barnard, op. cit., pp. 9, 117–18. Ricardo Newton was impressed by the ability of Australian graziers to offer liens on stock and produce, as security for loans, during his tour of 1882, and suggested that it become general practice in Argentina. Ricardo Newton y Juan Llerena, *Viajes y Estudios de la Comisión Argentina sobre la Agricultura Ganadería, Organización y Economía Rural de Inglaterra, Estados Unidos y Australia* (Buenos Aires, 1884) Tercera Parte, Tomo X, p. 80.

48. W. T. Easterbrook, 'Long-Period Comparative Study: Some Historical Cases', *Journal of Economic History*, 17 (1957) 576.
49. John P. Fogarty, 'Difusión de tecnología en áreas de asentamiento reciente: el caso de Australia y de la Argentina', *Desarrollo Económico,* No. 65, 17 (1977) 141.
50. Nathan Rosenberg, 'Economic Development and the Transfer of Technology: Some Historical Perspectives', *Technology and Culture, II* (1970) 555.
51. John Fogarty, 'Interpreting Australian History in the light of Argentine experience': Paper delivered at Section 26, ANZAAS Congress, Sydney 1982, pp. 4–6. W. T. Easterbrook, 'Uncertainty and Economic Change', *Journal of Economic History*, 14 (1954) 357.
52. M. M. Postan, *Fact and Relevance in History* (Oxford, 1971), p. 29.

2 Rents, Quasi-Rents, Normal Profits and Growth: Argentina and the Areas of Recent Settlement

GUIDO DI TELLA

I

My intention is to re-interpret, in economic terms, the dramatic expansion during the nineteenth century of the regions of 'recent settlement',[1] that is, the United States, Canada, Australia, New Zealand, Argentina, and South Africa (not to mention the notoriously similar, but neglected, case of Russia's Siberia). These countries and their development over the last century have some very interesting problems in common, although individual interpretation, which takes into account both economic and (most certainly) non-economic factors, is unavoidable. I can only acknowledge that the comments which follow are based on knowledge of one specific case, that of Argentina. All the same, Argentina seems to pose, even if in a somewhat extreme fashion, some of the peculiarities which have existed also for others, particularly the United States, Canada, and Australia.

We are talking about a group of countries which were discovered in relatively recent times, and which have had what seemed unlimited supplies of free land ('waste lands', in Adam Smith's phrase); they attracted massive movements of people, and similarly massive movements of capital. The description may sound peculiar to an economist, and particularly to an economist interested in international trade, as it conveys the idea that drastic increases in factor availability (even of land) and in factor movements of labour and capital were essential to their respective processes of growth. As we all know, standard economic history presupposes free movement of goods but international immobility elsewhere, while land is assumed to be constant; capital and labour are assumed to grow only as a consequence of savings and of the natural increase in population.

Although economic theory has long tried, even if with some difficulty, to incorporate international capital movements, it has not attempted to do the same with migratory movements and even less with increases in the stock of land, a *contradictio in adjectio*. In particular, the idea of an expanding land frontier is alien to most models of growth, even more so today than it was in Smith's time. To a large extent this is due to the fact that natural resources – of which land is but a particular case – played a fundamental role only in the nineteenth century, and in only a few places at that. In countries like the United States, it reached its maximum contribution by the last quarter of the century, having fallen from 36 per cent of GNP in 1870, to 27 per cent in 1900, and 12 per cent in 1954.[2] Although the dates and proportions are different, the trend has been the same in all areas of recent settlement. Actually it has been a world-wide trend that, in recent times, has diverged from the norm only in the case of the oil countries, particularly the new ones.

Little wonder, then, that economic theory has tended to play down the role of natural resources, and of land in particular, to the extent (as Schultz says with some chagrin[3]) of leaving them out altogether in most models of growth. One has to pick up a reference or search among the footnotes to find a mention of this 'passing' phenomenon. But my subject is precisely the analysis of the role of land, and the contrast between some of the characteristics of the growth process in the areas of recent settlement during the nineteenth and early twentieth century and alternatively some of the assumptions of economic theory.

I begin, in my first section, by analysing the concept of a frontier, and in particular the way in which it becomes inextricably linked with the existing technological level. In the second section we move to some peculiarities of frontier expansion, particularly those cases when significant, although not necessarily discontinuous, technological changes created economic opportunities that could not be taken advantage of immediately, and gave rise to an expansionary process in vigorous disequilibrium. In these instances the 'closing of the frontier' is a meaningful concept, and describes a situation when one might expect growth to falter if no substitute to land were found. In the third section I introduce the role of demand, when price movements exacerbated the expansion or, alternatively, tempered it for a while. Although prices have a bearing on the evolution of the frontier I argue, like many others, that changes in the supply side have overshadowed changes in demand and in fact preceded them. Finally, in the last section, I develop a broader view of the frontier problem, analysing it as just one instance, probably the first, in the search for abnormally high 'profits'. Entrepreneurs achieve these profits by the creation of rents, or, when unable to do so for scarcity of land, find a substitute in oligopolistic quasi-rents, either of an innovative or of a collusive character (the latter being the easier, but of limited utility).

These changes in the source of profits and rents, and consequently in the sources of accumulation, its interactions and shifts, are central to an understanding of the growth paths and of some of the problems of the areas of recent settlement.

II

Let us begin by exploring the nature and the particular circumstances of increases in the quantities of land. There are in fact quite distinct variations, with greater or smaller relevance according to place and time.

On the one hand we have instances of pure economic discovery – land previously unknown or of unsuspected productivity (a phenomenon most familiar for mineral lands). On the other, there are cases more common to nineteenth century expansion in which land had been known for a long time; in some instances the economic potential was not always perceived immediately, while in others it could not be exploited because of the high cost of development with the technology then existing. Although many technological advances were needed, different for each staple, the most important and widespread was the reduction in the cost of transportation by sea and land, engendered by steamships and railways. Canals were the first breakthrough in the reduction of the cost of land transportation, but in the United States their main impact was felt during the 1830s to 1860s with the river steamboat, when full use could be made of the magnificent natural network of rivers and lakes (a privilege denied both to Australia and Argentina). More significant for land transportation was the railway, rather later in date and more evenly diffused in all areas of recent settlement. The territorial expansion of Australia, Canada and Argentina employed different combinations of the various means of transportation, but they all depended ultimately on this unique technological advance.

Another factor of major importance was the improvement in sea transportation. Transatlantic freight charges, which had shown no noticeably downward trend until the 1880s, nearly halved in the following quarter of a century. Other innovations may have been less widespread, but they were quite as crucial to some areas and staples (like the cotton gin for the south of the United States, the reaper for the wheat and grain areas, refrigeration for Argentine and Australian meat, the mechanical saw for Canadian timber).

A contemporary element of equal or even greater significance (certainly for Argentina and the United States) was the improvement in military technology and military tactics, the consequence of the development of quick-firing, long range weapons, and in particular the substitution of muzzle-loading guns by breech-loading rifles (later improved still further with the introduction of magazines). These innovations, together with the improvement of transportation, transformed military tactics, permitted the greater and swifter deployment of armies, and made it much easier to gain control over the native, pre-existing populations. In Argentina, the new arms imported in the 1870s transformed the war against the Indians from a defensive operation on a stationary frontier to the offensive which, in a few years during the early 1880s, added many million acres to Argentina's market economy. In economic terms, 'pacification' meant a reduction in risks and uncertainty, and consequently a reduction in costs (at times quite dramatic).

If one looks at the areas of recent settlement one can see that initial discovery was followed by one or two centuries of painstakingly-slow expansion. Discovery was indeed a special case of innovation. The long period which preceded actual economic incorporation can be compared with the time span of the 'diffusion' process which characterised invention in general.

Technology continued to evolve and many, small technological changes were adopted; when accumulated over a long period the extent was not inconsiderable. But at some point in the nineteenth century, earlier in the United States and later in Argentina and South Africa, a significant change took place, the consequence of a coming together of the several elements described above. As was the case for all great expansionary processes, a certain 'clustering' of inventions (and in the application of those inventions) had occurred just previously. There was nothing in this that was necessary or inevitable. It just happened in the same way as it had at the beginning of the four or five identifiable industrial revolutions.[4] But those inventions to which I am referring had the peculiarity – based as they were on innovations in transportation and welfare – of being particularly appropriate for a process of physical, territorial expansion.

What can be seen, then, not only in the case of the major technological developments but also for many minor developments of the expansionary process, is an interaction between innovation and physical expansion. While innovation permitted, and provided the base for, expansion, some innovation was promoted by the discovery and existence of new territories so that a natural interaction took place between innovation and expansion.[5]

III

Peculiar to these expansionary processes was the speed at which economic opportunities, after a long process of maturing (or diffusion), were actually opened up. The downward shift in the cost curve was so intense, at least in Argentina, that around the 1880s it became economically feasible to incorporate most of the present-day pampas. In the short run the vast economic opportunities that were opened up far exceeded the possibility of exploitation. Expansion was frantic. It was known that if railroads were taken further, more land could be brought profitably into cultivation. But the incorporation of such vast expanses of land required time – time to bring immigrants from Europe to people the new cities and exploit the new land, time to build railways, roads, ports, villages and the whole infrastructure that goes with such a process. The actual physical frontier was moving all the time. For towns and communities the frontier was short-lived; the expansion went ahead, leaving the frontier town in an economically marginal situation, well within the frontier.

In fact, what was experienced was a *kinked* supply curve, i.e. costs gently rising with the greater distance from the port city, but at least for Argentina with a vertical kink at the frontier. This meant that rent was obtainable even there, which is indeed an indication of disequilibrium. It differs from the normal equilibrium of the Ricardian case, where the frontier is precisely the place where there is no rent. The fact that there *was* rent at the frontier is another way of saying that further expansion was seen as (and was) highly plausible – it was only a matter of time for new frontier land to become incorporated into the economy. The abnormality of rent at the frontier is the element which gave so extraordinary an impetus to this variety of expansion. Inherent to the process and to its dynamism was the fact that rents, so to speak, were lying fallow, and, as Adam Smith puts it, 'waste lands of the greatest fertility [were] to be had for a trifle',[6] open to appropriation by the first who could provide the minimum infrastructure required. The expansion, from a neoclassical point of view, should have taken place instantly, as soon as the cost-price relationship was 'right'.

All I am doing is to analyse the process of adjustment, far from instantaneous, which took from forty to eighty years in countries of recent settlement. This expansionary process might be described as an alternation of periods in which expansion was rather slow, maybe 'Ricardian', with small, marginal shifts in costs and/or prices, the frontier in disequilibrium, moving slowly forward or backward according to cost and price movements. It was followed by what might be called 'Schumpeterian' periods, in which the pace of expansion accelerated and the frontier was no longer in disequilibrium. In some cases the gently-rising cost curve, which we have assumed to be a consequence of increasing distances to the port city (or cities), was not so well-behaved. It is true that transportation costs in general increased, but along some of the rivers and lakes, in Argentina and Canada, or down the coast of Australia, these differences were minimal or non-existent as there was more than one export point. Moreover sometimes, even if further from port cities, the fertility of the land increased so that it lowered rather than raised costs. These were stages in the expansionary process where, instead of a tapering-off in the profitability of the expansion ('rentability' would be the proper term), it increased, and expansion intensified.

In any case, the frontier rent was bound to disappear at the close of expansion when the frontier stabilized. It is possible to think of present-day frontiers as subject still to change, expansion or even contraction. But unless a new, revolutionary and discontinuously significant innovation appears, one would be inclined to think more in terms of a slow reduction of costs and a cyclical movement of prices with no discernible trend, which allows for a slightly expansionary process, supply-induced, superimposed on a cyclical process, demand-induced, alternatively speeding up and retarding the expansion of a Ricardian frontier, always in a state of equilibrium.

It follows from this view of the expansionary process for new land that, at least in its dynamic disequilibrium variety, it cannot be expected to be a permanently continuing process. The opening of new lands contributed to a process of intense growth (for a while), but the growth tapered off as soon as the last frontier closed. At that point a qualitative change had to take place, which meant a lesser rate of growth; it was not easy to find alternative sources of growth that were new, absent until now, and capable of providing a source of accumulation equivalent to the expanding land rents of the past.

Innovations in familiar, land-using activities were, however, bound to be induced by scarcity; and new, non land-using activities which had been neglected – particularly among late developers – during the previous process because of their lesser potential for profit, might not be expected to receive attention in the absence of a better alternative. Yet it was one thing to grow as a consequence of 'Nature's bounty', so to speak, and quite another from human innovation which promised more evasive rents and profits.

What I have said of agricultural land can be extended very easily to mineral land, or, for that matter, to any natural resource. In our own century it would seem that new lands are unlikely to warrant significant agricultural expansion, although one should not underestimate what new agricultural technology can do to expand a frontier over very cold or mountainous territory, tropical lands, or areas of very low rainfall.

But what is not only possible but actually taking place all the time is the systematic search for, and discovery of, new mineral lands, of which oil fields are the most coveted. In this, clearly, we are nearer to the case of pure discovery followed usually by immediate exploitation. In economic terms, these are cases of the discovery of 'potential' rent. While the downward trend in the size of the contribution of natural resources to the process of growth is particularly applicable to an agricultural economy, in the case of minerals the picture is not so clear. In the particular case of oil the reality has been quite the reverse in those fortunate countries which are so endowed, both for the older oil producers (because of the price rise) and even more so among the new states in which oil has been discovered, such as Libya, Nigeria, etc. where oil revenue has promoted growth as dramatically as in any of the areas of recent settlement. If all the oil-producing countries are taken together, their share of economic rent increased from 24 per cent to 35 per cent of GNP (from just before to just after the rise, 1972 to 1976).[7] This may be compared with the falling percentages of rent in industrial countries, from an already low level of 4 per cent of GNP to about 1 per cent.

The difference between agricultural and mineral expansion is that, for agriculture, the closing of the frontier means an end to any increase in the stock of land, while the old lands maintain their productivity. In the case of mineral expansion, the closing of the frontier means not only that no more increases in land can be attained (or are too difficult or expensive) but that old resources will be depleted and their productivity reduced. No wonder that countries which base their growth on non-renewable resources are more aware of the transitory nature of their development. Such dissimilar countries as the United Kingdom and Iran, in our days, are examples of oil countries already concerned, even during their oil-boom days, about the prospect of a future decline in their sources of growth.

Among the areas of recent settlement, some, such as Argentina, have based their growth on agricultural expansion to the exclusion of all else. Others, such as the United States, Canada and Australia, have interspersed agricultural booms with mineral. Still others, notably South Africa, found that their agricultural development, so central to the formation of the national myth, was completely overshadowed by the exploitation of minerals, by gold and precious stones. The difference in the availability of various *kinds* of land goes far to explain some of the distinct growth paths of areas of recent settlement.

IV

The expansion of the frontier was a two-sided phenomenon. While its peculiarity is its association with a drastic downward shift in the supply curve, an upward shift in the demand for the various staples could conceivably have produced similar results. During the last century, as well as in our own, there was a quantitative change in demand, even if it was a consequence rather than a cause of the industrialization and the growth processes of the central countries. But neither the Malthusian notion of increasing relative scarcity and (consequently) increased prices of 'land intensive' goods, nor ECLA's prediction of secular deterioration of the prices of primary products, have taken place. Prices for most staples have moved in a cyclical manner, short and long cycles being superimposed, and long term trends have been difficult to ascertain. But the increase in demand has been felt, if not in prices, at least in the enormously increased quantities of primary goods that can be produced and sold without causing a glut on the market or a collapse of prices. Its evolution has been the consequence of the interaction of at least two different trends, operating at a different pace, on the supply and on the demand side. Both, supply and demand, have increased, but the downward shift in supply has at times been dramatic, particularly in the areas and periods that we are considering, permitting a postponement, or even a temporary reversal, of the Malthusian trend. Supply has increased not only because of the incorporation of resources – most significant in the nineteenth century – but also because of improved productivity of those same resources (more characteristic of the twentieth century). This has been, and is, a qualitative change with obvious quantitative results which, by contrast, have almost unlimited possibilities. The expansion of the frontier was a process in line with the former: more production from more resources. While the agricultural revolution, or to be more precise revolutions, has been in line with the latter: more production from the same resources.

On the demand side we have an income effect derived from the growth of the central countries, and a substitution effect which came from changes in the final demand of consumers. Moreover, demand has been influenced by technological improvements which have permanently reduced inputs and replaced those for which supply inelasticities were felt. Of these factors, those on the supply side, in addition to a substitution effect on the demand side, have offset the drastic increase in demand. The result has been a highly uncertain trend in prices.

Upward movements in the price of primary exports, during the expansion of the frontier, increased the pace of expansion, or, in the opposite case, acted as a deterrent. The 1854–73 deterioration of the *primary* terms of trade certainly did not help, while the brief improvement of 1873–81 was a significant boost, again to be reversed for the latter part of the century. Price changes were particularly crucial towards the end of the process of geographical expansion. They were, of course, crucial *during* the expansion, but became even more so at the closing of the frontier. If they rose at a time when agricultural products or minerals were experiencing increasing prices, rents could still increase and accumulation be helped at a delicate moment. If they fell, they added to an already difficult transition.

However, price changes may not have been crucial. While the terms of trade departed no more than ten per cent from the century's average, above or below, changes in costs and risks were far greater, moving in one direction most of the time and sustaining the extraordinary expansion of the economies over new lands. This is very much in line with Landes' view that most nineteenth century development can be seen as the outcome of large, cost-reducing innovations rather than long price movements.[8] It is, moreover, not entirely unrealistic to consider the expansion of the frontier as one of the most extraordinary 'innovations' of the century: a consequence of technological innovation, of course, but also in itself an innovation of a geographical nature.

While attempts to bring demand conditions into the analysis of areas of recent settlement must be welcomed, supply and demand changes cannot be considered as on the same plane, which would be to ignore the peculiarity of the expansion of the frontier and its crucial role in the development of such areas.

V

A broader perspective seems appropriate. This striving for rent, either agricultural land rent as in the past, or mineral land rent as at present, is part of the striving for 'abnormal' profits on the part of the entrepreneur. It is a way of saying that the Marshallian view that entrepreneurs are in business to search just for 'normal competitive profits' is utterly misleading. What entrepreneurs fear probably more than anything else is precisely such a situation, where profits are run down if not to zero (as a logical, even if extreme, consequence of the theory might indicate) – at least to that minimum which entrepreneurs require for taking the trouble to invest and risk their capital.

In the 'areas of recent settlement' it is clear that so large a capital was attracted not by the opportunity to earn a 'normal' Marshallian profit so much as to reap as much in rent as it could. This may indeed have been the behaviour of an imperfect market, but it is likely to be experienced at the frontier. The developer of the frontier, the entrepreneur responsible for its extension, behaved so as to reap a share of the rent that he was helping to create, and he did it by several methods. He could, for instance, buy part of the frontier land, as was done to a variable extent in all of the areas of recent settlement. The speculator in land, or the *empresario de colonización*, bought large tracts of land in order to develop them and then to sell.[9] This was done also by the railway companies which had bought, or been allocated, land on both sides of the track, sometimes to quite a significant extent. Another way has been to charge a monopolistic price for transportation services, and to attract thereby their share of the rent. In some cases, as in the case of the East India Company or the *Compagnie des*

Indes, exclusive trading rights have been obtained before the law. More recently trading companies, taking advantage of economies of scale, have been able to exert an equally efficient trade monopoly (perhaps oligopoly) by buying below standard prices and/or selling above. In the case of mineral lands, and of oil in particular, it is even clearer that the main purpose of exploration and of the ensuring exploitation of the fields is to reap the Ricardian rent.

But 'rent seeking' is just part of a more general entrepreneurial attitude.[10] If entrepreneurs are short of rents by which to add to their normal profits, they will try to replace them with quasi-rents, i.e. abnormally high profits stemming from oligopolistic situations of whatever kind. Schumpeter, who was capable of understanding (far better than Marshall) the nature of entrepreneurship, layed stress on the permanent striving after abnormal profits, which gave capitalism its dynamic character. While Schumpeter's emphasis on technological innovation was of a restricted kind,[11] the discovery of land can indeed be taken as a particular case of innovation. Entrepreneurs always strive to increase their profits; if discovery opens up new opportunities there may be a time when the priority becomes the full exploitation of new land. It is not that during the expansionary process entrepreneurs will stop innovating, rather that while land rents are within their easy reach, rents will be emphasized by entrepreneurs.

Once rents, or at least those which are easily attainable, are actually realized, the alternative path of sheer innovation will take first priority; it is a matter of where the greatest returns are to be made, whether by the opening up of new agricultural or mineral lands, or by the introduction of some new technology or product. But even if rents derived from geographical innovation, or quasi-rents derived from technological innovation, are two ways of increasing profits, there is a substantial difference between them. Agricultural rents provide a dynamic boost to the economy from the moment they are known to exist to the moment when they are returned. Once the new land is incorporated, they cease to be a dynamic factor; they contribute still to accumulation but they are quite static in character. Mineral rents are different from the outset, since they are exhaustible – a circumstance that induces strenuous search for new sources; they are therefore more dynamic in character, more like innovation. By contrast, quasi-rents, derived from innovation, are continuously at risk of being wiped out by new competitors, imperfect, Chamberlin-styled. This forces the entrepreneur to think of something new that will give him, if only for a while, an abnormal 'profit' (actually, an 'abnormal' quasi-rent). The transitory nature of quasi-rents, however, is of their essence, and it is not shared by rents. A great temptation, among late developers, is to replace rent-based growth once it begins to falter with a quasi-rent based development, not of the innovative Schumpeterian type but rather collusive mercantilist ('Colbertain', as it might be called). In fact, it is an easy way out for entrepreneurs, particulary when they can extract from their governments 'scarcity rights', i.e. transitory or permanent legal monopolies, subsidised inputs, transportation rebates, low interest credits, etc. In this way, quasi-rent can easily be created.

There is, however, a significant difference between the Schumpeterian quasi-rent and the 'Colbertian'. The Schumpeterian entrepreneur raises the level of efficiency in the use of resources, saves inputs, reduces costs, improves the quality, durability and performance of the product, and in so doing benefits the community, even if the lion's share or even the totality of the benefit may accrue to the innovator, at least in the initial stages. Sooner or later, according to the capacity (legal and technical) of the other entrepreneurs to copy and reproduce the invention, the benefit will spread to the whole of the economy. This will eliminate the quasi-rents that have accrued to the original innovator, who will be compelled to try repeating the process. But in so doing, he will contribute to the growth of the economy.

If, instead, the process is of a collusive character, although there may at first be some similarities the differences are more significant. In fact, even if a collusive quasi-rent does contribute to the process of accumulation, it is obtained at the expense of an optimal allocation of resources, and does not make any compensatory contribution either by cost reduction or improved product. Even more importantly, collusive quasi-rents are not dynamic in character: Colbertian entrepreneurs tend to have a defensive attitude – they try to keep what they already have. If the collusive quasi-rent is diffused, and this can only happen if the advantages or rights first granted to (or seized by) entrepreneurs become generalized, the economy will not benefit except by an increase in the stock of capital as a consequence of transitory quasi-rents.

Collusion contributes to accumulation – it is important to acknowledge this. But it does so at the expense of efficiency in the use of resources. If, however, innovation is beyond the capacity of entrepreneurs, the alternative is reduced to collusion and (modest) growth, or no accumulation and no growth. An initial, rent-based stage has been common to the growth processes of most areas of recent settlement. But they have differed in the evolution of rents as a source of accumulation. The United States, more than any other country, has relied rather on innovative quasi-rents, since many of the products required for expansion did not exist and had to be developed as the frontier spread. But the crucial question has been the ability to switch to innovation as soon as the frontier was closed (or lost its relative importance), both in the land-based sector and in the new capital employed in land. Those countries that chose to delay the necessary switch, or settled for collusion rather than innovation, put their growth in peril. Unfortunately it was Argentina that fell into the trap.

VI

My suggestions for the development process experienced by areas of recent settlement bring together part of the literature on the role of the frontier and also on innovation. They are indeed in line with the 'vent for surplus' element in Smith's and Mill's view of the role of trade, which emphasizes not so much the reallocation of resources as the effective use of previously under-employed resources, that is, an outward shift in the production possibility curve, rather than a movement along it. In each of the areas of recent settlement the role of land (free land) has received special attention. Foremost is Turner's well-known and forceful thesis, recently revived by North even for other areas and periods.[12] Canada has produced a more generalized version in the form of Innis' staple theory as refined by Watkins and others.[13] The theory (Innis) has the advantage of emphasizing the existence of different staples under those different technologies which have given their character to each of the various expansionary booms.

Oddly enough, both Argentina and Australia have been slower than the United States and Canada in understanding the peculiar nature of their processes of growth and the central role taken by natural resources. In Díaz Alejandro's work, for example, otherwise distinguished, the issue is set aside as an unnecessary diversion.[14] This is in line with the interpretation which maintains that the kind of development the country had enjoyed at the turn of the century could be the basis of continuous growth, and which attributed the difficulties later encountered to adverse international influence, to protectionism in the 1930s, to misconceived industrial policies in th 1950s, etc. While these, unquestionably, contributed, the fundamental issue has been the uniqueness an unrepeatability of a growth process based on the incorporation of land. Fortunately, new historiography since the 1960s has taken this into account,[15] and it is now beginning to be accepted even by some of those who had previously rejected it.[16] Australian scholarship has been more receptive than most, as Fogarty's contribution to the present book suggests,[17] and others have toyed with the idea.[18]

It would seem, in fact, that the alternation of agricultural and mineral expansion – two different kinds of 'land' exploitation – and the diffusion of mineral wealth, have blurred definitions of the role and peculiarity of frontier expansion. Australia, perhaps, still awaits a Turner, an Innis or a North. While the free land hypothesis which lies behind these models is not the same as Lewis's unlimited supply of labour model,[19] it is similar in spirit.[20] In Lewis's model the 'exhaustion' of the pool of unemployed in 'the industrial labour reserve', as Marx would have put it, marks a similarly qualitative turning point in the growth process, i.e. from a stage when the incorporation of labour is increasing productivity to another when labour's productivity improves as a consequence of a better reallocation of resources.

While my view is part and parcel of this tradition, I have tried to place it within a more general version of Schumpeter's view of innovation. I am arguing that innovation has to be seen more comprehensively so that it incorporates innovation; both discovery and technological innovation must receive similar treatment. Rents and innovative quasi-rents are the source of a sound growth process; collusive quasi-rents, on the other hand, can be only a temporary substitute – one that will soon encounter diminishing returns, at least if compared with those derived from technological innovation.

But one of the crucial differences between a rent-based or a quasi-rent-based process of growth is the different time paths. A process based on the appropriation of rents 'lying fallow beyond the frontier' is one that is bound to reach an end. Not that rents will disappear – the intramarginal producers will continue to enjoy them – but the frontier's entrepreneur will have lost his zest; he is operating now in a marginal, no-rent area with nothing beyond the frontier from which rent may be extracted, no matter how much is invested. This kind of area of new settlement was bound to see its rates of growth falter after initial colonization. Argentina behaved, to some extent, in this fairly predictable fashion. But the same was not true for the other countries. It must be acknowledged that the ability of the United States, Canada and Australia to continue a process of vigorous growth even at the end of the expansion of the frontier has been a most extraordinary feat, and one that could not be taken for granted.

At that point the successful cases were able to move to a quasi-rent-based stage – early for the most successful of all, the United States, less so for Canada and Australia, and rather later for Argentina; further development for the United States and Canada was more clearly based on innovation, and less so in Australia. For Argentina it arose exclusively from collusive quasi-rents. To the extent that development was based on innovation, these countries were switching to an alternative and unlimited source of growth. To the extent that it was based on collusion, it opened up a limited, alternative path.

It is possible to develop a comprehensive formula which includes rents and quasi-rents (of whatever source) as the basis for the process of accumulation. The analysis of such shifts and movements, forward and backward, and of the mingling of sources and their interaction, can help in explaining the process of growth in areas of recent settlement, i.e. the initial boom, and the problems encountered when a shift to a different source of accumulation had to be identified if growth were to continue. Failure was more probable than success. But it was the modern industrial revolution that shifted the odds and made possible the improbable. This turned out to be the case for most areas of recent settlement, but not, alas, for Argentina.

NOTES

1. R. Nurkse, *Patterns of Trade and Development* (Oxford: Blackwell, 1961).
2. J. Fisher and E. Boorstein, 'The Adequacy of Resources for Economic Growth in the United States', Study Paper No. 13 (Washington, DC: USGPO, 1959).
3. T. W. Schultz, 'The Declining Importance of Agricultural Land', *Economic Journal*, December 1951.
4. W. W. Rostow, 'Technology and Unemployment in the Western World' (mimeo), Oxford, November 1982.
5. H. J. Habakkuk, *American and British Technology in the XIXth Century* (Cambridge University Press, 1962), particularly ch. III.
6. Adam Smith, *The Wealth of Nations* (London: Methuen, 1950 edn), ch. VII, part 2.
7. C. W. Reynolds, 'The New Terms of Trade Problems: Economic Rents in International Exchange', in C. P. Kindleberger and G. di Tella (eds), *Economics in the Long View* (London: Macmillan, 1982).
8. D. S. Landes, 'Technological Change and Development in Western

Europe, 1750–1914', in *Cambridge Economic History of Europe*, Vol. VI, part 1 (Cambridge University Press, 1966).

9. A. Bogue and M. Bogue, 'Profits and the Frontier Land Speculator', *Journal of Economic History* (March 1957), and R. Swierenga, 'Land Speculator "Profits" Reconsidered', *Journal of Economic History* (March 1966).
10. The phrase comes from A. Krueger, 'The Political Economy of a Rent-Seeking Society', *American Economic Review* (June 1974).
11. J. Schumpeter, *The Theory of Economic Development* (Cambridge, Mass.: Harvard University Press, 1934; first pub., in German, 1911).
12. F. J. Turner, 'The Significance of the Frontier in American History', *Proceedings of the State Historical Society* (Wisconsin, December 1893); Douglass North, 'Location Theory and Regional Economic Growth', *Journal of Political Economy* (June 1955); North and R. Thomas, *The Rise of the Western World* (Cambridge University Press, 1973), particularly ch. 25.
13. H. A. Innis, *The Fur Trade in Canada* (Toronto University Press, 1956), particularly last chapter; M. Watkins, 'A Staple Theory of Economic Growth', *Canadian Journal of Economics and Political Science* (May 1963).
14. Carlos Díaz Alejandro, *Essays on the Economic History of the Argentine Republic* (New Haven, Conn.: Yale University Press, 1970).
15. Guido di Tella and M. Zymelman, 'Etapas del Desarrollo Económico Latino Americano', *Revista de Economía Latino-Americana*, II:2 (Abril/Junio 1961); di Tella, *La Estrategía del Desarrollo Indirecto* (Buenos Aires: Paídos, 1972) ch. 2; T. Halperín, 'La expansión de la Frontera de Buenos Aires, 1810–1952', in A. Jara (ed.), *Tierras Nuevas* (El Colegio de México, 1969); Halperin, 'Intimations of Mortality', in G. di Tella and D. C. M. Platt (eds), 'The Political Economy of Argentina, 1880–1950', to be published by Macmillan (London) in 1986; Roberto Cortés Conde, 'Algunos Rasgos de la Expansión Territorial de la Argentina en la Segunda Mitad del Siglo XIX', *Desarrollo Económico* (April/June, 1968); E. Gallo, 'Expansion and Industrial Development in Argentina, 1880–1930', R. Carr (ed.), *Latin American Affairs* (Oxford University Press, 1970); L. Geller, 'El Crecimiento Industrial Argentino hasta 1914 y la Teoría del Bien Primario Exportable', *Trimestre Económico* (October–December 1970).
16. Carlos Díaz Alejandro, ch. 5 in this volume.
17. J. Fogarty, ch. 1 in this volume.
18. G. Blainey, 'A Theory of Mineral Discovery; Australia in the XIX Century', *Economic History Review* (August 1970); J. W. McCarty, 'The Staple Approach in Australian Economic History', *Business Archives and History*, VI (1964).
19. A. Lewis, 'Economic Development with Unlimited Supplies of Labour', *Manchester School* (May 1954).
20. R. Caves, 'Vent for Surplus Models of Trade and Growth', in Baldwin (ed.), *Trade Growth and the Balance of Payments* (Amsterdam, 1965).

3 Land Tenure and Land Settlement: Policy and Patterns in the Canadian Prairies and the Argentine Pampas, 1880–1930

CARL E. SOLBERG

I INTRODUCTION

Argentina and Canada were two of a small group of historically favoured new countries that emerged in the nineteenth century. Although European settlement had existed in Argentina since the sixteenth century and in Canada since the seventeenth, both countries contained vast and rich grassland regions that remained virtually unpopulated until the nineteenth century. The prairies and the pampas made Argentina and Canada land-surplus rather than labour-surplus countries, and when the international trading economy expanded dynamically in the late nineteenth century, both regions and both countries underwent a dramatic transformation. Foreign capital, technology and labour poured in to develop the thriving agrarian economy that took root in both regions, and by the late 1890s, vast quantities of farm products flowed out to the hungry markets of Europe. As a result of the development of the prairies and the pampas, Canada and Argentina were among the leading world agricultural exporters by 1914, and both countries retained their primacy through the 1920s.

There were other historical similarities as well. Argentina and

Canada began their existence as organized states during the 1860s. A long series of civil and foreign wars followed Argentina's declaration of independence from Spain in 1816; it was not until 1862 that the national capital effectively established dominion over the interior provinces, previously largely autonomous. Canada became a self-governing Dominion in 1867, and acquired Rupert's Land, the vast territory of the Hudson's Bay Company that included the prairies, in 1869. By the mid-1880s, both the Argentine and Canadian governments had subdued the nomadic Indian peoples who roamed the prairies and the pampas – although Canadian Indians were placed on reserves, while pampa Indians were largely exterminated. Both governments also had to deal with *mestizo* horsemen (called *métis* in Canada) who long had inhabited the great open grasslands. In Canada, *métis* resistance was crushed during the Northwest Rebellion of 1885; in Argentina, its equivalent (better known as the *gauchos*) submitted to the Buenos Aires government by the early 1870s. In this way, both governments established unquestioned control over their open grasslands by the mid-1880s, and could then devote their attention to large-scale agricultural development.

Despite these parallels, there were also notable contrasts between prairie and pampa development, contrasts which reflected the distinct policies that Argentine and Canadian governments used to transform their grasslands into agricultural exporting regions. Argentina and Canada followed very different rural marketing, transport, and educational policies, but perhaps the most fundamental contrast was in their land policy. As a result, the prairies filled up with owner-operator farms, while on the pampas, large estates prevailed and most farmers were tenants. Very different patterns of social and cultural life resulted from these settlement patterns, but in the world wheat market the tenant farmers of Argentina were highly effective competitors with the smallholders of Canada.

This chapter examines and compares the land policies that the two governments formulated during the half-century that preceded the Great Depression. The analysis centres around the impact that distinct land tenure systems made on agrarian society and the agricultural economy in the prairies and the pampas. Although our focus falls primarily on the era of export expansion and generally high agricultural prices that ended in the late 1920s, we will also discuss how land tenure systems affected the economic viability of Canadian and Argentine agriculture when market prices collapsed in the 1930s.

II LAND POLICY IN THE PRAIRIES

Most prairie farmers owned their land (see Table 3.1), a pattern that resulted from the Homestead policy adopted by Canada's first Prime Minister, Sir John A. Macdonald, in 1872. This free land policy was a major event in prairie development, but it was only part of a much more ambitious development strategy, the famous National Policy, that Macdonald and the dominant Conservative Party had put into effect by the 1880s. Reflecting the expansionary interests of the financial and commercial élites of Ontario and Quebec, the National Policy aimed to keep the West out of the clutches of the United States and to create a viable trans-continental economy. To carry out this policy, Macdonald enacted tariffs to protect Canadian industries, built the Canadian Pacific Railway across the continent against formidable odds, and promoted the settlement of the West to produce a new export staple and to provide a market for the emerging industries of Ontario and Quebec.[1] The opposition Liberals, who theoretically opposed tariff protectionism, in fact continued the National Policy when in office between 1896 and 1911. Macdonald, in other words, by acting early and decisively, had shaped the economic structure of modern Canada.

To achieve the aims of the National Policy, the federal government administered the prairies as part of the Northwest Territories until Alberta and Saskatchewan became provinces in 1905 (Manitoba had become a province in 1870). And, until 1929, the federal government controlled the public lands in all three prairie provinces. It had alienated great expanses of this land by the time large-scale settlement began. Under the terms of the transfer of Rupert's Land to Canada, the Hudson's Bay Company had received 1/20 of the prairies as part compensation. The Macdonald government granted 25 million acres to the Canadian Pacific Railway, and later provincial administrations made grants to other railroad companies. Other lands were set aside for the *métis* (who soon lost most of them to speculators), for Indian reserves, and for the support of public education.[2]

But the vast bulk of prairie land remained in the public domain, and the Homestead Act made it available to any man who was head of a family or 21 years old. On payment of a $10 filing fee, he could apply for a quarter-section (160 acres) of land and, at the end of three years, could obtain title if he was or had become a British subject, and if he had met certain conditions of residence and of cultivation. Later

TABLE 3.1 *Land tenure in the Argentine and Canadian cereal belt, 1911–33 (numbers in '000s)*

Type of Tenure	*Prairies*[d] *1911*		*1921*		*1931*		*Pampas*[e] *1912–13*		*1923–4*		*1932–3*	
	Number	*% total*	*Number*	*% total*	*Number*	*% total*	*Number*	*% total*	*Number*	*% total*	*Number*	*% total*
Owners	180.0	89.3	202.9	80.0	198.8	69.2	24.4	32.6	42.1	35.7	47.8	35.8
Renters[a]	10.5	5.2	27.1	10.6	42.7	14.9	46.3	55.1	65.2	55.3	80.8	61.0
Others[b]	10.7	5.3	25.6	9.4	45.6	15.9	10.3	12.3	10.5	8.9	4.2	3.2
Totals[c]	201.2	99.8	255.6	100.0	287.1	100.0	81.0	100.0	117.8	99.9	132.8	100.0

[a] Includes cash and share renters in Canada.
[b] 'Others' includes sharecroppers in Argentina; part-owners and part-renters in Canada.
[c] Percentages may not add up because of rounding.
[d] In this and subsequent tables, the prairies include Manitoba, Saskatchewan, and Alberta.
[e] In this and subsequent tables, the pampas include Buenos Aires, Santa Fe, Córdoba and Entre Rios provinces as well as La Pampa territory.

SOURCES R. W. Murchie, *Agricultural Progress on the Prairie Frontier* (Toronto: The Macmillan Company of Canada, 1936) p. 102; Argentine Republic, Ministerio de Agricultura de la Nación, Dirección de Economía Rural y Estadística, *Anuario agropecuario: Año 1935* (Buenos Aires, 1935) p. 487.

amendments enabled farmers to 'pre-empt' and then purchase another quarter-section for $1 per acre.[3]

Despite this offer of land, before the mid-1890s the prairie population grew slowly and agriculture made little headway (see Tables 3.2 and 3.3). Political unrest, which culminated in the 1885 Northwest

TABLE 3.2 *Growth of population in the prairies and the pampas, 1891–1931*

	1891[a]	*1914*[b]	*1931*
Prairies	251 473[c]	1 328 121	2 353 529
Pampas	1 987 512	3 227 988	5 761 586[d]

[a] Argentine figures for 1895.
[b] Canadian figures for 1911.
[c] Includes Yukon and Northwest Territories.
[d] Estimate.

SOURCES Argentine Republic, Dirección General de Estadística, *Tercer censo nacional, levantado el 1º de junio de 1914*, vol. II (Buenos Aires, 1916–17) p. 109; Argentine Republic, Comité Nacional de Geografia, *Anuario geográfico argentino* (Buenos Aires, 1941) p. 151; Daniel Kubat and David Thornton, *A Statistical Portrait of Canadian Society* (Toronto: McGraw Hill-Ryerson Limited, 1974) pp. 12–16.

TABLE 3.3 *Area under cultivation in the prairies and the pampas, 1890–1927 ('000 hectares, cereals and flaxseed)*

	1890	*1915–16*	*1926–7*
Prairies	564	9 168	13 954
Pampas	1 738	13 020	15 969
Alfalfa	390	6 670	4 820

Argentine statistics for alfalfa are in addition to cereals and flaxseed area.

SOURCES Ernesto Tornquist & Cía., Ltda., *El desarrollo económico de la República Argentina en los últimos cincuenta años* (Buenos Aires, 1920) p. 22; Sociedad Rural Argentina, *Anuario de la Sociedad Rural Argentina: Estadísticas económicas y agrarias* (Buenos Aires, 1928) pp. 119–24; Canada, Census and Statistics Office, *Fifth Census of Canada, 1911*, vol. IV (Ottawa, 1912) p. 408; Canada, Dominion Bureau of Statistics, *Seventh Census of Canada, 1931*, vol. VIII (Ottawa, 1933–36) pp. 540, 592, 664.

Rebellion, along with a series of poor crop years, the attraction of neighbouring American states for immigrants, high transport costs, and low wheat prices, all combined to discourage settlement in the Canadian prairies. But after 1896, wheat prices rose and railway freight rates fell. Moreover, Dominion agricultural experiment stations developed and publicized new dry-farming techniques as well as new, quick-maturing strains of wheat, an important factor given the sometimes early prairie frosts. Once the economic and technical conditions for profitable wheat production were present, the 'greatest rush for farm lands in the world's history' took place as immigrants flocked into the prairies. By 1911, the population was 1.3 million, and 9.2 million hectares were under cultivation.[4]

III THE PRAIRIE CO-OPERATIVE TRADITION

A vigorous and dynamic group spirit and co-operative ethic emerged among the homesteaders. British, Scandinavian, and German immigrants, as well as migrants from Ontario, brought with them a rich heritage of experience in the consumer co-operative movement, and the prairie land tenure system of family-owned farms enabled the co-op tradition to become firmly rooted. Farmers were loyal to the co-operatives out of economic necessity, for they could reduce costs by pooling their efforts in joint concerns. This was an important consideration for prairie farmers, who were chronically short of capital and who were faced with a large initial investment when they started farming. By the 1920s, the co-operative movement expanded to include a giant farmers' wheat-marketing association, the Canadian Wheat Pools.[5] Prairie settlers formed not only economic co-ops but also social, recreational, and mutual aid associations of all kinds. The result was, as one rural sociologist pointed out, that Saskatchewan 'may in fact have the highest saturation of rural organizations of any region in the world'.[6]

The co-operative movement provided much of the economic framework for the material and cultural standard of prairie farm life. This standard grew rapidly and, by the early twentieth century, far exceeded the average for Argentine farmers. Although numerous exceptions existed, especially among newcomers and settlers in fringe areas, housing was decent if plain. In established farm communities the original sod or log house gave way to wood frame structures. Over 50 per cent of these farm houses had telephones by 1930. Another widespread convenience on prairie farms was the automobile – almost half the farmers in the Canadian West owned one in 1931.[7]

Public education developed rapidly; by 1931 the literacy rate was over 95 per cent in all provinces (see Table 3.4). Many farmers were

TABLE 3.4 *Social indicators, Argentine pampas and Canadian prairies, 1930s*

Indicator	*Year*	*Location*	*Measure*	*Pampas*	*Prairies*
A. Illegitimacy					
	1936	Saskatchewan:	per 1000 live births		36
	1937	Santa Fe Prov.:	ditto	203	
B. Illiteracy					
	1931	Prairie Provs:	% age 10 and over		4.0
	1943	Pampa Provs:	% age 14 and over	11.8–21.5[a]	
C. Infant mortality					
	1934	Saskatchewan:	per 1000 live births		55
	1931–5	Santa Fe Prov.:	ditto	83.8	
	1931–5	Córdoba Prov.:	ditto	111.7	

[a] Illiteracy rates for 1943: Buenos Aires province 11.8, Santa Fe 14.9, La Pampa 16.5, Córdoba 16.7, Entre Ríos 21.5.

SOURCES A. Illegitimacy.
Canada: G. E. Britnell, *The Wheat Economy* (Toronto: University of Toronto Press, 1939) p. 19.
Argentina: Carl C. Taylor, *Rural Life in Argentina* (Baton Rouge: Louisiana State University Press, 1947) p. 334.
B. Illiteracy.
Canada: Canada, Dominion Bureau of Statistics, *Seventh Census of Canada*, 1931, vol. I (Ottawa, 1933–36) p. 1068.
Argentina: Taylor, *Rural Life*, p. 316.
C. Infant mortality.
Canada: *Canada Year Book, 1936*, p. 176.
Argentina: Alejandro E. Bunge, *Una nueva Argentina* (Buenos Aires: Editorial Guillermo Kraft Ltda., 1940) p. 85;
Argentine Republic, Comité Nacional de Geografia, *Anuario geográfico argentino* (Buenos Aires, 1941) p. 174.

voracious readers in the off-season; the Saskatchewan government had a Travelling Library Service with over 100 000 volumes ('thank goodness' exclaimed one settler), and the *Grain Growers' Guide*, the premier farmers' newspaper and one of high quality, had a circulation of 120 000 by 1926.[8] Health care also was making notable strides. In Saskatchewan, it improved rapidly after the introduction of 'municipal doctors', supported by local taxes in 1916; in all three provinces the infant mortality rate fell steadily. Illegitimacy rates in the prairie provinces were lower than the national average.[9]

By the late 1920s, then, prairie farm society had become securely established around a solid co-operative framework. Living standards were improving. But meanwhile, mortgages and taxes were high, the Canadian tariff kept the cost of living above that in the United States, and debts were rising. The material and cultural standard of life could only be supported when the market price of wheat was high enough to cover the cost of wheat production – a cost that these very standards of a well-ordered and cultured community had helped to inflate.

IV LAND PRICE INFLATION AND MORTGAGES

The rapidly rising cost of land was one warning of the unstable economic foundations of prairie farming. Despite the apparently generous provisions of the Homestead Laws, they contained some major flaws. For one thing, vast amounts of land remained in the hands of the Canadian Pacific Railway, other railways, and the Hudson's Bay Company. A second problem was that the 1872 act had provided for purchase of land at $1 per acre up to 640 acres; this was, as one scholar puts it, 'an open invitation to land speculators'.[10] And speculation did indeed flourish. As a German traveller observed in 1909, 'in the Canadian West more or less everybody speculates in land'. Thousands of men who obtained homesteads had no intention of becoming farmers. Instead, they 'proved up', gained title, and then sold out. Land prices shot up rapidly – 123 per cent in Manitoba, 185 per cent in Saskatchewan, and 201 per cent in Alberta between 1900 and 1910.[11]

By the early 1920s, moreover, it was apparent that the original 160 or 320 acre homestead plots were too small for profitable grain farming, especially where environmental conditions were not optimal. Farmers who wished to expand had to resort to the private land market, and when they did buy more land (or in the 1920s, when people entered farming for the first time) they generally had to take out a mortgage. As a result, mortgages and other long-term debts were becoming a major burden throughout the prairie provinces.[12] As early as 1915, a Scottish traveller wrote of the prairies – that 'the whole country is shadowed by debt'. When depression and drought hit the prairies in the 1930s, mortgage debt as a percentage of the value of farm property was 49 per cent in Manitoba and 38 per cent in Saskatchewan and Alberta. Saskatchewan, wrote G. E. Britnell, was essentially a 'debtor community', an extremely perilous situation when wheat prices fell.[13]

The high price of land and frequent foreclosures stimulated a shift from ownership to renting among prairie farmers in the 1920s (see Table 3.1). Sharecrop tenancy on contracts of five years or less was the most common system used in Western Canada.[14] Many observers of the Canadian agricultural scene viewed the rise of tenancy with deep misgiving, and agreed that it resulted in soil destruction, especially when leases were short-term. Some observers, however, also pointed to one advantage of tenancy – during periods of low prices it allowed renters more flexibility and higher earnings than mortgage-laden landowners.[15]

V LAND TENURE IN THE PAMPAS

Indeed, high land prices and mortgage obligations were basic weaknesses of prairie wheat farming – they helped keep the cost of production high, especially in comparison with the very different land tenure system of Argentina. In the pampas, over 60 per cent of farmers were sharecrop or cash tenants (see Table 3.1), and tenancy was the central feature of Argentine farming. This land tenure system reflected the distribution of political power between the central and provincial governments. In Candada, Ottawa retained jurisdiction over disposition of prairie lands until 1929, and the Canadian federal government used this authority to promote the emergence of a smallholder society. But in Argentina, the 1853 Constitution gave the provinces authority over the public lands, while the central government lacked jurisdiction over land distribution except in the national territories. But with the exception of parts of La Pampa territory, the good farm lands of the pampas were all within Buenos Aires, Córdoba, Santa Fe, and Entre Rios provinces. The result, as one Argentine scholar put it, was a 'pulverization of authority'. Despite the desire of nineteenth-century statesmen like Sarmiento and Avellaneda to create a smallholder society, the Argentine federal government never was able to carry out a co-ordinated, land settlement programme.[16] The federal government did desire to promote agricultural production and exports, and to accomplish this end, it encouraged massive immigration and construction of a large railway network. But the central government had to leave land policy to the provinces.

Unlike the Canadian prairies, the pampa provinces contained a well-established landed élite whose holdings in some cases dated from the colonial period, and in other cases from the first half of the nineteenth century. This élite, which had specialized traditionally in cattle and sheep raising (activities that were land rather than labour intensive) became interested in promoting agricultural development and European immigration when world demand for grain increased late in the century. But these *estancieros* (owners of large estates) were not interested in promoting large-scale settlement of small farm owners. Instead, as we shall see, they viewed agriculture as an activity complementary and subsidiary to cattle raising.

Despite the prevalence of large estates, in the 1860s and 1870s the provinces steadily rolled back the Indian frontier, and in the process acquired vast expanses of publicly-owned land. But the provincial governments were in dire financial straits, partly because of the expense of the Indian wars. To raise funds, both Santa Fe and Córdoba adopted a policy of selling public lands, often in large chunks of a square league or more, to cattlemen or entrepreneurs who divided their large purchases and rented plots to immigrant farmers. In addition, governments granted land to railway companies, although to a much smaller extent than was occurring in Canada.[17]

Exceptions to this pattern of great estates and rented farms were found mainly in parts of Santa Fe, Córdoba and Entre Ríos. As early as the 1850s, the government of Santa Fe, motivated by a desire to populate the frontier as a buffer against Indians, began to provide public lands for immigrant colonization. These early plans, which were also tried in Córdoba and Entre Ríos, were successful, and thousands of the early settlers in immigrant colonies became farm owners by the 1880s. But due to the rapidly rising price of land and the continuing penury of the provincial treasuries, these land programmes virtually ceased by 1895.[18]

Buenos Aires, largest of the pampa provinces, gave practically no help to aspiring small farm owners. An 1887 law, the ostensible purpose of which was to promote growth of a smallholder class, did little more than aid speculators, and became a public scandal.[19] Land prices rose too fast for most tenants to buy. Between 1903 and 1912, average land prices in Buenos Aires quadrupled, while cereal prices rose only 28 per cent. As in the prairies, land in the pampas became an object of intense speculation. Georges Clemenceau, who visited Argentina in 1910, noted that 'the form of gambling which is special to Buenos Aires is unbridled speculation in land'.[20]

As a result of these land policies, by the 1890s, when large-scale agriculture began, land companies and *estancieros* owned most of the pampas. As late as 1924, 60 per cent of the total area of the four provinces and one territory in the cereal zone was in the hands of 12 673 landowners who owned 1000 hectares or more; 33.4 per cent was held in properties of 5000 hectares or more. In the province of Buenos Aires, 14 families possessed 100 000 hectares or more (one family held 412 000 hectares).[21]

Despite the difficulty of buying land, Argentina offered economic opportunity, and immigrants flocked into the pampas by the 1880s. Among the Southern Europeans who composed most of Argentina's immigrants were numerous, poor but ambitious individuals who were willing to enter agriculture as sharecroppers or renters. These people were aware that the tenancy system – at least if good luck and high prices prevailed – offered farmers the opportunity to make money which pampa immigrants often intended to use to move to the city or back to Europe.[22] This abundant supply of immigrant labour enabled the pampas to grow spectacularly. Indeed, as Tables 3.2 and 3.3 show, both population and the area under cultivation in the pampas were larger than in the Canadian prairies through the 1920s, although it should be noted that the urban population of the pampas was much larger than in the prairies. This extraordinary growth was in part due to the government's liberal immigration policy, which welcomed all able-bodied Europeans and which actively recruited Spaniards and Italians just at the time when Southern European emigration was reaching its height. In contrast, Canadian immigration policy was much more selective, and divided Europeans into 'preferred' and 'non-preferred races'. Spaniards and Italians were among the latter category.[23]

The pampas' relatively large population and cultivated area was also due to the earlier development of agriculture in the region than in the prairies where, as we have seen, the settlement boom did not get underway until the mid-1890s. During the 1880s, improved transportation, abundant labour, and the introduction of mechanization brought the onset of an agricultural export boom on the pampas. With few exceptions, wheat production and exports continued to expand during the 1890s, a trend that was due to the low price of Argentine wheat abroad. The relative cheapness of pampa wheat resulted in part from the depreciation of the paper peso during the 1890s, and partly from Argentina's low cost of production. Indeed, the *Financial News* of London noted in 1894 that the cost of wheat production in Argentina was so low that it would 'blanch the hair of American farmers'.[24]

Throughout this era of rapid expansion in the pampas, the land tenure system subordinated agriculture to the extremely profitable business of cattle raising. 'No business in Argentina of the same importance has shown such good returns as cattle breeding, and these results have been chiefly brought about by the introduction of alfalfa', wrote cattleman Campbell Ogilvie in 1910. Alfalfa, as he suggested, was a lucrative plant – steers fed on it could be sent to market sooner than those fed on native pampa grass. Indeed, the expansion of area under alfalfa from 400 000 hectares in 1890 to 6.7 million by 1915 (Table 3.3) enabled the spectacular growth of Argentine cattle-raising to occur. Cattlemen found that the land tenure system was ideal, for it enabled them, with little cost or risk, to rent land to tenant farmers on condition that they sowed alfalfa during the last year of their contract.[25] Alfalfa is a long lasting crop – up to 16 years in Argentina – but when it began to run out, estancieros would bring tenant farmers in again to sow grain crops and to prepare the land anew for alfalfa. As one Argentina writer pithily summarized this system, 'at one moment it may be more convenient to have more "cows than gringos" [a common Argentine term for Italians], and the next year to have more "gringos than cows" '.[26] In this respect, the Argentine land tenure system was a highly efficient mechanism that enabled flexible use of the pampas without requiring fertilizers or exhausting the soil.[27]

Although many Argentine tenants had begun as *medianeros* (share-croppers), by the end of the First World War the vast majority had accumulated enough capital to become *arrendatarios* (renters). The renter was a rural capitalist who often owned a variety of machinery and who rented large expanses (500 hectares or more). One result of the extensive nature of pampa farming was abuse of the soil: Rolf Sternberg, who farmed in Entre Ríos before moving to the United States to become a geography professor, noted that 'tenant farmers viewed land as something to be exploited and then to be left discarded'.[28] But extensive farming also meant that if prices were high, the grasshoppers stayed away, and the weather were favourable, *arrendatarios* could reap substantial profits. As early as 1904, one agricultural expert noted the 'fever of rapid enrichment' that encouraged land speculation among renters. Some of them even sublet part of their land to *medianeros*. 'These Italian peasants', concluded one English observer in 1911, 'living though they do in a very rough and uncomfortable way, appear to handle and to make a good deal of money.'[29]

The level of rents varied with prevailing land price trends which in turn reflected market circumstances for Argentine produce. During periods of prosperity, rents rose steadily – often faster than crop prices – but when markets showed a long-term downward trend, rents fell. In fact, between 1930 and 1933 the average cash rent in the cereal zone dropped 40 per cent, while average wheat prices also dropped 40 per cent.[30] This unprecedented decline in rents, however, forced numerous landowners to the verge of bankruptcy, for as in Canada, mortgages burdened Argentine rural property heavily. Total rural mortgage debt reached 2.3 billion by the early 1930s, or 35 to 40 per cent of the value of pampa rural property. In 1933, the government saved much of the landed class from what the *Review of the River Plate* called a 'carnival of foreclosures' by enacting a national mortgage moratorium over the strong protests of banks and insurance companies. This measure lasted from 1933 to 1938 and enabled rents to fall still more, to 50 per cent of the 1930 level in 1934 and 1935.[31] In other words, the cost of land – one of the principal determinants of the cost of crop production – was not a fixed cost as it was for so many Canadian farmers. Although at least one prairie province – Alberta – did enact a moratorium during the 1930s, the prairies suffered a wave of foreclosures. Of course, Argentine farmers also suffered, and often severely, when crop prices fell during the period of rental contracts. But the flexible rent structure was one reason why Argentina could undersell Canada in the world wheat market during the 1930s.

Numerous observers have concluded that many of the evils that afflict Argentine agriculture flow from this land system. They emphasize that short-term tenancy led to soil abuse, extensive and irrational cultivation, low yields, and the continuing impoverishment of the rural population.[32] Unquestionably many farmers were impoverished, and they did desire longer term contracts, compensation for physical improvements to the property, and rent reductions when crop prices fell suddenly. A 1921 tenancy reform law did in fact provide for minimum-term contracts and for compensation for improvements, but it contained numerous loopholes and was finally amended in 1932.

Certainly many tenants wanted to buy their land, and thousands of them did so, as analysis of cadastral records for the 1920s demonstrates and as Table 3.1 suggests. But most renters found it extremely difficult to accumulate the capital needed to become owners.[33]

Nonetheless, there is evidence that renters did not necessarily object to their temporary status. Many did not plan to remain in the pampas or even in Argentina. In a highly revealing comment, Esteban Piacenza, President of the Federación Agraria Argentina, the principal farmers' organization, confirmed this tendency. Farmers, he said, 'have migrated to this country . . . to work a few years, as few as possible, to make some money and then to return. . . . No-one has come here from his homeland with the thought of remaining'. This was an exaggeration, for numerous immigrants did desire to remain, but it does appear that during the era of international labour mobility prior to 1930, the land rental system did suit the economic interests of numerous immigrants.[34]

VI THE NOMADIC SOCIETY OF THE PAMPAS

The economic benefits of the tenancy system, then, were not necessarily limited to the landlords, but as H. S. Ferns notes, while the system 'did not necessarily impoverish the tenants . . . it tended to impoverish rural life'.[35] The prevalence of renters blocked formation of a close-knit society that could foster a sense of community and the emergence of strong rural organizations. And as time went by, the term of rental contracts grew shorter. In the nineteenth century they were often for five years, but by 1914, as Delich's study of Córdoba shows, the term of most contracts was three years or less. Because of the instability of tenure, 'the prevailing system of land leasing', as Sternberg argues, 'reduced tenant farmers to agricultural nomads'. Contemporary observers fully agreed; one likened the farmer to the 'wandering Jew', and another to an 'agricultural Arab'.[36]

With the farm population constantly in flux, co-operative organizations were much weaker in the pampas than in the prairies. Outside the area of the early colonization experiments where the bulk of the farmers had become owners, co-operatives or social and cultural associations were rare. Indeed, as late as 1937, there were only 106 rural commercial co-ops in all Argentina. Their total membership was 32 000. The first co-op grain elevator in Argentina began to operate in 1930; by that time there were well over a thousand co-op elevators in the prairies, and the Canadian Wheat Pools had 143 000 members.[37] The isolation of rural life did play a role in the weakness of these organizations on the pampas; in the prairies, organized farmers were able to overcome that problem – and in much worse weather conditions.[38]

Community life could hardly be expected to emerge on the pampas when few tenants bothered to build houses. 'They had no real houses, but merely uncomfortable adobe and mud hovels', wrote one English observer in 1911, 'yet there is plenty of money to be made.'[39] Few renters bothered to plant shade trees (despite the heat), a condition that shocked numerous observers of the Argentine rural scene. Even vegetable gardens were rare.[40] A poem by José Padroni expressed the bleakness of tenant farms:

No one planted a tree
And on the farms there were no sheep
Birds did not sing, the soft murmur
Of bleating lambs was absent.
Mothers raised sad children.[41]

Although the Argentine educational system improved greatly in the late nineteenth century, it remained inadequate to the task, and the illiteracy rate remained higher in the pampas than in the prairies (see Table 3.4). In part, the malaise of education was due to inadequate financing: in 1937 the Argentine economist Alejandro Bunge calculated that total government expenditures on education were 19.6 paper pesos per person in Argentina (the equivalent of 41.7 in Canada). Although these figures do not take regional variations into account, all evidence points to the generally poor situation of education on the pampas when compared with the prairies.[42] Moreover, unlike the situation in the prairies, farmers of the pampas did not read much. Antonio Diecidue, a Santa Fe agrarian leader, recalled that in 1912, 'with very few exceptions, it was difficult to find a book, a newspaper, or a magazine in the farmers' houses'. *La Tierra*, the newspaper of the Federación Agraria Argentina, had a circulation in the mid-1920s of only about one-sixth of that of the *Grain Growers' Guide*.[43]

If the standard of culture was not high, neither was public health particularly advanced for this period. The infant mortality rate, as Table 3.4 shows, was much higher on the pampas than on the prairies and, although rural towns had doctors, local *curanderos* (folk healers) practised among a large clientèle.[44] Yet another consequence of the rootless and insecure life of the rural population was a very high illegitimacy rate. Illegitimacy appears to have been higher among the native Argentine poor than it was among immigrants, but this trend was also true in the prairies, where the illegitimacy rate was higher among *métis* and Indians than among the rest of the population. In any case, Carl Taylor concluded of the pampas that 'thousands of farm people are living in a cultural no-man's-land' and numerous children grew up bearing what Argentine culture considered a serious social stigma.[45]

VII CANADIAN IMPRESSIONS OF PAMPA AGRICULTURE

Canadians were interested in Argentine farming primarily because Canada's wheat exports, the mainstay of the prairie economy, competed with Argentine wheat for the same overseas markets. But throughout the 1910s and most of the 1920s, Canadian analysts did not consider Argentina a particularly threatening competitor. Shocked by the low levels of social and cultural life they witnessed among pampa farmers, Canadians assumed that, as one 1913 writer in the *Grain Growers' Guide* put it, 'such nomadic farming can never build up a nation', especially when this factor was 'allied to a low order of intelligence and out-of-date methods of agriculture'. On the basis of these assumptions, Argentina could 'never rival Canada . . . in the production of strong wheat'. Indeed, Canadian observers often referred disparagingly to the ethnic origins of pampa farmers. As late as 1919, another writer in the *Guide* predicted that Argentina would not become a major competitor of Canada, for 'the genius of its Spanish [sic] population is all against grain growing'.[46]

W. J. Jackman, who was sent by the Canadian Wheat Pools in the 1920s to study Argentine wheat growing, and whose reports strongly influenced Canadian evaluations of pampa agriculture, constantly stressed the low living standards and insecurity of tenure in Argentina. Until the end of the 1920s, Jackman refused to take Argentina seriously as a major competitor in the world wheat market. He assumed that the itinerant nature of Argentine farming meant poor quality wheat and a lack of standards that would unfavourably impress European buyers. Moreover, the population of Argentina lacked 'that initiative and aggressiveness which distinguishes the northern races.

Southern European blood transplanted to a soft climate is handicapped in competing with Northern European blood transplanted to a hard and invigorating climate such as that of Canada'.[47]

What Jackman and other Canadian observers failed to notice was that this agrarian rootlessness also kept the Argentine cost of production down, and enabled Argentina to maintain a competitive position in the world wheat market. In 1929, Argentina had a bumper, high-quality, wheat crop. It was so large that it depressed the world wheat price, an event that contributed to the bankruptcy of the Canadian Wheat Pools in 1931.[48] Canadians suddenly awoke to the fact that Argentina was a ruthless competitor that could produce vast quantities of wheat at low prices.

Indeed, while the cost of wheat production in Argentina and Canada in the late 1920s was about equal, during the 1930s Argentina's (in terms of gold) fell much more sharply than Canada's. Currency depreciation did play a role in the decline of the market price of Argentine wheat, but falling rents and wages also brought the cost of production down. By 1932, the Buenos Aires firm of Gibson Brothers was able to assert that 'our cost of [wheat] production . . . is substantially lower' than in Canada.[49] The prairies enjoyed an advantage in transport costs, for the ocean voyage to Europe was shorter, railway rates in Argentina were higher (although the Argentine rail haul was much less than in Canada), and Argentina's cumbersome grain storage and handling system added heavily to the transport bill.[50] Wheat yields were also higher in the prairies than in the pampas. The Depression dealt both pampa and prairie agriculture staggering blows and forced thousands of farmers off the land in both regions; but on balance, the low cost of production in the pampas, sustained by government measures such as the mortgage moratorium, gave Argentina an advantage when wheat prices reached historic lows in the 1930s.

One of the first Canadians to appreciate this hard reality was E. Cora Hind, a veteran crop expert on the staff of the *Winnipeg Free Press*, who travelled to Argentina in the 1930s. This shrewd lady, 'who had a crop in her eye' and was famous in western Canada for her ability to predict yields, wrote *Seeing for Myself*, a book that W. L. Morton describes as of unusually 'tough competence'. She was impressed by what she saw in Argentina: 'The thing about these estancieros which strikes you at once is the air of efficiency, of things well done and done at the right time and no opportunity missed.' The world, Hind concluded, in a statement that struck at the heart of Canadian mythology, could get along without Canadian wheat. As for the cost of production in Argentina, 'physical, climatic, and labour conditions all point to it being less than in Canada.'[51]

VIII CONCLUSIONS

The distinct land tenure systems and patterns of rural settlement that emerged in the prairies and pampas reflected the divergent political systems and histories of Argentina and Canada. But another factor – the integration of cattle raising and agriculture in the pampa economy – also helps to explain the contrast between these two New World cereal exporting regions. And, on balance, the contrast did not imply that pampa agriculture was cost-competitive and adaptable to shifting market trends. Wheat yields were higher in Western Canada, but the land and debt structure left Canadian agriculture in a seriously exposed position when prices fell. Rural community life was superior in the prairies, but the mobility of pampa agriculture gave Argentine farmers certain economic advantages.

The evidence makes it difficult to agree with analysts who condemn the pampa land-tenure system as backward and inefficient. Although the tenancy system needed reform, it was the foundation of an agricultural export economy that competed effectively in world markets.

NOTES

1. There is a large literature on the National Policy, but two works by Vernon C. Fowke are especially useful for analyzing its impact on prairie development: 'An Introduction to Canadian Agricultural History', *Agricultural History*, 16 (1942) 74–90: and *The National Policy and the Wheat Economy* (University of Toronto Press, 1957).
2. R. G. Riddell, 'A Cycle in the Development of the Canadian West', *Canadian Historical Review* 21 (1940) 276–7.
3. For details of the 1872 act and later modifications, see Chester Martin, '*Dominion Lands' Policy* (Toronto: Macmillan, 1938) pp. 396–407; and the thorough discussion in Max J. Hedley, 'The Social Conditions of Production and the Dynamics of Tradition: Independent Commodity Production in Canadian Agriculture' (Ph.D. dissertation, University of Alberta, 1976) pp. 45–56.
4. For the quote, see Rollin E. Smith, *Wheat Fields and Markets of the World* (St. Louis: The Modern Miller Company, 1908) p. 153. Also see K. H. Norrie, 'The Rate of Settlement in the Canadian Prairies', *Journal of*

Economic History, 35 (1975) 410–27; and Robert E. Ankli and Robert M. Litt, 'The Growth of Prairie Agriculture: Economic Considerations', in Donald H. Akenson (ed.), *Canadian Papers in Rural History*, vol. I (Gananoque, Ontario: Langdale Press, 1978–80) pp. 33–64.

5. In 1900, an estimated $1000 to $1500 was the minimum capital required to buy the tools, animals, seeds, and shelter to begin farming. See Ankli and Litt, 'The Growth of Prairie Agriculture', p. 55. On the backgrounds and significance of the co-operative movement, see C. R. Fay, *Co-operation at Home and Abroad: A Description and Analysis* (London: P. S. King & Son, 1908) pp. 278–83; and John W. Bennett, *Northern Plainsmen: Adaptive Strategy and Agrarian Life* (Chicago: Aldine Publishing Company, 1969) pp. 207–9, 238–9, 280.
6. Donald E. Willmott, 'The Formal Organizations of Saskatchewan Farmers, 1900–65', in Anthony W. Rasporich (ed.), *Western Canada: Past and Present* (Calgary: McClelland and Stewart West, 1975) p. 28.
7. C. A. Dawson and Eva R. Younge, *Pioneering in the Prairie Provinces: The Social Side of the Settlement Process* (Toronto: Macmillan, 1940) pp. 154–5; W. A. Mackintosh, *Economic Problems of the Prairie Provinces* (Toronto: Macmillan, 1935) pp. 41, 149–54; G. E. Britnell, *The Wheat Economy* (University of Toronto Press, 1939) p. 179.
8. On education, see Dawson and Younge, *Pioneering*, pp. 159, 176, 190; Britnell, *The Wheat Economy*, pp. 113, 194. On libraries, see Lewis L. Lloyd, *Memories of a Co-operative Statesman* (No place or publisher noted, 1967?, University of Calgary Library) p. 17; and J. S. Woodward 'Wheat and Politics on the Prairies', *Queen's Quarterly*, 38 (1931) 741.
9. Dawson and Younge, *Pioneering*, pp. 262–4; Britnell, *The Wheat Economy*, pp. 19, 138.
10. Brian Robert McCutcheon, 'The Economic and Social Structure of Political Agrarianism in Manitoba, 1870–1900' (Ph.D. dissertation, University of British Columbia, 1974) p. 43.
11. The quote is from Wilhelm Cohnstaedt, *Western Canada 1909: Travel Letters by Wilhelm Cohnstaedt*, translated by Herta Holle-Scherer (Regina: University of Regina, Canadian Plains Research Centre, 1976) p. 27. Also see J. Burgon Bickersteth, *The Land of Open Doors: Being Letters from Western Canada* (London: Wells Gardner, Darton and Co Ltd., 1974) p. 85; and Paul F. Sharp, *The Agrarian Revolt in Western Canada* (University of Minnesota Press, 1948) p. 22.
12. Bennett, *Northern Plainsmen*, p. 104; R. W. Murchie, *Agricultural Progress on the Prairie Frontier* (Toronto: Macmillan, 1936) p. 127.
13. For the traveller's quote, see E. B. Mitchell, *In Western Canada Before the War: A Study of Communities* (London: John Murray, 1915) p. 155. Also see Britnell, *The Wheat Economy*, p. 79; Mackintosh, *Economic Problems*, pp. 12, 31, 259–66; and Canada, Dominion Bureau of Statistics, *Seventh Census of Canada, 1931*, vol. VIII (Ottawa, 1933–6) p. lxii. Murchie. *Agricultural Progress*, p. 78, presents statistics correcting the 1931 census data on mortgages.
14. Canada, vol. VIII, *Seventh Census*, p. xlix. For discussion of the move towards tenancy see Dawson and Younge, *Pioneering*, pp. 90–3; and Murchie, *Agricultural Progress*, pp. 117–25.

15. Saskatchewan, Royal Commission on Immigration and Settlement, *Report of the Saskatchewan Royal Commission on Immigration and Settlement*, 1930 (Regina: Ministry of Natural Resources, 1930) p. 31. One observer who pointed to the advantages of tenancy was G. H. Craig, 'Land Settlement and Tenancy in the Lomond and Vulcan Districts, Alberta', *Economic Annalist*, 7 (1937) 22–3.
16. Luis Rodolfo Cánepa, *Economía agraria argentina* (Buenos Aires: Librería 'El Ateneo', 1942) p. 61.
17. The basic historical study of Argentine land policy is Miguel A. Cárcano, *Evolución histórica del régimen de la tierra pública, 1810–1916* (Buenos Aires: Librería Mendesky, 1917). For a thorough and systematic analysis of Santa Fe's policy, see Ezequiel Gallo, 'Agricultural Colonization and Society in Argentina: The Province of Santa Fe, 1870–1895' (D.Phil. thesis, Oxford University, 1970) esp. pp. 22–56, 96–107. For a case study of Córdoba policy, see Aníbal Arcondo, 'Tierra y política de tierras en Córdoba', *Revista de Economía y Estadística* (Córdoba), 13 (1969) 13–44.
18. Gallo, 'Agricultural Colonization', pp. 22–4, 115–18; Rolf Sternberg, 'Farms and Farmers in an Estanciero World' (Ph.D. dissertation, Syracuse University, 1971) pp. 113–17, 135–8; Aníbal B. Arcondo, *La agricultura en Córdoba, 1870–1880* (Córdoba: Universidad Nacional de Córdoba, 1965), end fold-out (n.p.).
19. For thorough discussion of the 1887 Buenos Aires law and its results, see Noemí M. Girbal de Blacha, *Los centros agrícolas en la Provincia de Buenos Aires* (Buenos Aires: Fundación para la Educación, la Ciencia y la Cultura, 1980). Also see A. S. Morris, 'The Failure of Small Farmer Settlement in Buenos Aires Province, Argentina', *Revista Geográfica*, 85 (1977) 63–78.
20. Georges Clemenceau, *South America To-Day* (New York and London: G. P. Putnam's Sons, 1911) p. 161; Roberto Cortés Conde, *El progreso argentino, 1880–1914* (Buenos Aires: Editorial Sudamericana, 1979) pp. 166, 172.
21. Lázaro Nemirovsky, *Estructura económica y orientación política de la agricultura en la República Argentina* (Buenos Aires: Librería y Casa Editora de Jesús Meneńdez, 1933) p. 43; Jacinto Oddone, *La burguesía terrateniente argentina*, 3rd edn (Buenos Aires: Ediciones Populares Argentinas, 1956) pp. 182–5: Francisco J. Delich, 'Empresas agrícolas en gran escala', *Revista Paraguaya de Sociología*, 10 (1973) 119–76.
22. Italian immigrants perceived pampa agricultural conditions as much more favourable than those in Italy. See Kristin Ruggiero, 'Gringo and Creole: Foreign and Native Values in a Rural Argentina Community', *Journal of Inter-American Studies and World Affairs*, 24 (1982) 170. Also see Robert F. Foerster, *The Italian Emigration of Our Times* (Cambridge: Harvard University Press, 1919) pp. 235–6.
23. Carl E. Solberg, 'Peopling the Prairies and the Pampas: The Impact of Immigration on Argentine and Canadian Agrarian Development, 1870–1930', *Journal of Inter-American Studies and World Affairs*, 24 (1982) 183–212.

24. Gallo, 'Agricultural Colonization', p. 249, quotes the *Financial Times*. See also pp. 24, 59, 221–9, 247–8.
25. Campbell F. Ogilvie, *Argentina From a British Point of View and Notes on Argentine Life* (London: Wertheimer, Lea and Co., 1910) p. 9. On the relationship between alfalfa and cereal agriculture, see Simon G. Hanson, *Argentine Meat and the British Market* (Stanford University Press, 1938) pp. 113–16.
26. Emilio A. Coni, 'La colonización', *Revista de Ciencias Económicas*, 11 (1923) 363.
27. Miguel Teubal, 'Policy and Performance of Agriculture in Economic Development: The Case of Argentina' (Ph.D. dissertation, University of California at Berkeley, 1975) p. 109; John Fogarty, 'The Comparative Method and the Nineteenth Century Regions of Recent Settlement', *Historical Studies*, 19 (1981) 417.
28. Sternberg, 'Farms and Farmers', p. 242.
29. Walter Larden, *Estancia Life: Agricultural, Economic, and Cultural Aspects of Argentine Farming* (London: T. Fisher Unwin, 1911) p. 78; Ricardo J. Huergo, *Investigación agrícola en la región septentrional de la Provincia de Buenos Aires* (Buenos Aires: Compañía Sud-Americana de Billetes de Banco, 1904) p. 130. Also see James R. Scobie, *Revolution on the Pampas: A Social History of Argentine Wheat, 1860–1910* (Austin: University of Texas Press, 1964) p. 59.
30. For statistical series on land rents, see Argentine Republic, Ministerio de Agricultura de la Nación, Dirección de Economía Rural y Estadística, *Anuario agropecuario: Año 1935* (Buenos Aires, 1935) p. 503; and also Cánepa, *Economía agraria*, p. 80. Data on wheat prices are in Argentine Republic, Comité Nacional de Geografía, *Anuario geográfico argentino* (Buenos Aires, 1941) p. 207.
31. For the extent of mortgage debt, see *Review of the River Plate*, 6 January 1939, 12; and Cánepa, *Economía agraria*, p. 160. On the moratorium law, see *Review of the River Plate* 22 September 1933, 5; and 13 October 1933, 22. The moratorium, which lasted for three years, was extended for two more in 1936: ibid. 2 October 1936, 7.
32. Gallo, 'Agricultural Colonization', pp. 74–5, summarizes these arguments.
33. For a study of cadastral records and land subdivision, see Saturnino M. Zamboraín, *La verdad sobre la propiedad de la tierra en la Argentina* (Buenos Aires: Sociedad Rural Argentina, n.d.) pp. 39–58. Also see Mark Jefferson, *Peopling the Argentine Pampa* (New York: American Geographical Society, 1926) p. 142; and Carl C. Taylor, *Rural Life in Argentina* (Baton Rouge: Louisiana State University Press, 1948) p. 192. On the 1921 tenancy legislation, see Carl Solberg, 'Rural Unrest and Agrarian Policy in Argentina, 1912–1930', *Journal of Inter-American Studies and World Affairs*, 13 (1971) 47.
34. No date is given for this quote, which is in Tomás Carcía Serrano, *Esteban Piacenza: Apuntes biográficos*, 2nd edn (Rosario; Librería y Editorial Ruíz, 1966) p. 51. Also see Gallo, 'Agricultural Colonization', pp. 324–34.

35. H. S. Ferns, *The Argentine Republic, 1516–1971* (New York: Barnes & Noble Books, 1973) p. 94.
36. Sternberg, 'Farms and Farmers', p. 71. For the other quotes see Emilio A. Coni, 'Cuestiones agrarias', *Revista de Ciencias Económicas*, 26 (1926) 371; and Herbert A. Gibson, *The Land We Live On* (Buenos Aires: R. Grant & Co., Printers, 1914) p. 171. Also see Delich, 'Empresas agrícolas', 132–3.
37. On the Argentine cooperatives, see Domingo Bórea, *Tratado de cooperación* (Buenos Aires: Imprenta 'Gadola', 1927) p. 276; Bernardino C. Horne, *Política agraria y regulación económica* (Buenos Aires: Editorial Losada S.A., 1942) pp. 120, 249–50; and *La Prensa*, 13 July 1930, 13. Canadian Wheat Pool membership is reported in Canada, Royal Grain Inquiry Commission, 1936, *Submission by the Pool Organizations of Alberta, Saskatchewan, and Manitoba*, vol. I (no publisher, n.d. given) p. 20.
38. On the question of isolation, see Scobie, *Revolution on the Pampas*, pp. 61–2; and John Hirst, 'Respuesta de John Hirst a los comentarios', in John Fogarty, Ezequiel Gallo, and Héctor Dieguez (eds), *Argentina y Australia* (Buenos Aires: Instituto Torcuato di Tella, 1979) p. 110.
39. Larden, *Estancia Life*, pp. 78–9. Also see Gibson, *The Land We Live On*, p. 16; and Hugo Miatello, 'El hogar agrícola', *Boletín del Museo Social Argentino*, 3 (1914) pp. 565–7.
40. See, for example, Francisco Scardin, *La Argentina y el trabajo: Impresiones y notas* (Buenos Aires: Jacobo Peuser, 1906) pp. 232, 408; Jefferson, *Peopling*, p. 172.
41. This poem, 'María de Alcorta', is found in José María García, *El campo argentino a 60 años del grito de Alcorta* (Buenos Aires: Ediciones 'Centro de Estudios', 1972) p. 69.
42. Alejandro E. Bunge, 'Los gastos de la educación en la Argentina', *Revista de Economía Argentina*, 36 (1937) 269. Also see Ramón J. Cárcano, *800 000 analfabetos. Aldeas escolares* (Buenos Aires: Roldán-Editor, 1933) p. 9. The title of this book refers to the number of illiterates among school-age children in Argentina in 1932. Another study of the rural educational situation is Mariano Vélez, *La situación agrícola de La Pampa* (Buenos Aires: Imprenta 'La Vanguardia', 1934) p. 119.
43. Antonio Diecidue, *Netri: Lider y mártir de una gran causa* (Rosario: Federación Agraria Argentina, 1969) p. 117. According to Nemirovsky, *Estructrua económica*, p. 230, the circulation of *La Tierra* was 18 506 in 1926. This compares with the *Guide*'s circulation of 120 000 that year.
44. Scardin, *La Argentina y el trabajo*, pp. 244–5; Richard Wayne Slatta, 'The Gaucho and Rural Life in Nineteenth-Century Buenos Aires Province, Argentina' (Ph.D. dissertation, University of Texas at Austin, 1980) p. 89.
45. Gino Germani, *Estructura social de la Argentina* (Buenos Aires: Editorial Raigal, 1955) p. 44; Taylor, *Rural Life in Argentina*, p. 334. Also see Katherine S. Dreier, *Five Months in the Argentine From a Woman's Point of View* (New York: Frederic Fairchild Sherman, 1920) pp. 18–19.
46. Allan B. Hobbs, 'Agriculture in Argentina', *Grain Growers' Guide*, 3

December 1913, 7, 18; J. H. Haslam, 'The Future of Wheat Growing', ibid., 7 May 1919, 38.

47. W. J. Jackman, 'Wheatfields Under the Southern Cross', *Country Guide*, 15 May 1928, 35. Also see W. J. Jackman, *Wheat Growing and Rural Economic Conditions in the Argentine Republic* (Winnipeg: Canadian Co-operative Wheat Producers Ltd., 1927) pp. 10–12.
48. For the impact of Argentine competition on the Canadian wheat economy, see Harold A. Innis (ed.), *The Diary of Alexander James McPhail* (Toronto: The University of Toronto Press, 1940) pp. 192–210; and Duncan Alexander MacGibbon, *The Canadian Grain Trade* (Toronto: Macmillan, 1932) pp. 422–3.
49. For the Gibson quote, see *Review of the River Plate*, 13 May 1932, 57. For comparative analysis of the cost of production, see Paul de Hevesy, *World Wheat Planning and Economic Planning in General* (London: Oxford University Press, 1940), foldout facing p. 814. De Hevesy calculated that the cost of production in 1930 was 13.08 gold francs per quintal in the pampas and 12.24 in the prairies. The Argentine cost declined to 4.95 gold francs per quintal in 1934 and then rose to 6.64 in 1935. The Canadian cost fell to an average of 7.9 for 1931–7. An American agricultural expert familiar with Argentine conditions argued in 1926 that the cost of production in Argentina was significantly lower than in North America. See Leon M. Estabrook, *Agricultural Survey of South America: Argentina and Paraguay* (Washington: United States Department of Agriculture, 1926) p. 69.
50. Comparative data on transport costs from the prairies and the pampas to the British market may be found in Glenbow-Alberta Archives, Alberta Wheat Pool File, 818B.
51. E. Cora Hind, *Seeing for Myself: Agricultural Conditions Around the World* (Toronto: Macmillan, 1937) pp. xii, 271, 301. On Hind's remarkable reputation, see W. L. Morton, *Manitoba; A History*, 2nd ed. (Toronto: University of Toronto Press, 1967) p. 469.

4 The Social Origins of Industrial Growth: Canada, Argentina and Australia, 1870–1930

WARWICK ARMSTRONG

I INTRODUCTION

This chapter should start, perhaps, by stating what it is not. Given the limits of time and space, it is not an attempt to document in any economic, social or political way the detailed processes of modern, capitalist industrialization as they unfolded in the three societies during the six decades from 1870 to 1930. It has little specific empirical or factual material related to manufacturing development. Rather, it is an attempt to explain why a process of partial industrialization should have taken place in Canada, Argentina and Australia over the period. It thus presents an hypothesis – or a set of concepts – in which the elements leading to such a development can be examined. The paper is concerned also with the origins of the process, and stops arbitrarily (perhaps) at 1930. After that date, the manufacturing sectors of all three nations moved to a rather different level and pace of development.

The initial question is a simple one: why did industrial growth take place in these three outgrowths of European colonial or neo-colonial expansion in the late nineteenth and early twentieth centuries? However, it is an important issue because Canada, Argentina and Australia were quite distinctive from other, large imperial dependencies of the time. For a variety of reasons which will be examined in this chapter, they had begun, by the last quarter of the nineteenth century to exercise a sufficient measure of control over production and capital accumulation within their own national territories to ensure that the patterns of economic development would lead to the diversification and integration of their respective economies. By the 1920s their development levels were, by most social and economic indicators, closer to European industrial capitalist societies than to the majority of other raw material and foodstuff producers.

There were significant differences among the three in the course and nature of their development from 1870 to 1930, yet the overriding similarities, especially in comparison with the other dependencies of the time, permit some useful deductions to be drawn from their evolution (from production for export of specialized staples to partial industrialization).

II EXTERNAL AND INTERNAL FACTORS IN DEVELOPMENT

In setting out the reasons for their distinctive patterns of development, it is clear that external forces related to the growth of international trade and investment, as well as to the massive movements of people from Europe, must assume a focal role. The incorporation of the three economies into the rapidly-expanding, international commercial and financial system of the late nineteenth and early twentieth centuries provided both an impetus and a setting for their own dramatic growth in those decades.

The general nature of British and European commercial and financial relationships with Canada, Argentina and Australia are well enough known not to require elaboration here. Most studies on the 'white settler societies' or 'regions of recent settlement', by writers such as Nurkse, Meier and Kuznets,[1] in fact concentrate upon the external economic relationships as a means of explaining their distinctive evolution. The production of a specialized range of temperate foodstuff and raw material staples to meet the market demands of urban consumers in the industrializing societies of Europe is treated by these and other writers as the prime cause of the diversified internal development of the three societies.

This tradition has continued to the present. If the more conventional streams of international trade studies have treated the expansion of the international economy as the principal motor of economic growth in such economies, so the writers in the dependency school such as Frank, Sunkel, Paz and Dos Santos,[2] and underdevelopment theorists including Amin and Emmanuel,[3] have laid stress, equally, upon the adverse effects of such relationships on the societies of the periphery. For the dependency and underdevelopment writers, it is precisely the growing incorporation of the societies of Asia, Africa, Latin America and the Pacific into the evermore complex network of international trade and investment, that has led to the widening gap between the dominant capitalist centre and the subordinate, dependent periphery. From the mechanisms of military and political control in the classical empires to the informal yet even more encompassing economic influence of neo-colonialism, Europe, the United States and Japan have effectively appropriated a large part of the surplus produced by the peripheral societies. In this way, they have expanded their own sphere of capital accumulation to international proportions. This, in essence, is the basis of the unequal relationships which have characterized dependency, underdevelopment and the unfolding of a world order polarized economically and politically between the First and Third Worlds.

As a first approximation, this view of a world divided between a dominant, expanding industrial core and a dependent, underdeveloped periphery has thrown light on questions of global inequality and exploitation; and it has certainly stirred debate over the past twenty years. This paper, however, aims to move beyond the generalized level of discussion and, in doing so, to suggest that the bipolarized model of analysis, with its emphasis on external relationships, may be inadequate as a way of explaining the specific historical experiences of societies such as Canada, Argentina and Australia (which fit readily into neither category). In doing so, it takes the position of André Gorz that the most important social and economic divisions defining development and underdevelopment run *through* societies rather than between them.

To put such a proposition forward is not to ignore the profound and long term impact of imperial hegemony, nor the contemporary influence of the global operations of transnational corporations, particularly in the sphere of direct productive investment over the past three decades. It is rather to suggest that questions concerned with the internal social structure and relationships of nations be taken as the starting point for discussions on the nature of development, underdevelopment and inequality.[4] This emphasis is basic to the following interpretation of the patterns of development which evolved in Canada, Argentina and Australia between 1870 and 1930. The three countries were members of a group (which also included New Zealand and Uruguay) to which the present writer has given the designation 'dominion capitalist societies'.[5] It is not a completely satisfactory title, but one which is meant first to distinguish the five countries from other European dependencies, and second, to highlight the argument that only at the risk of overgeneralization can the societies which make up the international system be neatly divided into the two blocks of core and periphery.

III THE NATURE OF DOMINION CAPITALISM

Some characteristics defining the distinctive nature of the dominion capitalist societies will help to clarify the point. First, they were the consequence of the European colonization of temperate or semi-temperate and relatively unpopulated environments. In the process of land settlement, indigenous peoples were separated from their means of subsistence; they and their social organizations were largely destroyed and/or assimilated, and their lands were sold or granted to European commercial groups and settlers.

The fact of European colonization is of central importance. Having swept away the pre-capitalist handicaps,[6] the new inhabitants were left, relatively speaking, with a *tabula rasa* on which to create their modernized copies of European society, transferred along with the technology, institutions and attitudes that they had brought with them. Under such circumstances, the ruling groups in the new societies were particularly keen to maintain and extend those economic ties with the expanding industrial nations of Europe which would exploit the natural resources of their new country, and, at the same time, assure them of a satisfactory share of the profits.

Given these conditions, it is not surprising that, by the 1920s, many of the social indicators in these three societies – life expectancy, birth rates, literacy and urbanization among others – were equal to those of European nations.[7] At times during this period they were, indeed, superior, as were the income levels enjoyed by a working class in many ways similar to those of the industrialized economies. Sectorally, too, by the 1920s, the contributions to gross domestic product in each of the three were beginning to approach the patterns of European nations.

Certain characteristics, however, set Canada, Argentina and Australia apart from European and United States models. Their role within the international economy and division of labour was that of efficient and capital-intensive specialist producers of raw material and foodstuff exports. Most of the urban, commercial, financial and transport development which occurred was also associated with the staples export sector, so that, in effect, the prosperity of the national economy depended upon an expanding, though frequently unstable, export sector – as did the political stability of the ruling coalition of producers of staples and urban business.

The modern manufacturing sector, a later addition to economic activity – and for most of this period, a fairly minor one – also remained tied to the export sector, in its earlier phases. Industrial diversification consisted, first, of the early stages of primary processing – meat packing, dairy processing and milling in particular – or, to a lesser extent, the production of inputs – farm machinery, fertilizers and transport equipment – to serve the staples sector. The latter occurred more in Canada and Australia than in Argentina; on the other hand, in Argentina the open market economy associated with a free trade staples policy was responsible for the crushing of much provincial artisan manufacturing. Secondly, as the cities grew, small-scale, urban consumer industries based on individual and family capital sprang up to serve daily needs. Larger operations in manufacturing tended to attract foreign direct investment, especially in the early years of the twentieth century. Canada, in particular, was one of the earliest recipients of foreign (United States) production capital, but overseas firms also came to dominate the staples processing industries in the two other economies. Much of this occurred in the first decade of the new century, with a further extension of investment into the industries of the third industrial revolution – automobiles, rubber products and electrical goods – in the 1920s.

The above typology is essentially descriptive. It lists the elements that went to make up these societies. But it does not really help to explain how or why they evolved so distinctively from other colonial and neo-colonial dependencies of Europe. To attempt to answer the 'how' and 'why', this chapter proposes an hypothesis which employs the above elements, but which begins the analysis from within these societies rather than approaching them as peripheral elements in an international system. That they were integrated parts of that system is accepted as an important premise, but, then, so were most other societies in that period. Their distinguishing characteristics sprang more from the changes taking place in their social structures and relationships at the time.

IV AN HYPOTHESIS: SOCIAL FACTORS AND DEVELOPMENT

The hypothesis has a number of parts. First, it argues that there emerged a national ruling coalition whose economic influence was based on the production, trading and financing of a rapidly expanding, staples export sector. As a European élite, employing the techniques, institutions and attitudes borrowed from the advanced industrial societies, and adapted to local conditions and requirements, the national coalition gradually established itself, in each case, in a position of relative autonomy, *vis-à-vis* external pressures and forces. From this position it was able progressively to strengthen itself economically, socially and politically by retaining for its own purposes a significant portion of the profits (surplus) arising from the wealth-producing staples sector.

This capacity for domestic capital accumulation was, of course, enhanced by the generally high level of demand for raw materials and temperate foodstuffs. The international need for grains, meat and dairy products as well as wool, hides, lumber and, later, minerals strengthened the bargaining position of the three economies, allowing them to maintain profitable unit prices on the whole for their products throughout this period. Large-scale, mass-production techniques kept costs competitively low, while providing urban consumers in the industrialized societies with relatively cheap food and other basic requirements. This external demand, as will be pointed out later, was clearly a necessary condition for the emergence of relative autonomy in the three societies, but it was not a sufficient reason for its existence.

The strength of the national ruling coalition, together with the growth of the relevant institutions and legal and political structures, allowed it to increase the range of domestic capital formation (accumulation) by tapping overseas financial markets. In the first part of the period, up to the turn of the century, foreign investment generally took the form of loans to the state, local authorities and the private sector, especially the banks. The significance of a powerful financial sector in all three countries becomes clear, therefore, when their intermediary and allocative role in national development strategies is considered. In a sense, the banks became the national arbiters or determinants of the type and pace of internal development.

The achievement of political independence (formal independence for Australia in 1901 had been preceded by nearly half a century of effective internal self-government) gave each ruling coalition access to a national state apparatus whose political, legal and administrative powers it could call upon to defend its interests against both internal and external competitors.

Secondly, there also emerged a modern, wage-earning working class, mainly in the larger metropolitan centres, but in Ontario and New South Wales especially, and in some of the smaller towns as well. These urban workers shared some of the characteristics of the urban wage-earners of Europe and the United States, although the proportions to be found in commerce, administration and service generally were closer to those of the United States than Europe.[8]

Drawn largely from Western European societies – although from countries at different stages of modern industrial capitalist development – the workers of the three dominion societies inherited many of the attitudes (transferring with them the political philosophies and class organisational structures) which had been evolved in the social conflicts of nineteenth century Europe. In this sense, the working classes of Canada, Argentina and Australia were much closer to their equivalent in the industrial world than to those in the dependencies of Latin America, Africa or Asia.

As they became more effectively organized in their adopted countries, they were able to use their trade union and political strength to some advantage to lay claim to part of the retained surplus in the form of higher wages, improved working conditions and, to a limited degree, the provision of social services. Negotiation and confrontation were the main weapons used against both employers and the state – although, occasionally, class conflict did result in bloodshed. With relatively high levels of education, political awareness and social organization, the urban working classes were capable of wringing concessions from time to time in a way that the peasantry and rural workers of the period could not even begin to emulate.

If their gains do not appear impressive compared with the achievements of the post-Second World War years, the true comparison is with the working conditions and income levels of those other societies where an urban working class had not yet come into existence. Nor, indeed, did the standards of living of these organized working classes compare unfavourably with those of their counterparts in Europe at the time, as has been noted above. But it is necessary also to distinguish between the achievements of organized labour and the position of large minority groups which entered the labour force – women, ethnic minorities, recent immigrants (often from rural backgrounds), and rural workers. The latter were often far removed from the benefits won by their more powerful fellow workers.

Thirdly, between these two major social classes, there appeared an intermediate class composed of small businessmen, professionals (lawyers, doctors, accountants and teachers) and administrators; in other words, a stratum which made it possible for the modern capitalist state and society to function without heavy reliance upon external expertise. Politically, the majority of this class supported the ruling coalitions and their policies, although some of its members were involved in working with trade unions and radical parties to bring changes in direction from time to time. The armed forces formed an important component of this group in Argentina, a fact which distinguishes that society significantly from the other two. Its omnipresence may be seen as a major lacuna in the structure of social modernization that was evolving in this period, yet perhaps it was still part of a certain tradition of industrialization if the examples of Germany, Italy and Japan are also taken into account.

Finally, it becomes evident that one important consequence of the particular evolution of class structures and relationships in the three societies was the capacity to initiate and carry through a process of partial, domestic industrial development. It is necessary to emphasize this feature, because the generation of an indigenous manufacturing capability, which used modern technology and business organization, indicated the achievement of autocentric, industrial capitalist development – however limited and truncated that might have been.

Sections of the ruling coalition in each society undoubtedly used their profits to import capital and consumer goods directly from overseas. Others used their wealth for speculation and conspicuous consumption – travel and real estate expenditures especially – in imitation of current European fashions. But, even more, the surplus product was reinvested directly in the wealth-producing staples export sector, and indirectly in building up the infrastructure necessary for the transportation, storage, processing, commercialization and financing of the goods produced in the hinterlands of the three countries. These formed the backward and forward linkage activities, to use the terminology of the staples writers: the immediate effects arising from the export sector. But there were also the less immediate consequences, the final demand linkages, through which the multiplier effects of export sector growth were felt in the spread of wealth and in the growth of consumer demand throughout the society as a whole.

Rapid urbanization, concentrated especially around one or two major commercial and financial centres – Buenos Aires, Montreal, Toronto, Sydney and Melbourne – helped in the creation both of a growing consumer market and a source of labour for the ancillary commercial and service activities in the growing economies. This was also the basis for the emergence of a wide range of urban manufacturing industries, different in kind from those which had arisen to process the staples. Demand for the daily necessities of life by populations with increasing purchasing power in the metropolitan areas was the inevitable consequence of a modern society where few were independent, self-sufficient producers, capable of meeting their subsistence needs. These modern metropoles had given rise, early on, to a population which offered its labour in return for wages, and so provided the conditions for the growth of a rapidly-growing consumer market. Local businessmen were often able because of the nature of the demand – for clothing, footwear, basic daily foodstuffs, housing and construction materials – to compete with imports, especially if given some protection.

In the major cities, therefore, there arose a class of small and medium-scale manufacturers, employing few workers per factory, possessing relatively small capital resources, and usually lacking access to the major financial institutions for loans; moreover, this class exercised only limited political and social influence (particularly in cases where, as in Buenos Aires, the majority of factory owners were recent immigrants).[9]

Despite the relatively humble position of domestic, competitive manufacturers, their appearance – together with that of their larger, monopolistic brethren processing export staples – gives the three economies a qualitatively different character from most other dependencies of the times. F. H. Cardoso and E. Faletto have pointed to the difference between Argentina (and Uruguay) with their capacity for generating diversified sectoral development, and the enclaves of most other Latin American economies where the same pattern of relative autonomy could not take place or was prevented from doing so.[10]

The same was true for Canada and Australia, where modern, capitalist export sector growth was used by national ruling groups to generate internal diversified development. In both cases, the state also participated in the process of domestic capital accumulation as a partner and promoter of private sector expansion. The clearer perception of the need to encourage diversified national development, which was held by the ruling coalition and by the state in Canada and Australia, may be one of the elements distinguishing their evolutionary paths from that of Argentina. In turn, distance, combined with a rather more single-minded approach to national development, may have helped Australia to build a stronger indigenous manufacturing structure than that of Canada. In the latter, a deliberate policy to industrialize – the National Policy of 1879 – brought in US capital and branch plants to dominate the Canadian manufacturing sector, and US trade unions to organize their own branches.

Nevertheless, in summing up this section, it is clear that the development of the three societies was characterized by a significant degree of internally diversified, sectoral expansion; much of this was directly associated with the spillover effect of staples sector growth into related activities in commerce, finance, administration, transport and manufactures, supplying inputs or processing outputs. It was also part of a wider multiplier effect throughout the whole society, where the interaction of social classes within a relatively autonomous and modern nation-state provided the conditions for partial industrialization of the economy.

V STAPLES THEORY AND SOCIAL STRUCTURES

Much of this has been the subject of study by the staples theorists. The theory itself has largely been concerned with the examination of the economic linkages among different sectors; these include the multiplier mechanisms by which the surplus or profits generated in one sector can be transmitted to others, so creating the basis for a diversified, integrated national economy (or if there are obstacles to such mechanisms, to a fragmented, disarticulated structure).

Two questions, in particular, have exercised the staples theorists: the nature of the production function for different staples, and the patterns of income distribution associated with the staple. The two are closely related. If wealth and the ownership of production is concentrated in a few hands, as in plantation and enclave mining economies (or even in extensive livestock grazing sectors or lumber industries, to take examples from Argentina, Australia and Canada), the resulting multiplier effects on the rest of the economy will be limited. Consumer demand will be restricted, and supplied by imports (for the rich) and subsistence production (for the majority). Opportunities for domestic development will thus be leaked away through import expenditures, the remittance of profits, and the export of staples in their raw state. The leakages will thus be more in evidence than the linkages.

But in cases where the staples were produced by a wide range of medium-scale farmers, as in the case of grains or fruit or dairy products, the possibilities for domestic linkages were so much greater.[11] Middle-income producers tended to have less need for imported capital or (luxury) consumer goods, Family farmers, particularly in Australia and Canada, turned to local manufacturers for their fertilizers, fencing wire, and agricultural machinery; in this way smaller producers provided the basis for more diversified local development than did the plantations, mines, lumber companies, or, indeed, large-scale graziers and *estancieros*.

Backward and forward linkages developed, therefore, to meet the requirements of the export sector, while final demand linkages reflected the wider effects on consumer demand throughout society as a whole. M. H. Watkins has pointed out that higher average income levels, combined with a relatively equal distribution of that income, create strong links with the local mass production both of capital and consumer goods;[12] this process lies at the heart of the progressive industrialization of all three societies.

The staples theory explanation for industrial development is useful, particularly in the context of the recent tendency to emphasize the social elements in the argument. But this tendency can and should be pushed further, so that social forces are treated as the prime movers of economic and political change. The often technical discussions about linkages among different sectors become more comprehensible when they are considered as the consequences of actions taken by certain groups or classes. Changing balances within local ruling coalitions, with the emergence first of urban commercial and financial capital to challenge the traditional landed groups, and later, of an urban manufacturing group, led to shifts in influence and state policies on development.

VI THE HYPOTHESIS: SOME REFINEMENTS

In setting out the hypothesis above, much of the discussion is at a general level and some additional comments may help to highlight and clarify the argument. First, the favourable terms of trade (generally, though not always) enjoyed by the staples exporters, while providing a source of wealth for the producers and commercial/financial intermediaries, were not, in themselves, the cause of diversified economic development in Canada, Argentina and Australia. They were an extremely important contributory factor, certainly, and made the whole process a great deal easier. It must be noted, though, that the equally strong demand for tropical foodstuffs and minerals in other parts of Latin America, colonial Africa, and Asia rarely sparked the same domestic, integrated and diversified development. Often, the very success of the export sector led to greater disarticulation and widening social disparities within the country.

Explanations for the different course which was followed by the three societies must rest, therefore, rather on an approach which takes as its starting point the nature of the internal social structure and relationships among the classes of society. From there, it is a matter of considering the external factors and examining the patterns of development in terms of the interaction between internal and external forces which evolve and change over time. The character of these relatively independent societies altered during the six decades, with changes taking place both within the class alignments and among them.

Moreover, the external forces changed, with the United States coming to play a more influential role, especially in Canada, but also in Argentina after the turn of the century, and in Australia in the 1920s. Direct investment by US capital, and its encouragement by the governments of all three nations, altered the character of domestic industrial development, and was the harbinger of a much deeper and encompassing relationship than had been the case under conditions of British portfolio investment and commercial ties. A case might, in fact, be made that direct investment in production lessened the degree of autonomy enjoyed by the three societies.

Secondly, if this is taken a step further it seems that autonomy was not merely a consequence of formal political independence. Most other states in Latin America were as formally independent as Argentina, and more so than Canada and Australia in the latter part of the nineteenth century; but they probably had less room for independent economic action *vis-à-vis* the international powers of the era. Certainly, none enjoyed the relative freedom of action to create a similarly diversified and articulated economy. If anything, formal, political nationhood was gained by Canada and Australia in recognition of the economic independence of action achieved.

Thirdly, an important *caveat* on dominion manufacturing must also be entered. The existence of social and economic structures similar to those of the major European industrial nations did not mean that the three then automatically evolved into fully-fledged, industrial capitalist societies – as, indeed, writers such as Samir Amin have argued for Canada and Australia. Local manufacturers did not, in fact, become a significant element within the ruling coalitions or the wider society (except, perhaps, for powerful individuals such as Essington Lewis or W. L. Baillieu in Australia). Nor did they exert a strong and consistent influence on state economic policies, although again an exception might be made for Australia, where the new federal government adopted protectionist policies with the aim of stimulating national manufacturing (the issue, however, was by no means decided, and the free trade protection battle returned in the late 1920s).[13]

In Canada, the protective tariffs of the 1879 National Policy were intended less to promote an indigenous class of Canadian manufacturers than to encourage industries on Canadian soil. It was a policy that persuaded the larger and more dynamic US manufacturers to establish branch plants in Canada, many of which were financed in later years by powerful domestic banks.[14]

Argentine manufacturers, mainly foreign-born even into the 1920s, lacked sufficient influence to pressure governments into following a policy of industrial promotion. Tariffs there were, but they applied across the board, on raw materials needed as factory inputs, as much as on finished goods. And, for the most part, the manufacturers were without important allies in any group, either among landowning conservatives insisting on the benefits of free trade, or socialist workers pressing for cheap consumer goods.[15]

From 1870 to 1930, therefore, Canada, Argentina and Australia remained, first and foremost, producers and exporters of raw material and foodstuff staples to the industrialized societies of Europe and the United States. In return, they imported manufactured products, labour and capital. Their role in the international division of labour was firmly established and accepted by the ruling groups and the state.

The dominant social structures, in which well-developed commercial and financial groups combined to ensure the continued expansion of the staples export economy, explain why the specialist role should have been so acceptable for the three countries. The conventional wisdom was that the prosperity of all three sprang basically from the export sector, and not from a tariff-protected, domestic manufacturing sector. None of the three, therefore, moved into the category of an industrial capitalist society during this period, even taking into account the significant growth and diversification of manufacturing which took place after the turn of the century, and again in the 1920s. It is important to remember that the national ruling groups and their state institutions exercised *relative* autonomy in their management of the local economy. Clearly, the unassailable arguments were all on the side of a powerful, staples-export sector whose juggernaut march (before the international collapse of the 1930s) could scarcely be questioned. Their perceptions were reinforced by those of society at large, which accepted the established, and for the most part, highly profitable, specialized role that had opened up within the world division of labour. As Ronald Robinson has written, virtually every group in society supported those politicians and parties which maintained free trading and investment arrangements.[16]

Under such circumstances, the chances of a strong, national manufacturing class of entrepreneurs emerging out of the conscious decision of the state were found to be less than favourable. The encouragment of industrial growth by deliberate and selective government protection and promotion, and the fuelling of that expansion by credits and loans from the domestic banking sector (as happened in nineteenth-century France, Germany, the United States and Japan[17]), were largely lacking in Canada, Argentina and Australia – although certain Australian states did made efforts in this direction.

Even in Australia, however, the banks made little effort during this period to switch their emphasis away from traditional customers to the pastoral sector.[18] The same is true, in general, for loan priorities in Argentina and Canada, where credit was channelled into the export sector and into the transport and commercial infrastructure required to maintain it. This tendency was reinforced by foreign financial institutions which directed their loans into the Australian pastoral sector and into transport infrastructure in Canada and Argentina. In Canada, the powerful banking groups did invest in manufacturing, but in such cases the credit went principally to the expanding US branch plants in Ontario and, to a lesser extent, Quebec.[19]

Fourthly, there is yet one more reservation to be made. Most of the emphasis so far has been laid on the features common to the three societies. Given the main purposes of this chapter – to question the centre/periphery models of development/underdevelopment, and to explain why some societies were capable of evolving an economic structure sufficiently articulated to allow at least a partial industrial development – this is justifiable. The three societies were so obviously different from other dependencies of the time, and also from the industrial capitalist nations of Europe, that attention needs to be drawn to their own similarities – as, indeed, contemporaries did constantly.

Yet, within the general pattern of similarity which gave them their distinctiveness, there were also important differences. The key to such differences can, again, be identified in the nature of the social structures and relationships within the three. This, in turn, affected the way in which the economy of each interacted with others in the international system of trade and investment. The most obvious variation is to be found between Argentina on the one hand, and Canada and Australia on the other. In the latter two, the urban elements in the ruling coalition were stronger, and earlier assumed a dominance over the staples producers. By the 1880s and 1890s, the Australian squatters had become, in many cases, subaltern members of the coalition, indebted to, and dependent upon, the banking sector for their continued viability. The power of Canadian capital, too, was concentrated in the financial institutions and commercial enterprises of Montreal and Toronto, which exercised a clear economic hegemony over the staples producers, and especially over the grain farmers of Ontario and the Prairies. This economic weight was reflected also in political influence at federal level. In Argentina, the dominance of the urban groups was less evident. The landed oligarchy continued to wield much greater economic and political influence, even after the Radical Party's triumph in 1916, and acted as the principal arbiter of social, economic, and political change in a way that its Australian equivalent had ceased to do after the late nineteenth century. And in any serious confrontations, they could call upon the ultimate weapon, the armed forces, which had retained a special position in the administrative order ever since the nineteenth century.

One indicator of the relative capacities of the three ruling groups may be seen in railway construction. The railway networks, central to the opening up of the staples-producing prairies of Canada, the pampas of Argentina, and the outback of Australia, could be considered economic elements of national importance to each country. In Canada, the major part of the construction was carried out first by private capital, heavily promoted and subsidised by the state. Australia's federal government constructed its own system in the separate colonies, and later, federal capital remained responsible for construction and operation, although, as in Canada, it drew heavily upon foreign loans and expertise. In Argentina, however, the principal lines (and most profitable) were built and run by European companies, while the state was left with the task of undertaking the peripheral and less profitable sections.

The manufacturing sectors of the three societies reflected also the distinct capacity of the ruling coalition to branch out into new and innovative activity. In the 1850s Canada was already establishing a range of small-scale, manufacturing activities associated with agricultural production; these competed successfully with the later influx of US branch plants. Similarly, the steel industry of Southern Ontario remained essentially a Canadian national enterprise. By the First World War, these groups had formed a modern corporate élite, part of a powerful managerial structure.[20]

Australia diversified and industrialized later, and possibly more slowly, but its manufacturing sector was, if anything, more firmly based upon indigenous capital and entrepreneurship. The processing industries and small-scale urban manufacturers were joined, after the turn of the century, by large-scale corporate enterprises, especially in the mining metals sector. As in Canada, enterprises such as BHP and Collins House were no longer family-controlled; they were modern, twentieth-century industrial conglomerates with vertical control from mining to blast furnaces to wire-rope factories to shipping lines – and with links to foreign capital through joint ventures.[21] The Australian state, like its Canadian counterpart, was concerned directly with this phase of large-scale, corporate manufacturing expansion. And, in both societies, the work force assumed the character of a modern industrial proletariat by contrast with the craft workers of the small-scale, urban factories of the past.

It is rather more difficult to find an equivalent evolution taking place in Argentina during this period. The possibilities for backward linkages into agricultural machinery manufacture did not arise, and Australia, in fact, became one of the country's suppliers of such products. Staples processing was initiated by Argentine entrepreneurs, but fell rapidly into the hands of foreign firms. Consumer industries in the big cities were numerous, but the mainly immigrant factory owners remained socially, economically, and politically marginal within Argentine society.[22] The small, labour-intensive, factory sector continued to expand right into the 1920s, and provided more employment than the foreign-owned and larger-scale modern plants.[23] But corporate groupings of larger national industries similar to those of Canada and Australia failed to emerge. It may be significant that whereas the Australian ruling groups, in conjunction with the state, used the years of the First World War to restructure and create a new corporate industrialism, the Argentine manufacturing community, if anything, suffered from the shortages caused by war, as well as from the state's and its own inability to adapt and respond to the wartime challenges and opportunities.

VII CONCLUSION

For Canada, Argentina and Australia, despite differences compounded by regional variations within each society, the similarities in the pattern of development over this period of sixty years remain sufficiently striking. They are clear exceptions to the somewhat simplistic models which have divided world societies into two polarized groups within the world economy. This is not to deny the existence of inequality or exploitation, which have been associated all too clearly with the historical evolution of the modern international system. Rather, there is a change of emphasis. I am arguing that to understand the problems of development and underdevelopment, more specific and finely-honed studies of national cases must be undertaken. In undertaking such studies, the most important starting point must be the nature of the society itself – its social structures, its class relations, and the way that these have influenced state policies and so interacted with the forces of the international system of which each society forms part.

NOTES

1. R. Nurkse, *Patterns of Trade and Development* (Oxford: Basil Blackwell, 1962); G. M. Meier, 'The Problems of Limited Development', in A. M. Agarwala and S. P. Singh (eds), *The Economics of Underdevelopment* (New York: Galaxy Books, 1963) pp. 54–74; S. Kuznets, 'Underdeveloped Countries and the Pre-Industrial Phase in the Advanced Countries', in ibid., pp. 135–53.
2. A. G. Frank, *Capitalism and Underdevelopment in Latin America* (New York: Monthly Review Press, 1967), and 'Dependence Is Dead: Long Live Dependence and Class Struggle', *Latin American Perspectives*, I (1974); O. Sunkel and P. Paz, *El subdesarrollo latinoamericano y la teoría del desarrollo* (Mexico: Siglo XXI Editores, 1970); T. Dos Santos, 'The Crisis of Development Theory and the Problem of Dependence in Latin America', in H. Bernstein (ed.), *Underdevelopment and Development* (Harmondsworth: Penguin, 1973).

3. S. Amin, *Accumulation on a world scale*, 2 vols (New York: Monthly Review Press, 1974), and *Unequal Development* (New York: Monthly Review Press, 1976); A. Emmanuel, *Unequal Exchange* (New York: Monthly Review Press, 1972).
4. This is a point made also by P. J. O'Brien in 'A Critique of Latin American Theories of Dependency', in I. Oxaal *et al.*, *Beyond the sociology of development* (London and Boston: Routledge & Kegan Paul, 1975) p. 13ff.; also C. Bettelheim, 'Theoretical Comments', in A. Emmanuel, *Unequal Exchange*, p. 301, and N. Poulantzas, *Classes in Contemporary Capitalism* (London: New Left Books, 1975), p. 151.
5. The concept is discussed, *inter alia*, in 'Dominion Capitalism: a first statement', *Australian and New Zealand Journal of Sociology*, 24 (1978) pp. 352–63, 'Le Capitalism de Dominion', *Cahiers du Socialisme*, 3 (Université du Québec à Montreal, 1979) 163–211, and 'The Formation of Dominion Capitalism: Economic Truncation and Class Structure', in A. Moscovitch and G. Drover (eds), *Inequality: Essays on the Political Economy of Social Welfare* (University of Toronto Press, 1981). On the more specific issue of industrialization in the dominion societies, see 'The industrialization of staples producers: Australia, Canada and Argentina in the nineteenth century', *Occasional Paper* no. 8 (Planning Research Centre, University of Sydney, 1981), and 'Industrialization and Class Structure in Australia, Canada and Argentina: 1870 to 1980', in E. Wheelwright and K. Buckley (eds), *The Political Economy of Australian Capitalism*, vol. v (Sydney: ANZ Press, 1982).
6. This is more applicable to Canada and Australia than to Argentina, where cultural and social remnants of the colonial order were still to be found in the class relationships of the twentieth century. Quebec is another example of the continuation of an older, feudal order of relationships into the late nineteenth century.
7. C. Clark, *The Conditions of Economic Progress*, 2nd edn (London: Macmillan, 1951).
8. H. L. Browning and B. Roberts, 'Urbanization, Sectoral Transformation, and the Utilization of Labour in Latin America', *Comparative Urban Research*, VIII (1980) 86–103.
9. O. Cornblit, 'European Immigrants in Argentine Industry and Politics', in C. Véliz (ed.), *The Politics of Conformity in Latin America* (London: Oxford University Press, 1967), pp. 221–48.
10. F. H. Cardoso and E. Faletto, *Dependencia y Desarrollo en América Latina* (Buenos Aires: Siglo XXI Editores, 1969).
11. R. E. Baldwin, 'Patterns of Development in Newly Settled Regions', in J. Friedman and W. Alonso (eds), *Regional Development and Planning* (Cambridge, Mass.: MIT Press, 1964).
12. M. H. Watkins, 'A Staple Theory of Economic Growth', in W. Easterbrook and M. H. Watkins (eds), *Approaches to Canadian Economic History* (Toronto: Macmillan, 1978).
13. P. Cochrane, *Industrialization and Dependence: Australia's Road to Economic Development, 1870—1939* (St. Lucia: University of Queensland Press, 1980) ch. 5.
14. R. T. Naylor, 'The Rise and Fall of the Third Commercial Empire of the

St. Lawrence', in G. Temple (ed.), *Capitalism and the National Question in Canada* (University of Toronto Press, 1972) pp. 1–42.

15. J. Corradi, 'Argentina', in R. H. Chilcote and J. C. Edelstein (eds), *Latin America: The Struggle with Dependency and Beyond* (New York: Halsted Press, John Wiley, 1974).
16. R. Robinson, 'Non-European Foundations of European Imperialism: Sketch for a Theory of Collaboration', in E. R. J. Owen and R. B. Sutcliffe, *Studies in the Theory of Imperialism* (London: Longman, 1972), p. 124.
17. A. Gerschenkron, 'Economic Backwardness in Historical Perspective', in B. Hoselitz (ed.), *The Progress of Underdeveloped Areas* (Chicago University Press, 1952).
18. Cochrane, *Industrialization and Dependence*, ch. 4.
19. R. T. Naylor, *The History of Canadian Business* (Toronto University Press, 1975).
20. T. Traves, *The State and Enterprise* (University of Toronto Press, 1979).
21. R. W. Connell and T. H. Irving, *Class Structure in Australian History* (Melbourne: Longman Cheshire, 1980) p. 271.
22. Cornblit, 'European Immigrants', p. 226ff.
23. C. F. Díaz Alejandro, *Essays on the Economic History of the Argentine Republic* (New Haven: Yale University Press, 1970) pp. 284–5.

5 Argentina, Australia and Brazil Before 1929

CARLOS F. DÍAZ ALEJANDRO

I INTRODUCTION

Economic and political disturbances in the Argentine Republic during the 1970s and early 1980s have brought forth a renewal of fanciful assertions about the degree of Argentine progress before the 1930s, when allegedly the country fell from economic grace, even before the rise of General Perón to power, by engaging in massive state intervention in economic affairs. Journalists and even some academics find it irresistible to shock listeners with the claim that once upon a time Argentina was richer than Australia, and even as rich as the United States. This essay will briefly present the salient facts of the Argentine story until 1929, comparing it with Australian development, and restating that at least during the nineteenth and twentieth centuries Argentine per capita income has never been higher than that of Australia, a fact that has been known to serious scholars for quite a while.[1] Argentine progress since the middle of the last century was nevertheless remarkable, and that fact will be highlighted by comparing Argentine growth with that of Brazil.

II ORIGINS

Of the three countries considered in this chapter, Brazil is the oldest one, economically speaking. By the middle of the nineteenth century Brazil had already experienced a rich economic history characterized by export booms which left behind, besides splendid architecture, little but institutional arrangements inimical to development. The seventeenth century sugar boom of the Northeast yielded slavery and latifundia, plus a peripheral, low-productivity subsistence sector. The eighteenth century gold boom may have contributed to Brazilian national union, but its impact on sustainable per capita incomes was weak. The relatively painless way in which Brazil obtained independence during the 1820s could have been expected to facilitate the spread of the industrial revolution to the tropics, but by the mid-nineteenth century Brazil remained a patriarchal, rural society, its labour market shackled by the peculiar institution. In contrast with Argentina, however, the Brazilian state by 1850 had become a going concern which relied on reasonably firm institutions. At that time, only Chile in Latin America could match Brazilian institutional development. The Brazilian geographical vastness, and the heterogeneity of its regional economies, made the political achievements of the Brazilian monarchy the more impressive, although ambiguous regarding their impact on economic development. Reflecting perhaps certain faith in its manifest destiny, that state called itself an empire.

One may conjecture that Argentine per capita income at mid-nineteenth century was not far above the low Brazilian levels; by then, however, slavery had disappeared in the River Plate leaving practically no imprint either ethnically or culturally. Buenos Aires had come into its own only late in the eighteenth century as a result of the Bourbon reforms; other parts of what was to become the Argentine Republic had 'longer' economic histories, but mainly as peripheries to the mining centers of the Perus (including today's Bolivia). During the three decades following independence, what is today Argentina witnessed a good deal of political turmoil. In 1861 Argentina was more of an empty land than Brazil. This emptiness was regarded both as a key barrier to economic progress and as a potentially fatal, geopolitical flaw; Argentine leadership was to be marked by a compulsion to 'people the wilderness'. Before the 1860s what is today the Argentine Republic was made up of fragile coalitions of regional authorities, jealous of their autonomy, which might have gone their separate ways as in Central America. Threats from the North and the West, plus the growing hegemony of Buenos Aires, contributed to the establishment of national unity, a unity which may be viewed as a precondition for the rational exploitation of pampean land.

During the nineteenth century Australia was far behind both Argentina and Brazil in the development of sovereign political institutions. The Australian colonies did not become a federation until 1901, and even then the federation appeared to have less centralized control than those of Argentina and Brazil. Colonial status did not prevent Australia from achieving substantial industrialization and one of the highest per capita incomes in the nineteenth century, as will be seen below. Since the 1820s, even before gold, the expansion of the pastoral industry fuelled a sustained rise to prosperity in Australia.[2]

III OUTPUT AND ENGINES OF GROWTH

The export orientated growth made possible by an expanding international economy raised per capita income in a sustained and substantial way in Argentina from around the 1860s, and in Brazil from the beginning of this century. The vigorous São Paulo coffee boom of late nineteenth century was largely offset by the decline of other Brazilian export activities, such as sugar and cotton; in the River Plate the expanding export lines more clearly offset from an earlier period those in decadence, such as salted meat. The Argentine export quantum rose at a remarkable 4.8 per cent per annum from 1865 to 1912, and at 4.1 per cent from 1912 to 1928.[3] The expansion of the Australian export quantum reached 4.3 per cent per annum during 1870–1913.[4]

Table 5.1 presents estimates of per capita Gross Domestic Product for Argentina, Australia and Brazil. Brazilian per capita GPD growth could not have been very significant during the nineteenth century, given its 1901 level; Table 5.1 suggests significant Argentine per capita growth even before 1880. Australia by contrast was born rich; this point is often forgotten in comparing Argentina and Australia. Vast mineral resources and scanty population make the Australia of the second half of the nineteenth century comparable to some Persian Gulf nations of today, or to some of the mining states in the West of the United States also in the nineteenth century. As far back as 1861–5, Australian agriculture, livestock, dairying and fisheries contributed only 22 per cent of value added in the economy; mining and manufacturing together accounted for 19 per cent, and construction 9 per cent.[5] One may conjecture that value added in agriculture and livestock in Argentina and Brazil during 1861–5 must have accounted for no less than 40 per cent of GDP. The per capita income gap between Australia and Argentina, as shown in Table 5.1 for 1901, is similar to a Colin Clark estimate reported by Diéguez.[6]

Tables 5.1 and 5.3 illustrate the remarkable extent to which both Argentine population and per capita product made progress relative to Australia up to the late 1920s. Brazil advanced also in per capita product, but at quite a remove from the two temperate countries of recent settlement. Australia appears to have stagnated for surprisingly long periods. The aggregate figures, however, hide an impressive diversification from a rich but specialized mining and rural economy into a modern industrialized country, and may reflect an overestimation of the GDP around 1890.[7] Australia also suffered unusually harsh weather at the turn of the century.

TABLE 5.1 *Estimates of Argentine, Australian and Brazilian per capita GDP (in US $, of 1970 purchasing power)*

	Argentina	*Australia*	*Brazil*
1880	470	1520	211
1901	780	1360	190
1913	1030	1690	230
1928	1200	1590	340
1939	1170	1670	430

SOURCES AND METHOD Estimates projected back from the calculations for 1970 found in Kravis.[8] Argentine data on per capita growth since 1900 was obtained from Díaz Alejandro,[9] United Nations,[10] and International Monetary Fund.[11] Brazilian data since 1900 obtained from Haddad[12] and International Monetary Fund. Australian data came from Neil Butlin,[13] M. W. Butlin,[14] and International Monetary Fund (1981). The Argentine estimate for 1880 is a rough guess based on export quantum data. Data on Argentine export quantum are the revised series found in Diéguez.[15] The Brazilian 1880 estimate has been kindly provided by Professor Raymond Goldsmith, based on his forthcoming history of Brazilian financial development. It may be noted that the implicit use of the same purchasing-power-parity exchange rates obtained by Kravis *et al.* for 1970[16] during earlier years, probably overestimates the gap in per capita incomes between Australia and the Latin American countries. But this point is unlikely to be very significant for the Argentine-Australian comparison during the twentieth century.

TABLE 5.2 *Estimates of Argentine, Australian and Brazilian populations (millions)*

	Argentina	*Australia*	*Brazil*
1861	1.35	1.20	8.55
1880	2.47	2.24	11.55
1901	4.92	3.83	18.39
1913	7.60	4.75	23.66
1928	11.28	6.22	32.23
1939	13.95	7.03	10.29

SOURCES As in Table 5.1 plus national statistical sources; United Nations *Demographic Yearbook*, several issues; and IMF, *International Financial Statistics*, several issues.

TABLE 5.3 *Argentine and Brazilian GDP and population relative to Australia (Australia = 100)*

	Per capita GDP		*Population*	
	Argentina	*Brazil*	*Argentina*	*Brazil*
1861	–	–	113	713
1880	31	14	110	525
1901	57	14	128	480
1913	61	14	160	518
1928	75	21	198	573
1939	70	26	203	610

SOURCES As Tables 5.1 and 5.2.

Of the three countries, pre-1929 Argentina appears to have had the more adaptable and diversified export bill. During 1875–9 Argentine exports were still largely made up of wool, hides, and salted meat. By 1890–4 wheat had become a leading item; by 1900–4 both corn and linseed were (each) as important as hides; and by 1910–14 frozen beef exports were about as important as wool. Wool, hides and salted meat by 1910–14 amounted to only one-fourth of the value of merchandise exports. By contrast, coffee's share in Brazilian exports advanced secularly from the last century, so that by the late 1920s Brazil had become one of the classic examples of export concentration. Much of this contrast is explained by different natural endowments; Brazilian efforts since 1906 to support international coffee prices together with other policies may have reinforced the trend. Wool remained the leading Australian export, representing 54 per cent of all exports during the 1880s, and 43 per cent during the 1920s.[17] Gold plus mineral exports accounted for 27 per cent of exports in the 1880s, and 9 per cent during the 1920s; between those two decades the share of wheat in Australian exports rose from 5 to 21 per cent.

The ratio of exports to domestic product remained lower in Brazil than in Argentina: during 1925–9 it was about 14 per cent for the former and 24 for the latter.[18] Argentine growth was less handicapped by a low-productivity, subsistence sector than Brazil's. The corresponding Australian ratio was 18 per cent,[19] somewhat less than Argentina's despite Australia's lower population and the absence of a significant subsistence sector. A higher Australian per capita income, a more diversified productive structure, and differences in domestic relative price structures, may help to explain the contrast.

The socioeconomic linkages of Australian exports may possibly have been more desirable for long-term, economic and political development than those of Argentina, in spite of an apparently more diversified Argentine export bill. Gold and mineral exports relied on economic agents and forms of production sharply different from those for rural exports, and Argentina's export bill did not contain so powerful an alternative to rural exports. Australian mining exports generated interest in scientific and technical research; they provided a labour force which rapidly formed trade unions not only in mining but also among ranch hands; and Australian trade unions, as well as the entrepreneurs engaged in mining, coalesced into political groups which opposed the creation of a permanent land-owning class.[20] Both Australian and Argentine exports developed *some* direct forward and backward industrial linkages; in both countries, however, limited domestic processing of exported staples, and weak input demand generated by the export sectors, were viewed as flaws in the transmission mechanisms of the engine of growth.

IV INPUTS

We turn now to an examination of the inputs of land, labour, capital and technology that fed exports, as well as of those other goods and services that were generated by the pre-1929 economies. But first I want to say something about the institutional framework within which economic variables operated.

A political and social framework compatible with export-oriented growth was established in Argentina from shortly after the middle of the nineteenth century. During 1879–80, a series of military campaigns forced Argentine frontiers southwards, at the expense of native Indian and Chilean claims; Chile at that time was engaged in a war against Bolivia and Peru. Brazil was still experiencing important evolutionary changes in its institutional organization as late as the 1880s and 1890s, when slavery was abolished and the empire became a republic. Australia gradually evolved toward self-rule, but retained strong ties with the British crown. The external framework for all countries was that of the Pax Britannica until the First World War. Since both the internal and external environment were on the whole secure and satisfactory to hegemonic social forces, little public intervention was deemed necessary for outputs and inputs in the day-to-day operation of Argentine markets. The Brazilian state tended to have a more interventionist stance than Argentina's, partly because of the requirements of an orderly abolition of slavery. Brazilian tariffs were higher on average than Argentine, and the Brazilian commitment to the gold standard was less profound. Both countries, however, would frequently follow financial policies which foreign bankers found appalling. The Brazilian republic was inaugurated with an enthusiastic burst of credit expansion; Argentina also frequently floated her currency (a practice disparagingly labelled as an 'inconvertible paper standard'). In spite of declarations of economic liberalism, publicly-owned banks (provincial and national) expanded in late nineteenth-century Argentina, and influential landowners appear to have been the major beneficiaries. As for Australia, protectionism was the most pronounced departure from pre-1929 orthodoxy.

Both Argentina and Brazil were amply supplied with virgin land. The supplies were sufficient but they were not perfectly elastic: the upward tilt in the supply of economically homogeneous land was enough to generate large rents for intra-marginal landowners. Both on *a priori* grounds and on the basis of available information, one may conclude that pampean landowners were the major beneficiaries of the great Argentine expansion up to the 1930s. By 1880 the best land had been appropriated and land ownership concentrated into a few hands. Under these conditions, it was perfectly possible for an open and competitive land market to generate spectacular rents. While the Brazilian case is more complex because of its regional heterogeneity, similar conclusions seem to apply. Experiments with colonization schemes which centred around family-owned farms were carried out in some regions of Argentina and Brazil. Their beneficial socioeconomic consequences, unfortunately atypical for those countries as a whole, can be seen in the Argentine province of Santa Fe and in the Brazilian state of Santa Catarina. In both Argentina and Brazil, landowners, particularly those who produced exportable goods, became the most powerful agents in politics before 1929 with the most to say as to how newly-available land was to be distributed.

Australian land policies are in substantial contrast to those of Argentina. For many years the British government did not surrender ownership of Australian land and, before independence, the Iberian monarchies followed a similar policy in their American domains. Sheep ranchers failed to get clear titles to their enormous enterprises during the crucial, formative years of Australia;[21] opposition to their claims from miners, land-hungry ex-miners, and urban groups. Ranchers remained an important political force in Australia, but one which did not control the government machinery as did landowners in Argentina.[22] When cereals became an important Australian export, family-operated, medium-size farms were relatively more important than in Argentina, where tenant farming under contracts of about five years were more common than in Australia. A system of rural production, where tenant farmers moved frequently from one region to another, did not seem to damage Argentina's rural productivity and output growth before 1929, but it had deleterious effects on income distribution as well as on social and political life. The mediocre housing, poor social services, and lamentable infrastructural facilities in most of those melancholy little towns scattered across the pampean zone, were eloquent testimony to the rootlessness of Argentine farming and the weakness of the rural middle class. Landless tenant farmers had difficulty in obtaining credit, and in securing the marketing arrangements which they perceived as stable and fair.

With a pattern of land ownership dictated by political history, and with prices of exports, imports and capital determined fundamentally by international markets, total rents depended on the conditions of labour supply. Immigration policy became *the* critical policy variable which remained under the control of the governments of pre-1929 Australia, Argentina and Brazil, in the sense that public action could have an important influence on the levels of migration (which, in turn, had powerful effects on the growth and distribution of GDP).

The pre-1929 world witnessed massive migrations, but the 'international labour market' remained segmented by culture, policy and prejudice. Chinese and Indians migrated, but mainly to tropical regions, while north-western Europeans moved mainly to North America, Australia and South Africa. Argentina and Brazil (or one should say São Paulo) connected primarily with the labour markets of Southern Europe. Only via the Italian labour market were there significant indirect links with the broader, Atlantic labour market; Italian migrants moving back and forth between Santos and Buenos Aires provided also a link, albeit weak, between the Argentine and the Brazilian labour markets. Australia, in contrast, limited its connections to north-western Europe, primarily the British Isles. While it is not obvious that real wages in Ireland were above those in Lombardy towards the end of the nineteenth century, it is likely that on average real wages were higher in north-western Europe than in Italy and Spain. Emigrants had also the choice of migrating to the United States or the white dominions, which was a choice made often by Italians but not by Spaniards. On balance, Australia's more restrictive immigration policy placed a higher floor under home wages, and this variety of labour protectionism had probably a greater importance for the welfare of workers within Australia than the celebrated Australian tariff. For excluded migrants, however, the contemplation of advanced Australian social legislation must have proved poor consolation.

Argentine and Brazilian landowners favoured, and were able to obtain, more liberal policies for immigration. The Brazilian case is particularly interesting. After the abolition of slavery in the 1880s, a large pool of cheap labour existed within the country, yet São Paulo landowners put pressure on their state government to seek subsidized immigration from Southern Europe and even Japan. *Internal* migration into São Paulo remained surprisingly small until the 1920s. The São Paulo landowners experienced transitional troubles in dealing with free labour, and not only in the case of ex-slaves; the Italian government early this century imposed a temporary ban on subsidized emigration to São Paulo, after receiving reports of deception and maltreatment of migrants.

Migration into Argentina required fewer, if any, subsidies. The country, with a population of 2.5 million in 1880, received 3.2 million immigrants during 1880–1910, more than 80 per cent of whom came from Italy and Spain. The architects of the Argentine liberal program had hoped for immigration from northwest Europe, and framed laws after 1860 (including religious toleration) to accommodate them. Some came, but Argentina was to remain predominantly Latin. Of all immigrants who came, about two-thirds stayed. While Argentina's population increased by 5.1 million between 1880 and 1913, that of Australia rose only by 2.5 million. Under the influence of the interests of landowners and the urge to 'people the wilderness', many of the gains arising from export-led growth for Argentina took the form of higher population; the Australian government (under the influence of organized labour) 'chose' to maintain a high per capita income and a low, homogeneous population. Neither Australia nor Argentina received significant numbers of non-white immigrants although some Japanese went to Argentina, and more to Brazil. Internal migration in Argentina, as for Brazil, was surprisingly sluggish until the 1930s; it seemed easier to bring seasonal workers from Italy than from northern Argentina even when substantial pools existed of Argentine workers earning wages below those of transatlantic migrants. The coexistence of massive immigration in both Argentina and Brazil with persistent pools of domestic, cheap (or cheaper) labour, as in the case of the contemporary United States, indicates that *domestic* labour markets were segmented by culture and prejudice, and perhaps also by policy.

While little, apparently, was done either in Argentina or Brazil to select immigrants on the basis of their skills, pre-1929 Argentina took a lot of trouble over education, particularly at the primary level. The Argentine illiteracy rate, calculated as a percentage of the population fourteen years of age and older, dropped from 77 per cent in the 1869 census to 36 per cent by 1914. In 1920, comparable Brazilian illiteracy remained around 65 per cent. Yet in spite of Argentina's educational efforts, only half of children aged 6 to 13 attended school in 1914, when the corresponding figure for Australia was over two-thirds.

The pre-1929 domestic capital markets of Argentina, Australia and Brazil became closely interwoven with those in Europe, especially London, and later with that in New York. With cyclical ups and downs, savings generated both domestically and abroad were transformed into railroads, land improvements, houses, factories and social overhead capital. The presence of foreign capital was larger (relatively) in Argentina and Australia than it was in Brazil. It has been estimated that the stock of long-term, foreign investment in Argentina in 1913 was only eighteen per cent lower than the equivalent figure for Canada; by 1930 Argentina accounted for 12 per cent of all British, long-term investments overseas, while Canada took 14 per cent and Australia 13 per cent. Argentine creditworthiness, as measured by the market yield of her bonds, was not very different from those of Australia and Canada during the 1920s. As late as 1931 Argentina was able to roll over a loan at an interest only ninety basis points above the average rate paid by the government of the United Kingdom; in 1927 Argentine creditworthiness was ranked by British experts as seventh among foreign countries.[23]

Associated with foreign capital, but less tightly than in the 1950s and 1960s, came foreign technology and knowledge of various kinds. The tricks for running railroads and tramways, meatpacking and electricity plants, refrigerated ships and coffee warehouses, were first supplied by foreigners. They gave monopoly power, but of a wasting kind; too many people, including Argentines and Brazilians themselves, could provide them sooner or later. Meantime, it is likely that important quasi-rents were captured by foreign suppliers, fuelling the fires of nationalism. Much foreign capital was placed in activities which came close to being natural monopolies or monopsonies. Railroads and public utilities were obvious examples; less clear-cut were meatpacking, cereal-marketing, shipping and insurance. Such near-monopolies (railroads) and monopsonies (meat-packers) had intimate commercial and financial links with other foreign companies, so that competition was reduced not simply in the markets for their principal outputs and inputs, but also in a host of other related markets. British-owned railroads and public utility companies in Argentina are said to have bought coal, rails and many of their other inputs exclusively from those suppliers in Britain with whom they had common financial interests, and engaged also in what today would be called intra-firm transfer pricing.[24]

There were many mechanisms, other than foreign investment, by which the fruits of technological progress reached Argentina, Australia and Brazil. Imports of capital, intermediate and consumer goods incorporated much of nineteenth and early twentieth century advance, together with the more doubtfully useful products of fashion; migrants often carried in their hands and heads new knowledge; ideas moved freely in magazines and books eagerly sought in an age of faith in 'progress'. Of particular benefit were advances in medicine, hygiene and public health, the diffusion of which brought Argentine students, researchers, and other skilled personnel overseas.

In both Argentina and Brazil the production of exportable goods was predominantly in domestic hands, by contrast, say, with Chile and Cuba. But at least during the nineteenth century, international marketing remained controlled by foreigners to a large degree. Argentine cattlemen generated significant savings and diversified their portfolios, but they showed limited interest in investing 'downstream'. They had actively changed livestock technology, they steadily improved cattle herds, but they made only timid efforts to invest in meatpacking; Argentines took practically no part in the exporting of chilled meat (although their presence was greater in frozen meat exports). The behaviour of cattle ranchers contrasts with that of Tucumán landowners, who invested in sugar mills producing for domestic consumption. Argentine cattlemen, perhaps, let foreigners handle international marketing as a way of ensuring foreign markets, very much as some countries rely similarly today on transnational corporations. A few large trading companies dominated Argentine grain exports, some of which were started by Argentine entrepreneurs and quickly became international companies. Brazilian coffee-growers significantly expanded their marketing activities after the beginning of this century.

V SOME POLICY ISSUES AND CONCLUSIONS

Uneasiness about the presence of foreign capital was only one of the anxieties generated before 1929 by the export-led growth model. Industrial activities had made progress both in Argentina and Brazil, but not enough in the opinion of some critics (including members of the Armed Forces who associated industrialization with military strength and national greatness). As already noted, the Brazilian tariff seems to have been more protectionist than the Argentine, or at least on average. Both countries relied heavily on manufactured imports; machinery and equipment requirements were almost totally supplied from abroad. In the case of Argentina even textiles were predominantly of foreign origin; the Argentine textile industry lagged curiously behind those of Australia, Brazil and Mexico. Australian industrialization was encouraged not only by linkages from mineral exports but also by tariffs and other explicit forms of government support. Australian economic historians disagree as to whether those policies advanced or retarded Australian development before 1929; some see protection as a wasteful luxury that this early 'Kuwait' could afford.

Commercial and exchange-rate policies were debated in Argentina, Australia and Brazil with the usual arguments (and by the standard actors) by at least the second half of the nineteenth century. As suggested above, the long-run, developmental and distributional consequences of policy options were probably less than those for migration and have given rise to less debate and received less scholarly attention. The standard scenario naturally places landowners on the side of free trade (where one also finds the Argentine socialist party, but not the Australian labour party). Furthermore, it has been argued that, both in Argentina and Brazil, producers of exportable goods favoured flexible exchange rates whenever prices of their commodities were falling abroad, while they encouraged a return to the gold standard, as a check on appreciation, whenever world prices turned in their favour. Importers of goods and services also liked free trade, but they preferred an appreciated and stable currency. Central governments bound to service their external debt were among the major importers of services. They had to worry, too, about raising revenues in local currency, and found import duties an expedient mechanism for doing so. Landowners may not have been too displeased with moderate duties, as fiscal revenues may otherwise have had to come from property taxes. Memories of abuses of the inflation tax during the

1880s and 1890s in both Argentina and Brazil provided political support for the gold standard during the first three decades of this century; the Argentine socialist party was an eloquent defender not only of free trade but also of price stability and the gold standard. And both regional interests and politics in Argentina and Brazil may explain the adoption of protective tariffs.

Even if one considers landowners as the dominant influence on Argentine and Brazilian public society, their enthusiasm for completely free trade and flexible currency arrangements had certain, practical limits. Furthermore, in Argentina the middle class Radical party controlled the executive branch of government (but not the Senate) during 1916–30; Radical administrations introduced (mild) social welfare measures and expanded state investments in petroleum and railroads. This has not prevented some critics from tightly associating export-oriented growth with a skewed income distribution, oligarchical political dominance, a bias against industrialization, and a masochistic dependence on foreigners – a combination which was sharply in contrast with the classical English case that motivated David Ricardo.

To conclude this essay we might reconsider Argentina's position, relative to the rest, at the end of the Belle Epoque. As shown in Table 5.1, the narrowest gap between Argentine and Australian per capita incomes was experienced in the late 1920s. But the gap remained; *Argentine per capita income has never been higher than Australia's*. Other evidence supports this conclusion. Per capita Argentine exports were below those of Australia during 1925–9; Argentine per capita consumption of cement, so far as it can be measured, was about 60 per cent of Australia's in 1928–9; Argentine infant mortality rates were twice as high as Australia's during the 1920s, as reported by the League of Nations. The number of motor vehicles and telephones per capita in Argentina was significantly behind that of Australia (and, *a fortiori*, of Canada and the United States); so were literacy and the indicators for school attendance. With all this evidence, statements to the effect that earlier this century 'Argentina was richer than Australia' are quite puzzling. Perhaps comparisons of some unusual indicators, such as beef consumption, railway tracks, and gold stock per capita lie behind that statement.

One may also conjecture that the size, glitter, and cultural excellence of the city of Buenos Aires in the 1920s, unmatched by any Australian city, may have misled many a casual commentator on the Australian–Argentine comparison. The contrast between Buenos

Aires's glitter and Jujuy's poverty, or even the well-fed emptiness of pampean towns, is more revealing, and it is not found to the same extent in the more equalitarian Australia. Buenos Aires grandeur may even have misled some Argentine policy makers into confusing the city with the nation. It was a misperception compounded by Argentina's impressive record of growth after 1860, and it may have induced a delusion which was to have unfortunate consequences for Argentine domestic and international policies after 1929.

NOTES

Acknowledgements: Earlier versions of this essay received comments and criticisms from Pascal Arnaud, Edmar Bacha, Marcelo Cavarozzi, Juan Carlos de Pablo, Héctor Diéguez, Ronald Findlay, Albert Fishlow, Jorge Fodor, John Fogarty, Aleto Guadagni, Nathaniel Leff, Arthur Lewis, Ian W. McLean, Arturo O'Connell, and Gustav Ranis. The Oxford conference on Argentine economic history of July 1981 was particularly helpful. Virginia Casey bravely edited and typed these pages more times than she probably cares to remember. None of the named persons should be held responsible for any errors in this essay.

1. Héctor L. Diéguez, 'Argentina y Australia: algunos aspectos de su desarrollo económico comparado', *Desarrollo Económico*, 8 (1969) 543–63.
2. John P. Fogarty, 'Interpreting Australian history in the light of Argentine experience', mimeograph (Macquarie University, 52nd. ANZAAS Congress, 1982).
3. Héctor L. Diéguez, 'Crecimiento e inestabilidad del valor y el volumen físico de las exportaciones argentinas en el período 1864–1963', *Desarrollo Económico*, 12 (1972) 333–49.
4. Angus Madison, 'Long-run dynamics of productivity growth', *Banca Nazionale del Lavoro Quarterly Review*, 128 (1979) 1–30.
5. N. G. Butlin, *Australian Domestic Product, Investment and Foreign Borrowing, 1861–1938/9* (Cambridge University Press, 1962).
6. Diéguez, 'Argentina y Australia'.
7. Ian W. McLean and Jonathan J. Pincus, 'Living Standards in Australia 1890–1940: Evidence and Conjectures', Working Paper in Economic History 6, Australian National University, Canberra, August 1982.
8. Irving Kravis, Alan Heston, and Robert Summers, 'Real Gross Domestic Product Per Capita for More than One Hundred Countries', *Economic Journal*, 88 (1978) 215–43.
9. Carlos Díaz Alejandro, *Essays on the Economic History of the Argentine Republic* (New Haven: Yale University Press, 1970).
10. United Nations, *Series Históricas del Crecimento de América Latina* (Santiago de Chile: Naciones Unidas, 1978).

11. International Monetary Fund, *International Financial Statistics* (Washington, DC: IMF, 1981).
12. Claudio L. S. Haddad, *Crescimento do Producto Real no Brasil 1900–47* (Rio de Janeiro: Editora da Fundacao Getulio Vargas, 1978).
13. N. G. Butlin, *Australian Domestic Product, Investment and Foreign Borrowing.*
14. M. W. Butlin, 'A preliminary annual data base 1900/01 to 1973/4', Research Discussion Paper 7701, Reserve Bank of Australia, 1977.
15. Diéguez, 'Crecimiento e inestabilidad'.
16. Kravis *et al.*, 'Real Gross Domestic Product'.
17. Ernst Boehm, 'El desarrollo económico australiano a partir de 1930', in John Fogarty, Ezequiel Gallo and Héctor Diéguez, *Argentina y Australia* (Buenos Aires: Instituto Torcuato Di Tella, 1979), p. 151.
18. Data obtained from Haddad, *Crescimento do Producto Real*, and Díaz Alejandro, *Essays*.
19. Butlin, *Australian Domestic Product, Investment and Foreign Borrowing.*
20. John Hirst, 'La sociedad rural y la política en Australia, 1850–1930', in Fogarty *et al. Argentina y Australia*, pp. 87–8 and pp. 110–12; Ezequiel Gallo, 'Comentarios', in ibid., pp. 66–7.
21. Gallo, 'Comentarios', pp. 100–2.
22. Hirst, 'La Sociedad Rural', pp. 83–4.
23. Charles Wortman, 'Argentina, Australia and Brazil: Bonds in the London Capital Market, 1929–39', unpublished mss., Yale University.
24. Jorge Fodor and Arturo O'Connell, 'La Argentina y la economía atlántica en la primera mitad del siglo XX', *Desarrollo Económico*, 13 (1973) 3–66.

6 'Who Are We?': the Search for a National Identity in Argentina, Australia and Canada, 1870–1950

J. C. M. OGELSBY

'Who are we? What are we?' are questions that have dogged new nations. Domingo Faustino Sarmiento posed that problem to his compatriots; he hoped that Argentines would throw off their Spanish roots and emulate the (North) Americans. While (North) Americans seemed to have confidence in their own nationality, two other offshoots of the British Empire – Australia and Canada – were not so fortunate. They, too, were searching for a national identity. It is likely that Argentina, Australia and Canada are not certain as yet that they have found it. But in the process of the struggle to achieve a national identity, the period 1870–1950 demonstrates how serious a problem it can be.

The three countries have long been recognized as having much in common. They are 'new' countries whose wealth has been based on pastoral and agricultural activity, while mining and forestry have taken a varying role in economic life. These natural resources lay in the largely unsettled interiors that seemed to overawe, if not frighten, those who lived at their edges. As recently as 1951 a major Canadian Royal Commission opened its presentation with the uncharacteristically dramatic remark that 'Canada's scattered regions are dominated by the mysterious expanses of the Canadian Shield, with the still more mysterious Arctic beyond pressing down and hemming in the areas of civilized life.[1] Sarmiento, who provided the epic analysis of Argentina as a struggle between 'civilization' and 'barbarism', began by referring to Argentina's 'vast tract. . . . Its own extent is the evil from which the Argentine Republic suffers; the desert encompasses it on every side. . . . Immensity is the universal characteristic of the country . . .'[2]. On the other hand, W. K. Hancock, whose classic *Australia* was published in 1929, could declare that 'Australians are not depressed by the contemplation of their vast open spaces. The great majority of them live in a genial environment, and their hopeful gaze has been fixed on nearer frontiers.'[3]

Whatever the bias, those who wrote about the countries or expressed their feelings elsewhere were affected by the land, and by the sense of space. The pampas, which are slightly larger than the island province of Newfoundland, or which might fit comfortably into southern Alberta or the eastern half of the state of New South Wales, seem to have had as great an impact on the mind of Argentines as did the 'bush' on Australians. And these two peoples have tried to develop a national identity from that vastness. Canadians, aware occasionally that they inhabit the second largest country in the world, do not appear to have done so; the rocks, lakes and forests of the Laurentian Shield blocked expansion, and when the Northwestern prairie region opened up it was largely immigrants from Britain, Continental Europe, and the United States who came to fill the void. They would have difficulty identifying with the East.

The land dictated the form of settlement, and this contributed to shaping the way the inhabitants came to view themselves. In Argentina and Australia the land was conducive to pastoral activity. It was the 'Big Man's Frontier' of the nineteenth century,[4] where the *estanciero* and his Australian equivalent, the squatter, ran their cattle and sheep stations. By 1870 they depended upon a rural proletariat to do the manual work: in Argentina it was gauchos; in Australia, stockmen and shearers.

The independence enjoyed both by gaucho and stockman in the 1840s was by 1870 little less than a memory. In 1845 Sarmiento could describe the gaucho as 'a man independent of every want, under no control, with no notion of government . . .';[5] almost simultaneously an Australian was describing life in the Bush as a 'sensation of absolute freedom, which is one of the chief attractions of this sort of life . . .'.[6] In neither case was the individual attracted to agriculture. The horse was part of him, and he disdained those who worked on the ground. But barbed wire had come to limit freedom, and the gaucho was in the process of being permanently tamed. The poet who spoke for him was José Hernández, who began publishing his *Martin Fierro* in 1872.[7]

Martín Fierro was intended to represent the past; he was a 'rebellious and solitary man . . . of an essentially individualistic epoch'.[8] He demonstrated the essential masculinity and 'mateship' that was also characteristic of the Australian Bushman. His Australian contemporaries were men like Ben Hall and Ned Kelly, who were not fictional characters but outlaws who rode their way into myth as symbols of the 'real Australia'. Kelly died on the gallows but, as the ballads suggest, it was not the police who should be honoured.[9]

This sentimental approach to illegality would not have appealed to Canadians, who also have a continent to tame. In 1867 Canada achieved Dominion status and control over its internal affairs; two years later it acquired the Hudson's Bay Company territories in the Northwest. In 1873 the federal government established the North-West Mounted Police, whose red jackets came to symbolize law and order on the vast prairies and in the Arctic. Moreover, the Mounties became representative of the nation, and of how many of the world's police forces can this be claimed?

While the Mounties ensured 'peace, order and good government' in the Northwest, several Canadians in the East established 'Canada First' in 1868 as a means of coming to grips with the new Dominion status and the question 'Who are we?'. They wanted to develop a new, non-colonial identity which incorporated the Northwest and British Columbia into a great northern nation, standing side-by-side in equality with Britain and strengthened *vis-à-vis* the United States.[10]

'Canada First' faded into oblivion in the 1870s, and some of its supporters transferred their energies to the Imperial Federation Movement. These Imperialist–Nationalists of the 1880s and 1890s found themselves challenged by Canadian Nationalists and Continentalists. It proved immensely difficult to find a national identity in such a competitive atmosphere.

Canada emerged before its people had refused to become citizens of the United States. The Loyalist emigrés and former French colonists had demonstrated both in the American Revolution and in the War of 1812 that they did not want to be absorbed into the American Republic. Confederation in 1867 was in part a response to fear of attack by the victorious North after the US Civil War, but it was also a means by which the French-speaking populace could control their provincial destinies. The *Canadiens* did not want to be assimilated into an Anglo-Saxon society. Therefore it was the *Canadiens* who were foremost in challenging both the Continentalists and the Imperialists during the period 1880–1914.

The Continentalist position had few supporters. Goldwin Smith, an expatriate Oxford don, was the most articulate in urging union with the United States because he saw North America as 'an economic whole'.[11] His arguments were virtually drowned in those between Imperial and Canadian Nationalists.

The idea of Imperial Federation, a British concept, was particularly attractive to those who believed that Canada's development as a nation depended upon its links with the British Empire, whether for economic, emotional or security reasons. The Imperialists, in essence, were Canadians who also wanted to be, and indeed were, British. They believed in the superiority of British institutions, and wanted to use the weight of British power and influence to Canadian advantage. Federation, as they saw it, was the means to eliminate any vestiges of colonial status which would advance Canada under the Imperial umbrella. It was an argument that *Canadiens* recognized to be as assimilationist as the Continentalist solution.

Henri Bourassa was the best-known spokesman for the *Canadien* position. Indeed he spoke not so much for *Canadiens*, as Canadians, in that he looked forward to a Canada that was a duality, Anglo-phone and Franco-phone, but not British. He lamented the fact that so many British immigrants and their descendents still thought of the British Isles rather than Canada as 'home'. Stirred by Canadian participation in the South African War (1899–1902), Bourassa was worried that overly close ties with Britain would ultimately drag Canada into other wars. In this he was joined by J. S. Ewart, who proudly called himself a 'Canadian nationalist'. Ewart hoped, as he wrote in *The Kingdom Papers*, that Canadians would declare their independence from ties to British foreign policy and become a Kingdom of Canada whose 'English, Scotch, Irish, French, Americans, etc. . . . ought to be Canadians.'[12] Ewart was talking to the wind. Within two years the British Empire went to war with Germany.

The Canadians who went to war in Europe could take their hockey sticks and wear 'Canada' shoulder patches on their uniforms, but otherwise it was only their accent (when the soldiers were actually Canadian and not immigrant Britons) which could differentiate them from the British forces. And those with hockey sticks were left to play among themselves, which might be useful for establishing a national identity if only non-Canadians would watch. The Australians, on the other hand, had begun to build their sense of identity by taking on the British at their own games and done rather well at it.

Australia, unlike Canada, remained a continent of separate self-governing colonies during the last three decades of the nineteenth century. In that period, cricket had become an important 'test' against Britain, and the colonies united in selecting 'Australian' teams to compete against the British. The Sydney *Bulletin* claimed in 1898 that cricket had done 'more to enhance the cause of Australian nationality than could ever be achieved by miles of erudite essays and impassioned appeal'.[13] But cricket was a game, and many Australians had to work for a living. It was work, or at least a type of work, that fostered an image of what an Australian was. And that image came from the Bush.

The Bush ethos established itself in print. The Sydney *Bulletin*, founded in 1880, became a major outlet for balladers and writers. From 1887 Henry Lawson, the proponent of 'mateship' (the belief that the individual, living exposed to Nature, 'must cooperate with other men or die'),[14] published many of his works in the *Bulletin*. Lawson reproduced the Bushman's view of life, and he was supported (also in the *Bulletin*) by A. B. ('Banjo') Paterson, a squatter and horseman. Lawson and Paterson represented the 'voice of the country, speaking through two different men, but with one recognizable accent'.[15] These two and others brought the Bush to town, and it was urban Australia, where the majority of the nation lived, that absorbed the Bushman's values.[16]

A distinct Australian alternative was now on offer. Australia's colonies had separate governments, were isolated from each other, and viewed the others as foreigners and rivals,[17] but the Bush was common to all. It was this commonality that the writers expressed, and they proved right when it came to establishing a federation. It was the Bush-vote that brought New South Wales, Queensland, and Western Australia into federation. The Bushman had clearly established who and what was 'national' in that splintered environment of isolated metropolitan capitals.

Perhaps it is not strange to find the capital cities without a sense of national identity. They tended to be the first stop for newly-arrived immigrants, who were reluctant to move on. Moreover, as one Australian urbanologist suggests, the residents of cities in new societies found no 'emotional sustenance' in a local past; they lacked an 'historical distance and historical romance'.[18] To what could they turn if they were to feel a part of the new society? They could identify themselves with the outback even if they themselves had no wish to join it. Hence the residents of Australia's colonial capitals looked to the Bush, and the residents of Buenos Aires turned to the pampas.

In *Martín Fierro*'s time there were some 1.8 million Argentines, about one-fourth of whom lived in urban areas. This would alter considerably during the period 1880–1914 when a flood of immigrants, especially from Spain and Italy, entered the country; few settled in rural areas. As a result, 53 per cent of Argentine's eight million inhabitants lived in towns in 1914, half in greater Buenos Aires.[19]

With this large, Eurocentric population one would have thought that 'civilization' would have dominated over the 'barbarian' values of the hinterland, but this was not apparently the case. The second-generation, growing up in city streets and alleys some distance from the pampas, did not want to be identified as 'gringos' and so adopted *criollo* values that would differentiate it from its parents. The government helped that generation by providing Argentine history and geography in the public schools.[20]

The gaucho had been tamed, but his legend and his ways lived on. To be seen as an Argentine one dressed as a gaucho, drank *maté*, sang *payadas*, and went to clubs like 'La Pampa' or 'Los Rastreadores'.[21] The tango provided a *criollo* element in the entertainment of all classes.[22] The theatre and the literary world of the first decade of the century 'joined hands with Argentine popular fashion on a common ground: the gaucho tradition.'[23]

Argentina's 1910 centenary offered opportunities for reflection; and probably the most important spokesman for recognition of Argentine values was Ricardo Rojas. Rojas published his *La restauración nacionalista* that year and subsequently went on to write, among others, a multi-volume history of Argentine literature.

Rojas used his writings to emphasize the rural qualities of Argentina as formed by the pampas and its gaucho: '. . . genuine Argentine thought has been born in him; he is dominant in the oral tradition of folklore and in the written form of a more complex literature in prose and in verse, in criticism and in art'.[24] It is a theme which Rojas would continue to espouse over the next four decades, perhaps itself an indication that the position had not been wholeheartedly accepted by the nation.

Manuel Gálvez joined Rojas in the auto-analysis promoted by the centenary of 1910. In *El diario de Gabriel Quiroga*, Gálvez was concerned for the nation and the dichotomy between urban and rural life. Gálvez could see the Europeanized, material life of urban

Argentina, particularly of Buenos Aires, and he did not believe that this was his country's destiny. His works in the period 1910–25 reflected his vision of a people who could absorb the best of both worlds into an *Argentinidad* which Rojas had declared was 'constituted by a territory, by a people, by a state, by a language, [and] by an ideal that tends to define itself better each day'.[25]

If the frustrations post-1910 are any evidence, then *Argentinidad* was not a success. The struggle to reach some consensus between 'civilization' and 'barbarism' continued in Argentina's intellectual world into the 1920s and 1930s. Martín Fierro became a symbol for a group of young writers, and *Martinfierrismo* was defined as 'a movement on an international scale for the ultra modernization of aesthetic expression'.[26] The group founded a journal, *Martín Fierro*, and sought to counter imitators of European models, although paradoxically, they were not opposed to new foreign trends. Gálvez allied with them because he was attracted to their Argentine vision and to their desire to stress indigenous themes on the model of José Hernández.[27]

The writer who promoted the gaucho as 'in essence, a true Argentine'[28] was Ricardo Güiraldes, whose *Don Segundo Sombra* has become an international classic since publication in 1926, even if it has not necessarily provided Argentines with a national identity. Güiraldes, *estanciero* by birth, was in Ceylon when he discovered what he believed to have gone wrong with his own country. His argument was that 'everything in my country was imitation, apprenticeship and submission, and [that] Argentina had no personality of its own, except in the case of the gaucho who still stood upright and firm and who expressed himself in a bold new manner.'[29]

Few Argentines could be Don Segundo, as Carlos Alberto Erro pointed out. By focusing on the gaucho, Erro believed that all those who sympathized with Güiraldes were trying to tie Argentines to the past; the future of the nation lay both in city and hinterland.[30] The response of some Argentine intellectuals was to reemphasize Europe and North America. Thus Victoria Ocampo and her circle established *Sur*, and in its first issue she wrote: 'To turn one's back on Europe! Don't you feel the infinite absurdity of that phrase?'[31] Jean Franco remarks that Ocampo and her colleagues were worried because they could not identify with 'either the gaucho tradition or with the urban immigrant'; they saw the debasement of their civilization and wanted to identify themselves with a larger, more cosmopolitan world.[32]

Ocampo, Borges and others probably felt more at home in Paris and

London than they did in Buenos Aires. Gálvez, Rojas, Eduardo Mallea and Ezequiel Martínez Estrada, on the other hand, spoke for 'barbarism' as they continued to promote rural values over urban within the framework of the impact of the pampas on man and the nation. They denied an imported identity.[33]

There were both Australians and Canadians who could sympathize with that approach. They lived in Dominions, an inferior status to nationhood, in which British influences continued to predominate. However, the 1914–18 war offered both Dominions an opportunity to establish in the world at large that they were indeed nations, while at the same time developing their sense of identity.

Until the war, Canadians were more apt to think of themselves as Nova Scotians, Ontarians, Albertans etc., while Australians emphasized their regionality as New South Welshmen, Tasmanians, or Victorians. The war forced volunteers into national units, and broke down regional sensibilities. As a result of their experience and their achievements, they returned to Canada and Australia more conscious of their national identity.[34] But in Canada the racial split caused by the 1917 conscription crisis had a correspondingly negative effect, and in both Dominions the imperial relationship still weighed heavily.

The Imperial Conference of 1926 might have agreed that the Dominions and the United Kingdom were 'equal in status, in no way subordinate one to another . . .', but British values and British points of view continued in fact to be inculcated through the educational system. The route to international stature was through Britain or the United States (which was beginning to rival Britain as an attraction for those who wanted, like their Argentine counterparts, to identify with a larger, more cosmopolitan world).

After 1918, Australia found itself bombarded with the viewpoints and culture of Britain and America, through film, radio, the press and theatre. In reply Rex Ingamalls tried even to carry Australian identity back beyond the Bush worker to the Aboriginal experience.[35] He founded 'the Jindyworobaks, a youth club whose members, glorifying the aboriginal, cultivated the pre-European heritage of Australia'.[36] This proved too much for other students and urban intelligentsia who, like Ocampo and her circle, were unhappy with the emphasis on 'barbarism'. They formed the 'Angry Penguins' in 1940 to educate Australians in what was going on abroad and at the same time to introduce readers to Australians who imitated foreign ways. The Jindyworobaks and the Angry Penguins, as W. F. Mandle has said, represented

> the division in Australian literature [which, since the 1890s] had been between those who looked to a metropolitan, English tradition and those who sought to discover specifically Australian roots. Angry Penguins and the Jindyworobaks were the decadent successors of the two approaches.

But he went on to stress that Australian literature by the end of the 1940s, had achieved an identity without the 'need [of] a boomerang as a trade mark', and cited Patrick White as an example of what he meant.[37]

Canadians during the period 1919–50 were certainly less sure of themselves than Australians. Canada was inundated with foreign publications, British and American. Like Australians, Canadians read British and American authors in preference to their own. In order to attempt to preserve a Canadian point of view, whether in French or in English, the Canadian government established the Canadian Broadcasting Corporation in 1932, the same year as the Australians. But what was the point of view? Two leading literary critics in the early 1940s saw English Canadians as utterly colonial in their view, whether British, (North) American, or both.[38] Highly educated French Canadians were no less colonial; they studied the French and British classics, and departed to British, French or US universities, while the limited education of the French Canadian majority meant that it remained parochial in both a secular and clerical sense.

No doubt French Canada derived some advantage over English Canada from the very fact of its struggle for the *survivance* of language and culture in a sea of Anglo-Saxondom. But what culture? Was it indigenous or not? One of the foremost spokesmen for a *Canadien* point of view was Abbé Lionel Groulx, the first professor of Canadian history at the Université de Montreal (the date of this appointment, 1915, provides a clue). Groulx influenced a whole generation of university students to think of *l'appel de la race*, founded on a past exemplified by the French empire in America.[39] He urged *Canadiens* to draw both on Roman and French culture to be themselves.[40]

Groulx remained a strong figure in clerical and clerical-intellectual circles for more than three decades, but Quebec *nationalistes* were moving away from the clerical dominance that had characterized French Canadian society since the expulsion of France.[41] The Church had always emphasized rural values, and its strength lay in the parishes. It saw an industrial, materialist, urban civilization as a danger both to it and to the *Canadien*, because such a civilization identified urban life with the Anglo-Saxon.[42] But there were Quebecois who, while recognizing the disadvantages and discomfort which urban life brought to *Canadiens*, believed that *Canadiens* could no longer be educated and prepared for a way of life which had already passed; they would have to learn to live and compete in the present. In the 1930s one way to strengthen the French identity was to have a grasp of what was going on in contemporary France.[43]

The Second World War forced Canada to assert itself more vigorously if it were to avoid being overly-dominated by British leaders, only to find that the War had brought the United States to the forefront as the natural leader of the allied cause. And as part of that advance, US economic and cultural influences on Canada proved all the greater. Blair Fraser, a sound commentator on the Canadian scene, reflected on this influence as it affected Canada at the end of the war:

> When some fifteen million speak American, watch American TV, read American magazines, follow American fashions . . . what, if anything, distinguishes them from Americans? The conventional wisdom . . . was that Canada had a distinctive national character perceptible to the most myopic observer, but the distinction was embarrasingly difficult to describe, let alone define.

The passage comes from Fraser's introduction to his study of the 1945–67 period, entitled *The Search for Identity*![44]

By 1950 Canadians had not yet found a national identity. They were not unlike the Argentines, who were still searching for it. Australians seemed more secure in knowing who they were, but in 1950 Australians were only in the process of opening up their country to non-British, and even non-white, immigration. How they dealt with that influx might provide a clue as to the strength of their identity. Both Argentines and Canadians have tended to the mosaic approach, rather than the melting pot; strong, often vibrant, ethnic communities have survived to the detriment of the development of a national identity.

On the other hand, Argentina did not share the imperial tie with the mother country that made it so difficult for Australians and Canadians to break away. Some influential Argentines tended indeed to link themselves intellectually with other imperial powers, and when Argentina did not live up to the expectations of these 'civilized' individuals, they despaired of the 'barbarism' that engulfed their country, whether Rosas for Sarmiento or Perón for Borges.

All three nations suffered from this colonial mentality. Those who fought it had the frustration of finding that their compatriots could not believe that something produced in their own country could possibly be of any intellectual or material value.

All three nations had the rural-urban dichotomy, but it was most marked in Argentina and Australia. These two, which had employed their hinterland to provide them with the rural values with which many identified, were, paradoxically, the most metropolitan. Canada remained relatively rural. Only Montreal seemed to have the materialistic, alienating characteristics attributed to Buenos Aires, Melbourne or Sydney. The cities stood for 'civilization', and 'civilization' was foreign; it was hardly the base on which to establish a national identity.

The fact that all three countries were not actually secure in their identity by 1950 is understandable, but an Argentine, an Australian and a Canadian identity certainly existed. The search for an identity proved more of an intellectual exercise. No matter what one's regional affiliation within a country, outside it the individual tends to reflect his national being. Only those with superior capacity for imitation can change their heritage, and the chances are that there will usually be something that gives one's origins away. But in trying to find an identity the searchers have done, and continue to do, a service by forcing individuals to think about themselves and their nation. And the search between 1870 and 1950 demonstrates the importance of that task. It shows also that a people does not necessarily have a unique experience. There is much in common in the search of Argentina, Australia and Canada; but just as certainly it has been the differences between them that have ensured that each of the three peoples is identifiable in its own right, if not in its own image.

NOTES

1. *Report of the Royal Commission on National Development in the Arts, Letters and Sciences, 1949–1951* (Ottawa: King's Printer, 1951), p. 11.
2. Domingo F. Sarmiento, *Life in the Argentine Republic in the Days of the Tyrants or, Civilization and Barbarism* (New York: Collier Books, 1961) p. 25.
3. W. K. Hancock, *Australia* (Brisbane: Jacaranda, 1961) p. 9. See also Claude Bissell, 'A Common Ancestry: Literature in Australia and Canada', *University of Toronto Quarterly*, 25 (1956) 131–42.
4. This was an expression used by Brian Fitzpatrick in *The Australian People, 1788–1945* (Melbourne: Melbourne University Press, 1946) chs 18 and 19.

5. Sarmiento, *Life in the Argentine Republic*, p. 53.
6. Quoted in Russel Ward, *The Australian Legend* (Melbourne: Oxford University Press, 1958) p. 53.
7. José Hernández, *Martín Fierro* (Barcelona: Ed. Bruquero, 1967, amongst others).
8. Carlos Mastronardi, *Formas de la Realidad Nacional* (Buenos Aires: Ediciones Culturales Argentinas, 1961) p. 17.
9. See Ward's chapter on the 'Bushrangers', in Douglas Stewart and Nancy Keesing (eds), *Australian Bush Ballads* (Sydney: Angus & Robertson, 1957) pp. 135–66.
10. Carl Berger, *The Sense of Power: Studies in the Ideas of Canadian Imperialism, 1867–1914* (University of Toronto Press, 1970) pp. 49–77.
11. W. L. Morton, *The Kingdom of Canada* (Toronto: McClelland & Stewart, 1963) p. 377.
12. Carl Berger, *Imperialism and Nationalism, 1884–1914: a Conflict in Canadian Thought* (Toronto: Copp Clark, 1969) p. 84.
13. W. F. Mandle, *Going it Alone, Australia's National Identity in the Twentieth Century* (Ringwood, Vic: Allen Lane, 1978) p. 30.
14. Peter Coleman (ed.), *Australian Civilization, A Symposium* (Melbourne: F. W. Cheshire, 1962) p. 4.
15. Vance Palmer, *The Legend of the Nineties* (Melbourne University Press, 1963) p. 109.
16. A. A. Phillips, *Henry Lawson* (New York: Twayne, 1970) p. 21.
17. Palmer, *Legend of the Nineties*, p. 142.
18. J. W. McCarty, 'Australian Capital Cities in the Nineteenth Century', in J. W. McCarty and C. B. Schedvin (eds), *Australian Capital Cities* (Sydney University Press, 1978) pp. 19–20.
19. The figures were drawn from James Scobie, *Argentina: a City and a Nation* (New York: Oxford University Press, 1964), p. 276, and E. Gallo and R. Cortés Conde, *Argentina, La República Conservadora* (Buenos Aires: Editorial Paidós, 1972) pp. 165–8.
20. James Scobie, *Buenos Aires, Plaza to Suburb, 1870–1910* (New York: Oxford University Press, 1974) pp. 231–2 and 240–1, and Giovanni Previtali, *Ricardo Güiraldes and Don Segundo Sombra, Life and Works* (New York: Hispanic Institute, 1963) p. 28.
21. Previtali, *Güiuraldes*, and Scobie, *Buenos Aires*, p. 240.
22. Tomás de Lara and Inés Roncetti de Panti, *El tema del tango en la literatura argentina* (Buenos Aires: Ministerio de Educación y Justicia, 1961) pp. 191–2.
23. Previtali, *Güiraldes*, p. 29.
24. Ricardo Rojas, *La Restauración Nacionalista* (Buenos Aires, 1910) p. 82.
25. Myron I. Lichtblau, *Manuel Gálvez* (New York: Twayne, 1972) p. 51; the quotation is from Rojas, *Restauración Nacionalista*, p. 34.
26. Previtali, *Güiraldes*, p. 71.
27. Ibid.
28. John F. Garganigo and Walter Rela, *Antología de la Literatura Gauchesca y Criollista* (Montevideo: Ed. Delta, 1967) p. 403.
29. Previtali, *Güiraldes*, p. 35.
30. Martin S. Stabb, *In Quest of Identity: Patterns in the Spanish American*

Essay of Ideas, 1890–1960 (University of North Carolina Press, 1967) p. 152.
31. From the editorial in the first issue of *Sur*, 1 (1931) 11.
32. Jean Franco, *The Modern Culture of Latin America, Society and the Artist* (New York: Praeger, 1967) p. 261.
33. H. Ernst Lewald, *Eduardo Mallea* (Boston: Twayne, 1977) pp. 54–5.
34. Geoffrey Serle, 'The Digger Tradition and Australian Nationalism', *Meanjin*, XXIV (1965) 150.
35. A. A. Phillips, *Australian Tradition* (Melbourne: Cheshire, 1958) pp. 82–7; and Mandle, *Going it Alone*, p. 152.
36. John Thompson, Kenneth Slessor, and R. G. Howarth (eds), *The Penguin Book of Australian Verse* (London: Penguin, 1958) p. 17.
37. Mandle, *Going it Alone*, pp. 160, 162.
38. Northrup Frye, *The Bush Garden, Essays on the Canadian Imagination* (Toronto: Anasi, 1971) pp. iii, 143; and E. K. Brown, 'Canadian Poetry', in Eli Mandel, *Contexts of Canadian Criticism* (University of Chicago Press, 1971) p. 40.
39. Mason Wade, *The French Canadians, 1760–1945* (Toronto: Macmillan, 1956) pp. 868–70; and J. Lacoursière, Denis Vaugeois and Jean Provencher (eds), *Canada–Québec, Synthèse Historique* (Montréal: Éditions de Renouveau Pédagogique, 1977) p. 498.
40. Wade, *The French Canadians*, pp. 870–1.
41. Lacoursière, *Canada-Québec*, p. 509.
42. Ramsey Cook, *Canada and the French-Canadian Question* (Toronto: Macmillan, 1967) p. 86.
43. Lacoursière, *Canada-Québec*, p. 509.
44. Blair Fraser, *The Search for Identity: Canada, 1945–1967* (Toronto: Doubleday, 1967) p. 3.

7 The Fiscal Motive for Monetary and Banking Legislation in Argentina, Australia and Canada Before 1914

CHARLES JONES

I

Because people have expected so much from banking systems, their evolution has invariably been a subject of great controversy in developing economies. The result of this is that the historian of banking has a hard time of it discounting a historiography replete with the deceptions of generations of publicists; and the problem is if anything made worse by the readiness of many readers in countries with mature financial systems to regard banking as a technical, and hence a non-controversial, matter. Comparison of the banking history of countries with broadly similar patterns of development, like those considered here, offers one solution to this historiographical problem. It throws into relief some of the more outstanding variations between national interpretations, and so suggests where close questioning might best be directed. Since variations only make sense in relation to established themes, this paper begins by outlining four common patterns of interpretation of banking history against which the history of each country is then set.

When not directly concerned with the history of some particular institution, or with the evolution of those routine market activities which are the chief foundation of commercial banking business, the historian of banking commonly strays off along one of four well-trodden paths. In the first of these four styles of interpretation stress is placed on the ordered evolution of a stable system. The historian begins with the lamentable frequency of bank failures in the early years, and proceeds to recount the development of a more or less stable oligopoly. This is collusion, but collusion that serves the public interest, as the banks evolve clearing procedures and agree on standard rates for routine business, and a disinterested government imposes regulations governing capital requirements, reserves, and the publication of accounts. The concluding chapter in this version applauds the emergence of a central bank to buttress the private system, and takes very seriously the independent and apolitical character of the central bank. Where political influence is too evident to be ignored, it is censured and treated either as a sign of institutional immaturity and individual immorality or as a legitimate but temporary response to national crisis.

The second version, and one which has been much more fashionable than the first over the past fifteen years, is obsessed with economic development. Wildcat banking, however reprehensible for the private losses which fall upon note-holders, depositors, and shareholders, is discovered to have been beneficial to a more broadly defined public. The history of banking becomes a contest between heroes, such as the Pereires, who lent long, and those tiresomely orthodox commercial bankers who stuck firmly to short-term financing of trade along existing lines. The first played their part in engineering important structural changes in the economies within which they worked; the second merely confirmed existing structures, however anachronistic.[1]

A third interpretation, less often seriously entertained these days but with a long and intriguing ancestry, casts banking as a manifestation of the Old Corruption, a conspiracy against the public interest. This is, *par excellence*, the view of the agrarian populist who believes himself as much exploited by the refusal of city banks to lend to him as by their reluctance, when they *do* lend, to forego repayment. Bray Hammond records that this spirit was strongly voiced in opposition to Alexander Hamilton's proposal for a national bank, quoting an agrarian representative from Georgia, James Jackson: ' "What was it drove our forefathers to this country?", Jackson demanded. "Was it not the ecclesiastical corporations and perpetual monopolies of England and Scotland? Shall we suffer the same evils to exist in this country . . .?" '[2] Amongst those who were to adopt this view must surely be numbered Papineau, Mackenzie, and the Canadian rebels of

1837. To Mackenzie, banking corporations represented a double threat to civil society. Their powers of note issue and discrimination in lending policy gave bankers an ability to corrupt public officials and politicians; at the same time, opportunities for procuring extra-parliamentary revenue could tempt governments to engage in banking for their own account. Banks, he declared, 'are the infamous means of preventing your government from confining itself to its appropriate functions, the protection of life and property'.[3]

Finally, there is a fourth view of banking history which alike rejects the naïve acceptance of state disinterestedness and belief in progress which generally characterises the first view, the over-sanguine belief in the efficacy of banking which distinguishes the second school, and the malign and conspiratorial portrait of the banker which informs the third. This last view accepts banks as economically neutral or facilitatory, and takes as its main theme the importance of banking to the public finances of growing but impecunious states. It is an interpretation particularly appropriate to the experiences of Australia, Argentina, and Canada in the fifty years before the First World War. It fits more closely than any of the other interpretations with the known facts of public banking and monetary policy. It is most consistent also with the patchy record of private banking history, that is to say of history written from the archives of banks rather than from government publications, parliamentary proceedings, and the press.[4]

II

Here, in Argentina, Australia and Canada, were governments called upon by commercial and landed interests to carry out extensive programmes of public works on the basis of an inadequate system of taxation.[5] Governments borrowed heavily, and much of their borrowing was in London. This meant that public finances became doubly dependent on the vagaries of the metropolitan business cycle. First of all, customs receipts – a significant proportion of revenue – were vulnerable to any fall in the volume of external trade. So too were receipts from those railways and other primary, commodity-related, infrastructure projects directly controlled by the state. Furthermore, in Argentina any fall in the earnings of the privately owned railways below a fixed rate brought claims for guarantee payments from the state. Second, the state was vulnerable to the cessation of foreign lending which commonly accompanied any more general commercial crisis. But at the same time debt service payments continued to fall due.

The tourniquet thus applied to public finance by successive crises – 1837, 1857, 1873, 1889–93 – was not felt equally on each occasion or in each state. Canadian governments were badly caught out in 1837, Argentine governments in 1876 and 1890/91, Australian governments in 1871 and 1893. This meant that lessons were learnt and remedies applied at different and more or less propitious times in each country. This in turn has made it fruitless to compare the histories of banking in the three countries by the superimposition of one chronological sequence upon another, as though comparing mutant growths of the same genus. Yet there are some common themes. For in all three countries the range of possible solutions included resort to the domestic banking system for short-term accommodation at the height of the crisis and, in the long run, attempts to evolve a wider range of domestic sources of revenue and borrowing. This suggests three principal categories of encounter between banks and states. The state, more obviously, might seek short-term accommodation from the banks or enlist their help in floating internal bonds when London funds were tight. Second, the state might seize upon note issue or solicit savings deposits as, effectively, a means of securing extra-parliamentary funds. This might be done either by the state (as monopolist or competitor with existing banks) issuing notes through some wholly official agency, in which case it would have to meet the not inconsiderable costs of managing the note issue, or it might be done through a free banking law on United States lines which obliged the banks to back their note issue with relatively low-interest government bonds. Third, the state might engage directly in banking through some more or less official institution which would carry on a business big enough to permit it to provide generous accommodation to the Treasury without endangering overmuch its own position in the market.

In advocating legislation to effect these policies, governments and publicists were not above resorting to stratagems which have done much to obscure and complicate the historiography of banking, and which it is the chief purpose of this paper to expose. The proclivity of the historian for veering into erroneous and misleading interpretation may be considerably encouraged by the availability of evidence. Thus the creation of a government bank such as the Commonwealth Bank of Australia could be represented, in accordance with the first of our four styles of banking history, as the foundation of a proto-central bank. State banks in Argentina were traditionally portrayed by their advocates as engines of economic development in line with the second style of banking history. They could be – and the Commonwealth Bank certainly was – perversely and deceptively presented to populist elements as devices to break the monopoly of the Money Power of the privately-owned banks. In short, any consideration of nineteenth-century banking controversies will constantly have to take account of all four interpretations – orthodox, developmental, populist, and statist – but it is a contention of this paper that where commercial banking entered the public realm in our period and became a subject of government policy and legislation, it is generally statist considerations that hold the key to satisfactory explanation; an essential first stage in any comparison of the banking systems of the lands of European settlement must be to lay some of the more obvious ghosts which have haunted the Argentine, the Australian, and – much, much less – the Canadian mind.

For Argentina it will be argued that the notion that Rosas revoked the charter of the Banco Nacional in 1836 and stripped its successor, the Casa de Moneda, of banking functions out of populist, anti-bank motives of the kind which moved the Canadian radicals, or because of his lack of concern for economic development, is not tenable. Furthermore, it will be said that the Banco de la Provincia de Buenos Aires was not a proto-development bank, and the Guaranteed Banking Law of 1887 was not primarily aimed at preventing bank failures or stimulating economic development. For Australia it will be maintained that the creation of a government savings bank in New South Wales cannot be convincingly presented as a mere technical improvement, and that the Commonwealth Bank was not and was never originally intended to be either an instrument of anti-Big Money populism or a proto-central bank.

III

Central to Argentine history in the second quarter of the nineteenth century was the dominant figure of Juan Manuel de Rosas. The advent to power of Rosas coincided with the failure of many of the economic experiments of the *unitario* regime that he replaced. The Banco Nacional which had been established as successor to the earlier Banco de Descuentos de Buenos Aires, with the object of fostering strong, private-sector economic development, soon became almost entirely a government agency. Commercial discounts amounted to only a third of the bank's loans to the state at the start of 1827, and fell thereafter.[6] The Bank remained, until its dissolution in 1836, an agency for the issue of inconvertible currency notes which more or less met the costs of this note issue by restricted lending activities.[7] When Rosas revoked the charter of the Banco National and made its successor so unambiguously the instrument of a public finance policy based on inflationary issues of paper money, he was not acting against a true bank at all, though he was undoubtedly working off some grudges against the Bank which dated back to the time when, under *unitario* control, it had been used to promote a model of political organization obnoxious to himself.[8] He cannot therefore be construed as a backwoods populist, mistrustful of banking and credit in a general way. Further, Rosas did not interfere with the private firms which provided Argentina with banking facilities throughout his ascendancy, although as the opponent of Big Money that he has sometimes been portrayed, he might have been expected to have done so.

If the banking history of the Rosas era fails to support the populist model of an heroic conflict between Big Money and the metropolis on the one hand and on the other the small rural capitalist, it equally fails to sustain a second, developmentalist version of the story. Miron Burgin, in his classic account of the Argentine economy in this period, allows himself at one point to be overwhelmed by federalist rhetoric. He rightly observes that while the Banco Nacional was portrayed by *unitario* publicists as the 'motive power of the country's growth', it was seen by their opponents as 'the symbol and source of power of the money aristocracy and of the unitary party'. But he then falls into the trap of accepting the notion that such credit as the Banco de Descuentos and the Banco National supplied went to private firms and individuals, favoured city merchants and speculators, and was of no use to *estancieros* and other producers in the countryside because it was provided entirely in the form of discounts on 90-day bills. This hypothesis lacks credibility. Bills, notoriously, may be renewed; nothing can be inferred from the charter of a bank alone. More important, it is not possible to distinguish a group of leading merchants in Buenos Aires at this time who were not also engaged in rural production. Money loaned on *bona fide* commercial paper could easily be diverted to industrial or speculative investment. Conversely, substantial *estancieros* could get access to short-term commercial credit through city firms with which they were connected, and divert it to rural activities. As a close associate of the banker-*estanciero* Anchorena family, Rosas knew the extent of vertical integration of international trade and rural production, and he cannot have been under any illusion that the Banco Nacional favoured city over countryside in any such straightforward way as Burgin supposed.[9] The divide, such as it was, might be construed in economic terms as a split between those with cattle *estancia* and *saladero* interests, and the newer, more cosmopolitan and *unitario* generation engaged in the growing sheep-breeding industry. But it may just as easily be interpreted as a factional division with no precise economic rationale.

In short, attempts to view the cessation of public banking in Argentina under Rosas as heroic, anti-Big Money chauvinism or as a crime against economic development, are alike doomed to failure. Private banking went on regardless. The institutional reforms which transformed the rump Banco Nacional into the more accurately named Casa de Moneda were simply the expression of a decision, prompted by the depressed condition of the Buenos Aires market at the time, to abandon the issue of short-term government bonds (*fondos públicos*) in favour of note issue as the principal instrument of public finance.

The next opportunity to impose a developmentalist bias on Argentine banking history centres upon the Banco de la Provincia de Buenos Aires which was established (originally as the Banco y Casa de Moneda) in 1854, just two years after the downfall of Rosas. Well into the twentieth century the Banco de la Provincia, which collapsed in the crisis of 1890/91, was still widely credited with having been a major, if not the major, cause of Argentine economic development. One early example, not untypical, must suffice to illustrate this almost reverent attitude. A contemporary, Pedro Agote, claimed that

> In the Province of Buenos Aries, not excluding the capital, there is not a firm or industry, whether big or small, not one political or social organization of more or less influence upon the progress and wealth of the country, which does not owe [to the Bank] its creation or development, less because of the credit in itself than because of the way in which it was provided and distributed.[10]

Agote emphasizes the provision of personal credits repayable at 5 per cent, and draws attention to the large number of branches in rural centres. Banking and economic growth were indivisible for Agote as for many of his generation. 'Among us', he concluded, 'the history of banks *is* the history of our social progress, in that it is in proportion that the former grow and multiply that public wealth multiplies, freed [*desenvuelta*] by the efficient mechanism [*acción*] for credit.'[11]

But this idealized portrait is largely false. In the only major recession which the Banco de la Provincia survived, that of the 1870s, it failed in one of the crucial tasks of a development bank. It was unable to nurse its clients through the cyclical crisis, and it was unable to do so not because it was fundamentally weak, but because its management believed their first duty to be the sustenance of the provincial government. Ironically, not even the appeals of the developmentalist incumbent at the Finance Ministry, Rufino Varela, could prevent the Bank fron instituting a review of private accounts at the worst point of the recession, raising a storm among landowners who had come to regard it as 'an institution specially created to supply them with funds without their being compelled to refund in due course'.[12] The Banco de la Provincia was government bank first, development bank only second and imperfectly.

The closing years of the long if rather unsteady boom of the 1880s coincided with the swansong of this spurious developmentalism. Modelled on the United States' earlier free banking legislation, the Argentine Guaranteed Banks Law of 1886 provided for the creation of a multiplicity of banks of issue emitting standard federal currency notes. Banks were to buy 4.5 per cent national government internal bonds which they would then deposit with the Banco Nacional (established in 1872) in exchange for banknotes. After two years the gold received by the national government was to be applied to the amortization of the external debt. External government debt was to be internalized, while at the same time new foreign investment in the banking sector was to be encouraged. The intended effect was to convert fixed to variable-interest external obligations and thereby ease the Argentine foreign exchange position in times of reduced economic activity. Simultaneously it placed the Banco Nacional in a position strong enough to be able to assure the government of ample, short-term facilities from the banking system in future.

Yet in Congress and in public debate, these public finance considerations were often neglected, and the free banking system was presented by its advocates largely in terms of the stimulus it would provide to national development. Underlying the whole discussion was the assumption that an increase in the number of banks would mobilize fresh resources which would automatically be directed into productive investment. It was left to critics of the Bill to address its merits and demerits as a fiscal measure. In the last resort, however, public finance considerations proved paramount. As the storm clouds gathered, the government abandoned its long campaign to nudge the private banks into its new scheme in exchange for their support in raising a new internal loan to support the official banks, and without the private banks, the Law proved a dead letter.[13]

In the prosperous years that followed the crisis of 1890/91, the idea of free banking was never revived, partly, no doubt, because it had been discredited by the abuses of the 1880s, but also, surely, because money was cheap and available, and any repetition of the sort of public finance dilemma of the 1870s, which the Law of 1886 had been designed to prevent, no longer appeared probable.

IV

As in Argentina, so in Australia, it was not until the period following the Second World War that historians got a firm grip on the evolution of the banking system before 1914 and pruned back overgrown orthodox and populist side shoots.

Two incidents stand out. In a most persuasive paper Gary Wotherspoon has taken issue with the orthodox interpretation of the establishment in 1871 of a government savings bank in New South Wales.[14] A history of the savings bank by Noel Griffiths, published in 1930, had maintained – as had the government of New South Wales in 1870 – that the principal motive was to overcome a technical deficiency in the existing Trustee Savings Bank (1832), namely its inadequate branch network. Yet this problem could have been overcome just as easily by allowing the post office to act as agent for the existing bank, as it was to initiate the new state bank. Noting the mounting demand in the Lower House for public expenditure on utilities and amenities, and the extreme difficulty in finding new sources of revenue, Wotherspoon paints a picture of an executive driven to desperation. An attempt to increase rents paid to the Crown by squatters failed in 1867. Recession in 1870/71 provided a further twist. In these circumstances the government found it extremely provoking to be declined assistance by the Trustee Savings Bank which, with between 10 and 15 per cent of deposits in the colony, was an institution of some weight. In 1863 and 1864 the Bank transferred substantial deposits from the Treasury to the trading banks, in search of higher interest. Some of this money was returned in 1865, but only after the government agreed to a stiff increase in the rate of interest.

It appears that the reluctance of the Savings Bank to assist government was not motivated entirely by commercial considerations, but was explicitly political. Eleven of the twenty-seven members of the Legislative Council, the upper house of the colonial legislature, were also trustees of the savings bank, and their action in this capacity was clearly consistent with their public opposition to the growth in public expenditure thrust on the executive by popular pressure. Government and the Legislative Assembly, feeling that Council was, in effect, opposing their will by extra-parliamentary means, responded by creating a source of extra-parliamentary funds. The new savings bank paid only 4 per cent on deposits, at a time when the nominal rate on government debentures (which usually stood below par) was 6 per cent.

A second confusing episode in Australian banking history is the founding of the Commonwealth Bank in 1911. Orthodox historians, predictably, have viewed the creation of the Bank as a deliberate step along the road to central banking. The selection of Denison Miller, a former official of the Bank of New South Wales, to head the new bank led to the adoption of policies which, by and large, avoided conflict with the trading banks, and after 1920 the bank did indeed start to develop into a modern central bank.[15] Yet this was to some extent fortuitous and was neither intended nor foreseen in 1911, when, as Baster remarks, few people in the Dominions even knew what a central bank *was*.[16] Baster accepts a less-obviously anachronistic version of the orthodox interpretation, married with a slight trace of populism. The motives behind the creation of what was, in form, a state-controlled commercial bank, were to provide a bulwark against any repetition of the grievous banking crisis which the country had suffered in 1893, and to break the alleged monopoly created by collusion between the trading banks. While the trading banks had shown an ability to co-operate in fixing rates, they had failed dismally and had set off a serious panic by a hamfisted attempt to prevent the failure of one of their number in March 1893.[17]

Baster may have overestimated the success of past attempts by the trading banks to fix rates.[18] This said, his account is accurate, but it is only part of the truth and does not touch on the fiscal motives of government. What is more, Baster was so much the orthodox interpreter of banking history that he was happy to dismiss as an aberration what he rightly identified as a main motive for the establishment of the Bank:

> It is *unfortunate* that the desire to set up a banking standard and the fear of a banking monopoly led the government then in power to give the Commonwealth Bank full powers of competition, to the injury of its 'reserve bank' functions because as a result, it is not nearly so well fitted by its constitution as it might be, to take charge in a banking crisis like that of 1893.[19]

But if Baster's rather patronising view of the Bank as a small step in the direction of technical maturity spoilt somewhat by the ignorance and political motives of its creators is wide of the mark, so too – and by a greater margin – is the old radical view of the original purpose and antecedents of the Bank, a view originally publicised by King O'Malley and only finally stamped out in the 1960s by S. J. Butlin and Kim Beazley.[20] After settling in Australia on the advice of his doctors, O'Malley, a flamboyant American, had risen high in the Australian Labour Party. In the 1920s, more than a decade after the event. O'Malley put it about that he had had to fight against strong opposition from prime minister Fisher and other members of the cabinet in order to force the project for a Commonwealth Bank into the government programme. This fraud by O'Malley (for Beazley demonstrates from contemporary records that fraud it was) came to be accepted and repeated in a number of later histories.[21] The error was all the more pernicious as it seemed to lend weight to the view that the currency and banking legislation of the Fisher government, passed in the teeth of moderate Labour opposition, must obviously have been bitterly resented by bankers and by conservative opinion in the country.

On the contrary, Butlin argues persuasively that the state banking movement of which the Commonwealth Bank was a manifestation took root in Australia in the year following the crisis of 1893, well before the young Labour Party had become seriously concerned with the issue, and received substantial support in the mid-1890s from political moderates and from farmers' organizations anxious to harness reforming enthusiasm to their narrow interest in cheap money. Nor did the trading banks offer serious opposition to the Fisher reforms. They were sceptical certainly, but no longer felt that the once profitable privilege of note issue was worth fighting about.[22] In fact, all the seven Commonwealth governments which preceded Fisher's had had plans of some sort for a federal note issue, and:

> Labour's legislation might well have come from any of the early governments, for all saw in note issue – Fisher's government most

> frankly of all – not a matter of high principle but a cheap source of funds. Note issue, whether government or bank, was in effect an interest-free loan from the general public.[23]

Similarly, doubt is cast on the notion that the Commonwealth Bank was highly controversial by the fact that the opposition Conservative programme in the 1914 election campaign left it largely untouched, advocating only that it be given direct control of the new government note issue and power to take over the banking business of the state governments.[24]

V

In dealing with Argentina and Australia it has been necessary to clear away misconceptions in order to see clearly the constant fiscal motive of banking and monetary legislation. These misconceptions turned out to result from the imposition on past events of the preoccupations of a later period, the rantings and fantasies of contemporaries who were not in fact party to, or influential in, the decisions they sought to influence, and the lame and transparent rationalizations of politicians who wished to represent as systematic action in the public interest what was often no more than pragmatic response to an empty treasury. In Canada many of the less wise experiments which would later be tried in Argentina and Australia had been seen to fail quite early in the century. That loss of innocence regarding the permanence of a great and trusted state bank, which came to Argentina only in 1891, was safely stored in the Canadian memory a generation before, when the Bank of Upper Canada finally closed its doors in 1866.[25] Federalization came earlier to Canada than to Australia, and gave the national government a clearer and more emphatic mandate to control banking than could be derived from the 1854 Argentine constitution. Canada was able to experiment with United States free banking ideas and bond-backed government note issue, first under the Provincial Acts of 1850 and 1866, and then under the Dominion Bank Acts of 1870 and 1871 and their subsequent revisions, at a time when asset-backed notes of private (Australian) or private and mixed-capital banks (Argentine) were still deeply entrenched. So, while orthodox apologia, radical ranting, and developmentalist agitation were never wholly absent from Canadian banking and monetary politics, the fiscal motive had been so evident for so long that the first generation of Canadian banking historians, writing at the turn of the century, were deeply sceptical, and worked hard to prevent the establishment of mythologies such as those which surrounded banking legislation in Argentina or Australia. Moreover, the early strength of Canadian banks – attributable partly to the careful scrutiny of their charters by the British Treasury, and partly to the predominance among their staff of experienced, Scottish-trained officials – meant that by mid-century they were a match for government, able to defeat Lord Sydenham's proposal for a bank of issue on Currency School principles in 1841 and to ignore and frustrate the Free Banking Act of 1850, with an ease and impunity that the private banks in Argentina forty years later, foreigners in a hostile land, could not match.[26]

For Breckenridge, writing in the 1890s, the 'real purpose' of the Free Banking law had been the sale of bonds.[27] The 'ultimate object' of Provincial Finance Minister A. T. Galt in proposing a bank of issue in 1860 was 'assistance to the public finances'.[28] The same minister's Provincial Note Act of 1866, presented as a move to render the currency more secure, was simply an acknowledgement of 'the primary cause of all paper currencies emitted by government – government need', and the bank of Montreal only acquiesced in it because it could see no other way of recovering the large debt of the Provincial Government than by replacing its own notes with those of the Province.[29] In short, Breckenridge provides what is, in essence, a Banking School broadside against what he sees as repeated attempts to further the narrow and particular interest of the state under the guise of Currency School theory. In answer to the contention of John Rose, successor to Galt at the Dominion Finance Ministry, that 'it is the duty of the Government not to interfere with banking proper, but to see that the circulation which the public at large is bound to take, should be placed on as sound and wholesome a footing as possible', Breckenridge firmly declares that 'we cannot accept the Finance Minister's implication that the note issue is not a function of banking in the strictest sense of the term.'[30]

VI

The constant theme of this chapter has been that the view taken by Breckenridge, by Wotherspoon and by Butlin concerning the fundamentally fiscal motivation of the three states considered here in their banking legislation before 1914 stands up far better than any of the three alternative interpretations outlined in section one, whether orthodox, populist, or developmentalist.

In the market conditions prevailing in frontier economies of the mid-nineteenth century there could be little peace between state and bank, and this was shown constantly in contests between private and official or semi-official banks and in bank opposition to government legislation. If government appeared eventually to triumph through the Dominion note and the Bank of Montreal in Canada, the Commonwealth note and the Commonwealth Bank of Australia, and the peso 'moneda nacional' and the Banco de la Nación of 1891 in Argentina, this was less because of a growth in state power than because bank opposition had fallen away. By the end of the century note issue had ceased to be important or profitable to the banks, while larger and better-organized money markets made it possible for official banks to survive in competition with private commercial banks as they had been unable to do a generation before. After 1914 convertibility, which had been the great shibboleth of the nineteenth century, lost its sanctity, and the principles of public finances were revolutionized by the needs of the belligerents. It soon became hard to recall quite how seriously sound money had been taken before 1914, and the ground was laid for interpretations of the past which would rudely push these debates to one side in pursuit of more modern concerns.

NOTES

1. For a less caricatured contest between these two views, see Fritz Redlich, 'American Banking and Growth in the Nineteenth Century: Epistemological Reflections', and Richard Sylla, 'Economic History "von unten nach oben" and "van oben nach unten": a Reply to Fritz Redlich', *Explorations in Economic History*, x (1973) 305–14, 315–18.
2. Bray Hammond, *Banks and Politics in America from the Revolution to the Civil War* (Princeton, 1957) p. 116.
3. *The Constitution*, 24 May 1837, quoted in Margaret Fairley (ed.), *The Selected Writings of William Lyon Mackenzie, 1824–1837* (Toronto, 1960) p. 21. See also Fernand Ouellet, *Papineau* (Laval, 1958) pp. 66–8.
4. Substantial archival material has survived for a few Argentine banks and for quite a number of Australian ones. See David Joslin, *A Century of Banking in Latin America* (London, 1963); C. A. Jones, 'British Financial Institutions in Argentina, 1860–1914' (unpublished Ph.D. thesis, Cambridge, 1973); Geoffrey Blainey, *Gold and Paper: a history of the National Bank of Australasia Limited* (Melbourne, 1958); S. J. Butlin, *Foundations of the Australian Monetary System, 1788–1851* (Melbourne, 1953), and *Australia and New Zealand Bank: the Bank of*

Australasia and the Union Bank of Australia Limited, 1828–1951 (London, 1961), and R. F. Holder, *Bank of New South Wales: a history*, 2 vols (Sydney, 1970). These are all based substantially on bank archives. Very little work on Canada appears to share this characteristic. Merrill Denison, *Canada's First Bank: a history of the Bank of Montreal* (Toronto, 1966) is unfortunately the work of a playwright. The author of an anonymous centenary volume, *The Bank of Nova Scotia, 1832–1932* (Toronto, 1932), may have had access to the firm's archives, but while his work is useful it is not thorough or substantial. I have not been able to consult V. Ross, *A History of the Canadian Bank of Commerce*, 2 vols (Toronto, 1920), and have not come across any other works on individual Canadian institutions. In short, there appears to be quite a serious variation in the quality of the sources on which history of the banking systems of the three countries must be based. This bedevils comparisons.

5. My view of the state in Canada owes much to D. G. Creighton, 'The Economic Background of the Rebellions of 1837' *Canadian Journal of Economics and Political Science*, III (1937) 322–34 and V. C. Fowke, 'The National Policy – Old and New', in the same journal, XVIII (1952), both of which are reprinted in W. T. Easterbrook and M. H. Watkins (eds), *Approaches to Canadian Economic History* (Toronto, 1967). For Australia I have relied on S. Encel, 'The Concept of the State in Australian Politics' *Australian Journal of Politics and History*, VI (1966), 62–76 and N. G. Butlin, 'Colonial Socialism in Australia, 1860–1900', in H. G. Aitken (ed.), *The State and Economic Growth* (New York, 1959).
6. Miron Burgin, *The Economic Aspects of Argentine Federalism, 1820–1852* (New York, 1946) p. 95.
7. Ibid., p. 216.
8. Rosas complained of the Bank that, 'created at the moment of triumph of the *unitario* faction, it was organized to help that party and to impose its yoke upon the Republic': quoted in *El Banco de la Provincia de Buenos Aires: estudio histórico y constitucional* (Buenos Aires, 1957) p. 8.
9. Burgin, *Economic Aspects*, p. 95.
10. Pedro Agote, *Informe del Presidente del Crédito Público Nacional* (Buenos Aires, 1881–8) p. 118.
11. Ibid., p. 117. On the Banco de la Provincia see also Baring Papers, London, Baring Brothers & Co., Ltd., HC4.1.65, Part 1, N. Bouwer to Head Office, 13 Jan. 1877, p. 4; Vicente Fidel López in C.S.N. *diario de sesiones*, 17 Jan. 1891, p. 83; Norberto Piñero, *La moneda, el crédito y los bancos en la argentina* (Buenos Aires, 1932) p. 209. Compare, especially with Bouwer's comments cited above, the account given of the Bank of Upper Canada in R. M. Breckenridge, *The Canadian Banking System, 1817–1890* (New York, 1895) pp. 166–7.
12. Baring Papers, HC4.1.65, N. Bouwer to Head Office, 1 May 1877.
13. Archives of Mandatos y Agencias del Río de la Plata (formerly in Buenos Aires, now destroyed), records of the English Bank of the River Plate, Buenos Aires to London, 5 March 1891; Bank of London and South America Papers, University College, London, D75, telegrams, 5–9 March 1891.
14. Gary Wotherspoon, 'Finance and Politics: A New Look at the Establish-

ment of the Government Savings Bank of New South Wales in 1871', *Australian Journal of Politics and History*, XXI (1975), 62–72.
15. R. F. Holder, *Bank of New South Wales*, p. 560.
16. A. J. S. Baster, *The Imperial Banks* (London, 1929) p. 145.
17. Ibid., p. 150.
18. Holder notes that successful agreements on exchange rates oprated during the period 1893–1914 with only two interruptions. Butlin, on the contrary, finds that most agreements collapsed: Holder, *Bank of New South Wales*, ch. 26; Butlin, *Australia and New Zealand Bank*, pp. 258–60.
19. Baster, *The Imperial Banks*, p. 158 (My emphasis).
20. Butlin, *Australia and New Zealand Bank*, pp 323–54 *passim*; Kim E. Beazley, 'The Labour Party and the Origin of the Commonwealth Bank', *Australian Journal of Politics and History*, IX (1963) 27–38.
21. Much of the O'Malley version is evident in the accounts of L. F. Giblin and Leslie Jauncey. The latter, indeed, appears to have been one of self-proclaimed 'Bishop' O'Malley's acolytes. Yet even S. J. Butlin's otherwise excellent and critical account bears traces of O'Malley's audacious falsehoods. L. F. Giblin, *The Growth of a Central Bank: the Development of the Commonweatlh Bank of Australia, 1924–1945* (Melbourne, 1951) ch. 1; Leslie C. Jauncey, *Australia's Government Bank* (London, 1933) ch. 3; Butlin, *Australia and New Zealand Bank*, p. 343.
22. Butlin, *Australia and New Zealand Bank*, pp. 325, 330, 340–1.
23. Ibid., p. 341.
24. Ibid., p. 351.
25. R. M. Breckenridge, *The Canadian Banking System, 1817–1890* (New York, 1895) p. 169.
26. Ibid., pp. 112, 146–7.
27. Ibid., p. 142.
28. Ibid., p. 162: 'his solicitude insincere, his monetary theories false'.
29. Ibid., pp. 178 and 180.
30. Ibid., pp. 240–1.

8 The Financing of City Expansion: Buenos Aires and Montreal Compared, 1880–1914[1]

D. C. M. PLATT

I

Thomas de Quincey once spoke of the 'burden of the incommunicable'. It is a hideous burden which we must all bear. But here the question is quite simple – who paid for the expansion of Buenos Aires and Montreal? The population of Buenos Aires in 1869 was 177 787; it was 1 575 814 in 1914 and had risen by 786.3 per cent.[2] Montreal was far smaller and the increase less dramatic; but the town of 107 225 in 1871[3] had become a city of 540 000 by 1914.[4] In fact, the natural increase of population for both Buenos Aires and Montreal put them in a class of their own; the rates of increase for Buenos Aires of 18.66 per 1000 and of 18.22 for Montreal shortly before the First World War, were several points ahead of any other city.[5]

Expansion was expensive, and it must soon become obvious that simple, conventional explanations for the funding of expansion, such as 'foreign capital', are insufficient. The comparison of two cities, Buenos Aires and Montreal, suggests some answers, and in most cases the answers go well beyond the two cities discussed; they apply, *mutatis mutandis*, to a whole generation of Western cities for the half century before 1914.

II

Naturally, differences existed. In 1914, for example, Montreal spent $346 010 on snow clearance[6] (a regular item on the city budget unknown to the finances of Buenos Aires). Then, although the population of both cities was markedly international, Buenos Aires did not suffer from the antagonism between nationalities, between Franco-phone and Anglo-phone, which, as Terry Copp says, meant that

> Politics [in Montreal] increasingly tended to focus on emotionally charged nationalist issues which, however important in the larger sense, militated against the development of strong public interest in municipal affairs.[7]

Raymond Préfontaine, indeed, with the support of the French Canadian 'masses', 'erige la corruption et le patronage en système'.[8] Buenos Aires, before the First World War, showed little evidence of such conflict, and was spared some part of that corruption which Edward Gibbon described as 'the most infallible symptom of constitutional liberty'.

These are differences – a serious difference in the case of national antagonism – between the experience of Buenos Aires and Montreal. But the parallels are even more substantial, and perhaps more illuminating.

We are accustomed nowadays to accept that a very large proportion of city services and development is likely to be undertaken by the municipality itself. Yet a salient feature of cities everywhere during the period with which I am concerned is the diminutive size of city revenues. Small revenues merely reflected the obligation to supply limited services, and it is true that the range of functions undertaken by municipalities was infinitely more restricted than it is today. Buenos Aires, for the financial year 1884, budgeted for only £416 571. By the end of the century municipal outgoings, net of debt service, of share of the national educational budget, and of arrears, were 10.2 million paper pesos (just over £900 000). Within this minute amount the government of a city of 800 000 had to meet its entire responsibilities for cleaning, lighting, hospitals, public assistance, paving, parks, *paseos* and so forth, that is, 'las mil necesidades de un municipio . . . extendido en una vasta superficie territorial de 18 000 hectáreas, donde todo lo fundamental está por hacerse'.[9] Montreal's revenue in 1900, at $3.2 million (£640 000), was even more modest.

Obviously, city revenues rose very rapidly during the great expansion of the 1900s. The revenue of Buenos Aires in 1912 was nearly 46 million paper *pesos* (£4 million), although Montreal's was still only $8 million (£1.6 million). The experience, both of a rapid rise of revenues and of a traditionally limited role for municipal government, was common to all Western cities. Municipal responsibilities were not evenly divided. In some cities before 1914 municipalization (city ownership of public utilities) went much further than in others, and, in general, muncipalities took greater responsibility for some services (notably water and drainage) than for others (transport, light and power). On the whole, education was financed by charity, by religious bodies, or by the Federal Government, while municipalities paid merely a contribution to costs. Charity and the Church funded the hospitals. Only in Britain was much progress made towards worker housing by the municipality, and even then the scale was small compared with the inter-war years. For both Montreal and Buenos Aires, as the principal national ports, the main harbour developments were undertaken at the expense of the federal government, and in Buenos Aires, as national capital, the State paid for the police.

III

Before the First World War the major contribution of the municipality was to paving and lighting, street widening and drainage. For both Buenos Aires and Montreal, revenues were drawn from a somewhat similar range of taxes, with property taxes heading the list by a wide margin. Deficits and miscalculations in budgets were common enough, but seldom disastrous. The key was the rise in the value of real estate. The assessment values of Montreal real estate rose from $78.4 million in 1880 to $219 million in 1905, and to $792 million in 1913.[10] The same dramatic increases were experienced in Buenos Aires; during the boom of the 1880s, houses which were rented at 100 pesos a month in 1880 produced a monthly rent of up to 500 pesos by the time of the Census of 1887.[11] Rising property values brought increased tax receipts, so that Montreal's revenue more than doubled between 1900 and 1910.

Normal expenditure, then, was covered by rising tax receipts. Major projects for city improvement, such as modern drainage, water supplies, street widening, new avenues, plazas and parks, which were beyond the range of current revenue but of permanent value to the city, were paid for either by levies on interested citizens or by borrowing (at home or abroad).

Buenos Aires and Montreal, like all other cities at the time, were able to draw on proprietors for contributions to the cost of those public works which might be expected to increase the value of private property. The details varied, but the principle was the same. The cost of street improvements was offset against the increment in site values; better streets brought improved conditions, more business, and hence higher prices for real estate.

But it was municipal credit, rather than the contributions of proprietors, which supplied most to this kind of permanent improvement. Neither Buenos Aires nor Montreal found it difficult or expensive to borrow for worthwhile, productive purposes. Financial crises tightened credit from time to time. Argentina suffered severely for a decade after the Baring crisis of 1890/91. But Argentina could borrow, both at home and abroad, at 6 per cent in the 1880s, and although the rate was up slightly to 6.5 per cent by 1900, it had fallen to 5.25 per cent in 1904, and reached a low point, early in 1909, of 4.75 per cent.[12] Canada could borrow more cheaply even than Argentina. Canada in 1888 was the first British colony to place a 3 per cent loan on the London market (at 95.05); the loan was heavily oversubscribed.[13] By the beginning of the twentieth century, 1901–2, the net rate on new borrowing was only 2.6 per cent. Credit became more expensive during and after the financial crisis of 1907, but by early 1910 the Dominion could borrow in London at 3.5 per cent.[14]

Municipal credit followed national credit. In the mid-1900s both Montreal and Toronto paid just under 4 per cent on their borrowing at home and abroad, and even after a period of some financial difficulty in world markets, Montreal could still borrow in London (in 1913/14) at 4.5 per cent.

IV

Of course, the availability of social services was extraordinarily limited by comparison with what is on offer today. The city subscribed to hospitals, night refuges and education, but it took no direct responsibility. Nor did it build houses. Charles Sargent has described the few private attempts in Buenos Aires to supply subsidised worker housing before the First World War; the first public housing project was undertaken only after 1915.[15] A 'brief flurry of public interest' in municipal housing in Montreal subsided with the war. Terry Copp explained that:

> For all practical purposes the supply of housing in the City of Montreal was in the hands of the private contractor, as indeed it was in all other North American cities.[16]

The tendency in both Europe and the Americas was for government intervention in housing to be limited to regulation – sanitary inspection and controls, building by-laws. Little attention was paid to construction.

More generally, Scobie is right in saying, for Buenos Aires, that the family, particularly the extended family, served to provide for its members' welfare at all levels of society.[17] There was no alternative. Dr Francisco Alcobendas, *intendente* of Buenos Aires from 1896 to 1898, called attention to the absence of a charitable tradition in Buenos Aires by contrast with the United States; the city was responsible for the administration of not a single institution 'que acredite en ella esa generosidad traducida en donaciones cuantiosas que ennoblecen, como el timbre más preclaro, la vida de los potendados yankees'.[18]

Charities were of more importance to Montreal. Although the Municipality itself did little directly to supply social services, it made an annual grant to charitable institutions which (in 1913) amounted to $160 000. Furthermore, and again in 1913, it committed itself to the payment of nearly $500 000 for the relief of destitute persons.[19] It is true that the large number of charities which operated in Montreal substantially replaced the responsibilities of municipal government. In 1910 the Director of Municipal Assistance himself admitted that public assistance in Canada, until a few years before, had fallen entirely to private charity.[20] Up to the mid-1900s such public assistance as Montreal was prepared to afford, in the form of poor relief, was limited to uncared-for children and the insane; the homeless who applied to the City Hall for a night's shelter were sent to gaol![21]

In the same tradition, Montreal city government made no contribution to hospitals before 1895, when the Council first acknowledged its responsibility to provide hospital accommodation for cases of infectious disease; previously it had taken charge simply of the small 'Civic Fever Hospital' (100 beds), built after the epidemic of 1885 for the treatment of smallpox cases. In a city so deeply divided by religion, Catholic and Protestant hospitals existed to serve the faithful, while others, such as the Montreal General Hospital and the Royal Victoria Hospital, served privately a wider constituency. Even by 1910, Montreal's Muncipality owned nothing other than the Civic Fever Hospital. Otherwise, its contribution to hospital services, other than ambulances, was limited to contracts with the St Paul and Alexandra Hospitals to reserve and finance 25 beds apiece for the city's contagious diseases (diphtheria, scarlatina, measles and erysipelas).

In this respect, however, the municipality of Buenos Aires behaved more responsibly, probably because Buenos Aires, after a series of exceptionally unpleasant epidemics, felt more at risk from contagious disease. Its attitude to the provision of hospital beds, but rather more to general hygiene, meant that whereas the death rate in Buenos Aires (15.5 per thousand in 1913) was one of the lowest in the world, Montreal's (at 21.5 worse even than that of St Petersburg) was among the highest in the West.[22]

It is true that a Public Assistance Department had been established within the Municipality of Buenos Aires as early as 1883. Its first director, Dr José Maria Ramos Mejía, took steps immediately to centralise the city's five municipal hospitals, which, even at the time, were caring for over 850 patients. Subsequently, other hospitals came into operation and, at the turn of the century, the Municipality was supporting eight institutions.[23]

All the same, it would only be realistic to say that, for a population the size of Buenos Aires's, the municipal contribution to hospital services merely touched upon the problem. For Buenos Aires, as for Montreal, the main burden was taken by religious institutions, private charities and immigrant communities. And in this, of course, both cities reflected common practice elsewhere.

V

Bearing in mind the limited responsibilities accepted by municipal administrations at the time, the question remains: Who paid for the expansion of these huge cities?

As yet, neither Buenos Aires nor Montreal had been touched by the fashionable move towards muncipal ownership and administration – the 'municipal socialism' which currently afflicted so many of the larger cities in the United Kingdom.

Charity, as we have seen, accounted for the major part of the cost of such limited social services as existed. Private citizens, private business and the municipality shared the cost of paving, water and drainage. Private companies operated the utlities. Private individuals, speculative builders and private contractors built the houses. In the end, the really huge costs of city expansion were met not by the foreign company, the foreign investor and the foreign contractor, but by the citizens themselves.

This was at its most obvious in building, the largest of all calls on urban finance. For Buenos Aires the peak periods of new building were the second halves of the 1880s and 1900s. New building, in linear metres of street frontage, increased from 4289 in 1881 to a high point of 32 377 in 1888.[24]

In 1904 the total was down to 18 939 metres (after years of economic recession). But it was up again to 55 126 in 1907, just before another recession, and new buildings were valued at 79 million paper pesos (about £7 million) for that single year.[25] Similarly, the annual value of building operations in Montreal reached its first peak of $4.8 million (£960 000) in 1887, remained thereafter in the range of $1 million to $3 million until the mid-1900s, and then rose very sharply indeed, from $5.5 million in 1905 to $27 million (£5.4 million) in 1913.[26]

The money had to come from somewhere. Buenos Aires, by 1914, was still a one-storeyed city (105 500 buildings out of its 132 000).[27] Public buildings were financed by the Federal Government and by the Muncipality, largely by loans, domestic and foreign. The huge profits of land ownership and speculation paid for the *palacios*. Electric trams pushed out the radius of the city. Sargent believes that the introduction of *venta por mensualidades* – sales of building lots on monthly payments, spread over as many as ten years – 'must rank with the introduction of the trolley itself [the electric tram] as one of the major 'technical' innovations in urban residential development'.[28] For different reasons, the very rich and the very poor remained in central Buenos Aires; it was the middle-income office worker and the skilled worker, as Sargent says, who migrated to the new suburbs of Buenos Aires, who could afford to buy a building lot on time payments and with a very low first instalment, and who could borrow money for construction or purchase from 'an increasing number of national and foreign mortgage companies, building societies and land development groups'.[29] The scale was modest, starting (at the bottom) with the one-room dwelling of the artisan built at the cost of 1000 paper *pesos*

(£88). And although (before the mid-1900s) the cost of living in Buenos Aires was exceptionally high, and wages relatively low, wages began to rise so that, by 1910, skilled labour, earning from 2.5 to 3.5 gold *pesos* per day, was much better paid in Buenos Aires than in Southern Europe, and more so even than in most parts of Britain and the United States.[30]

Montreal experienced much the same phenomena, except that Canadians were even better off than Argentines just before the First World War. In 1912 the total savings deposits in Canadian chartered banks, government savings banks, post office and special savings banks, building societies and land and trust companies, amounted to about $700 million (£140 million), averaging $100 per head of population.[31] For Montreal as for Buenos Aires, the great boom came after the mid-1900s; the loans of Canadian loan companies and building societies rose very steeply from $140.7 million in 1904 to $302 million in 1913.[32] With total deposits in Canadian chartered banks (in 1913) at $1.1 billion,[33] loan company and building society assets at $479 million,[34] and real estate assessment values in Montreal at $792 million,[35] the origins of the money to pay for the building boom in Montreal are not in doubt.

VI

It is scale which is important for an analysis of the separate elements in financing the modernization of cities. A public utility company – whether it takes the form of a large electric tramway system, a water works, a gas or electricity plant – will need, over the years, a capital of several million pounds. And, if the business were promising, as it was at the turn of the century, it could attract cheap capital from abroad.[36]

The municipal borrowing of Montreal, at home and abroad, brought its funded debt to $83.8 million (£16.8 million) for 1913. The municipal debt of Buenos Aires, in circulation in January 1910, amounted to £8 million.[37] These are large sums, and they are often dramatically presented. But they do not seem quite so overwhelmingly large when compared with the £22.4 million spent on building operations in Montreal alone over the years 1905 to 1913.[38] And the assessed valuation of Montreal in 1913 was £158 million.[39]

Francisco Latzina, former director of Argentina's *Estadística Nacional*, calculated that, at the beginning of 1910, the collective national wealth in Argentine real estate (land and buildings) could be taken as 8.9 billion paper *pesos* (£784 million).[40] Only part of this was in Buenos Aires itself, but Buenos Aires was by far the largest and wealthiest city in Argentina, with huge sums invested in urban real estate. Then, to take a much smaller element in the cost of a great city, the expense simply of paving Buenos Aires (5.2 million square metres) for the fifteen years 1895–1909 – most of which was raised internally from the proprietors, from an annual percentage tax on tramway revenues, and from municipal revenues and borrowing – amounted to 59.4 million paper *pesos* (£5.2 million).[41]

The conclusion can only be that the huge costs of modernizing and expanding a city, so far as the experience of Buenos Aires and Montreal can serve as a guide, were met piecemeal and over a long period; they were financed, to a surprising extent, by the citizens themselves.

NOTES

1. As a rule of thumb, gold *pesos* (Argentine) and dollars (Canadian) can both be taken at the exchange of five to one pound sterling. 'Paper' *pesos* have been converted throughout into sterling at the current rate.
2. Alberto B. Martínez, 'Consideraciones sobre los resultados del Tercer Censo Nacional de Población', *Tercer Censo Nacional 1914*, vol. I (Buenos Aires, 1916) p. 80.
3. *Census of Canada, 1911*, vol. I (Ottawa, 1912) p. 554.
4. Projected figure in the report of the Hygiene and Statistics Department for 1914: *Montreal City Reports* (Montreal, 1915) p. 16.
5. Ibid. p. 21.
6. Report of the Chief Engineer and City Surveyor for 1914, *Montreal City Reports* (Montreal, 1915) pp. 22–3.
7. Terry Copp, *The Anatomy of Poverty: the Condition of the Working Class in Montreal 1897–1929* (Toronto, 1974) p. 147.
8. Paul-André Linteau, 'Montreal 1850–1914', *Urban History Review*, I (1975) 35.
9. Alberto Martínez's introduction to the *Anuario estadístico de la ciudad de Buenos Aires, 1899* (Buenos Aires, 1900) p. xxxii.
10. William Henry Atherton, *Montreal 1835–1914*, vol. II (Montreal, 1914) p. 661.
11. Manuel C. Chueco, 'Estudio sobre los resultados del censo de edificación', in the *Censo Municipal de Buenos Aires 1887*, vol. II (Buenos Aires, 1888) pp. 85, 102.
12. *Memoria del Departamento de Hacienda, 1909* (Buenos Aires, 1910).
13. Report of the Deputy Minister, Public Accounts, *Canadian Sessional Papers*, vol. II (1899) p. ix.
14. Public Accounts for the fiscal year ended 31 March 1913, *Canadian Sessional Papers*, vol. II (1914) p. 75.

15. Charles S. Sargent, *The spatial evolution of Greater Buenos Aires, Argentina, 1870–1930* (Tempe, 1974) p. 83.
16. Copp, *Anatomy of poverty*, p. 83.
17. James R. Scobie, *Buenos Aires: plaza to suburb, 1870–1910* (New York, 1974) p. 226.
18. *Memoria del intendente, 1896* (Buenos Aires, 1897) p. 12.
19. Report of the Municipal Assistance Department for 1913: *Montreal City Reports* (Montreal, 1914) pp. 35, 37.
20. Annual report on municipal assistance for 1909: *Montreal City Reports* (Montreal, 1910) pp. 34–5.
21. Annual report on municipal assistance for 1907: *Montreal City Reports* (Montreal, 1908) p. 30.
22. Report of the Hygiene and Statistics Department for 1914: *Montreal City Reports* (Montreal, 1915) p. 20. The age structure of the population should also be taken into account.
23. *Anuario estadístico de la ciudad de Buenos Aires, 1899* (Buenos Aires, 1900) p. 313.
24. *Memoria de la intendencia municipal correspondiente a 1889*, vol. I (Buenos Aires, 1891) p. 64.
25. Ibid. for 1908 (Buenos Aires, 1909) p. xiii.
26. Report of the superintendent of buildings for 1913: *Montreal City Reports* (Montreal, 1914) pp. 5–6.
27. 'Censo de edificación: capital federal', in *Tercer Censo Nacional, 1914*, vol. X (Buenos Aires, 1917) p. 485.
28. Sargent, *Spatial Evolution of Buenos Aires*, p. 76.
29. Ibid., p. 82.
30. Scobie, *Buenos Aires*, p. 137.
31. *69th report of the Council of the Montreal Board of Trade, for 1911* (Montreal, 1912) p. 4.
32. *Canada Yearbook for 1914* (Ottawa, 1915) p. 591.
33. Ibid., p. 577.
34. Ibid., p. 592.
35. Atherton, vol. II, *Montreal*, p. 661.
36. City Comptroller's report for 1913: *Montreal City Reports* (Montreal, 1914) p. 125.
37. Enrique Ruiz Guiñazú, 'Finanzas de la Municipalidad de Buenos Aires', *Censo Municipal de Buenos Aires 1909* (Buenos Aires, 1910) p. 481.
38. Report of the Superintendent of Buildings for Montreal for 1913: *Montreal City Reports* (Montreal, 1914) pp. 5–6.
39. Report of the Assessment Department of Montreal for 1913: ibid., p. 7.
40. Quoted (as an underestimate) by Alberto Martínez, 'La fortuna colectiva del pueblo argentino', *Tercer Censo Nacional 1914*, vol. VIII (Buenos Aires, 1917) p. 432.
41. Carlos María Morales, 'Estudio togográfico y edilicio', *Censo General de la Ciudad de Buenos Aires 1909*, vol. III (Buenos Aires, 1910) p. 538.

9 Some Notes on the Industrial Development of Argentina and Canada in the 1920s[1]

ROBERTO CORTÉS CONDE

I INTRODUCTION

Many reasons exist for comparing the economic evolution of Argentina and Canada between 1910 and 1930. Both countries had enormous natural resources (primarily land) but lacked people; once idle resources were employed, vast surpluses became available for export. Furthermore, for reasons connected with contemporary international markets for goods and capital, both countries were closely linked to the British economy.[2]

The favourable ratio of land to population, unlike that for older countries (and different even to countries of the Andean area), should have produced similar effects in both countries. First of all, needless to say, it gave them a special interest in foreign markets. Secondly, it compelled them to obtain from abroad factors of production (capital and labour) that were locally in short supply.

Great Britain was the principal supplier of capital goods to both countries, and the largest industrial market for their exports of raw materials and foodstuffs. It was also the main source of capital for financing the infrastructure.

In summary, both countries were similar:

(a) in their high ratio of land to population, and the availability of huge export surpluses;
(b) in their orientation towards foreign markets (and vulnerability, in consequence, to fluctuation);

(c) in their recruitment of capital and labour from abroad, their high production costs, and their close ties with the English market. Countries with such huge open spaces incurred enormous transport costs when they tried to put those spaces to productive use.[3] A very large, initial capital investment was required to reduce the cost of production (and in subsequent calculations, this cannot be overlooked).

In 1933 the Canadian Royal Commission on Banking and Currency defined the Canadian economy as follows:

> Canada presents a number of prominent economic characteristics which determine the special nature of her financial problems. These characteristics are mainly:
> 1. Excess production in relation to population;
> 2. Dependence on international trade;
> 3. Specialised production and local diversity;
> 4. Heavy cost of development;
> 5. The burden of debt, internal and external;
> 6. Relative economic instability.[4]

Those characteristics were shared equally by Argentina.

II ARGENTINA AND CANADA AFTER THE FIRST WORLD WAR

I will now discuss the evolution of the more relevant economic variables during the 1920s so as to identify the parallels. I am starting from the assumption that, for both economies, after a period of rapid growth based on the *mise en valeur* of fertile lands when no changes had occurred in other sectors of the economy, a decline in the rate of growth might be expected. Then, both countries were open to changes in the world economy in the 1920s, and mainly to those affecting the British economy.

The most important variables were population, the area under cultivation, the mileage of railways, and the size of exports and industrial production. By comparison with what had gone before, there was a slight decline in the inflow of immigrants during the 1920s. In Argentina the figures give an annual average of 81 000 for 1925–9, by contrast with 169 000 from 1910–12; in Canada the annual average was 113 000 for the five years 1925–9, compared with 274 000 for 1910–12. Thus total population increased at a slightly lower rate: 2.3 per cent per year for Argentina from 1914 to 1929, as against 3.8 per cent for 1895–1914; and 1.4 per cent annually in Canada, 1914–31, as against 2.3 per cent over the period 1891–1914.

A circumstance common to both countries was the rapid increase in the size of areas brought under cultivation, made possible largely by the construction of an extensive railway network. From the end of the war the increase in land under cultivation lost momentum, and finally stopped altogether. Simultaneously, the construction of new railway track almost ceased. Obviously, the high growth rate of exports during the pre-war period was not maintained. Exports reached their maximum in 1920 both in Canada ($Canadian 149 per capita) and Argentina (95 gold pesos). Between 1920 and 1930 there was a slowdown in the export by Argentina of traditional export items, while for Canada there was even a slight fall in exports overall.

But the most important factor in the post-war period which differentiates the two countries was the rise of non-traditional exports from Canada – newsprint, wood, nickel, etc. (Table 9.1) – while

TABLE 9.1 *Principal exports (Canada), 1890–1930 ($Canadian, millions)*

Commodity	*1890*	*1920*	*1930*
Wheat	0.4	185	216
Newsprint	–	54	146
Nickel	–	9	25
Wood pulp	0.2	41	45
Planks and boards	18	75	49

SOURCE *Canada Yearbook* (Ottawa: Bureau of Statistics).

Argentina's more diversified (but more traditional) exports – principally meat, hides, wool and cereals – remained at roughly the same level as before (Table 9.2).

According to Carl Solberg's paper of 1981,[5] the differences between Argentine and Canadian industrial development developed out of the dissimilar industrial policies adopted by each country. Canada, on the one hand, chose a 'national policy' of protectionism so as to check penetration of the Canadian market by the United States. Argentina, on the other hand, supported Free Trade – a policy which has been attributed to the political influence of the Argentine landowner.

TABLE 9.2 *Principal exports (Argentina), 1910–30 (gold pesos, millions)*

Commodity	*1910*	*1920*	*1930*
Livestock	172	286	196
Meat	48	119	97
Leather	41	46	35
Wool	59	73	35
Agriculture	196	639	241
Corn and flax	195	633	231
Forestry	11	18	12
Mining	3	6	0.5
Hunting and fishing	1	1	0.2
Manufacturing	0.1	20	1.0

SOURCE Roberto Cortés Conde, Tulio Halperí Donghi and Haydée Gorostegui de Torres, *Evolución del Comercio Exterior Argentino* (Buenos Aires: Inst. di Tella, 1965), mimeo.

The feeble development of Argentine industry has been explained similarly by many writers, and it may be useful at this point to seek out some empirical evidence for the process of industrialization in both countries during the critical, post-war period.

For both countries industry was undoubtedly a dynamic sector. However, industrial production increased more rapidly in Canada than in Argentina. Between 1911 and 1930, manufacturing production rose by 194 per cent in Canada (5.8 per cent per annum) and 103 per cent in Argentina (3.8 per cent per annum). Although the rate of growth was much higher in Canada than it was in Argentina, it was high also in the Republic. But it is worth noting that in Canada the greatest period of growth was during the war years, while during the 1920s it was higher for Argentina (80 per cent) than for Canada (60 per cent).

The differences in industrial growth during the war owed something to the shortage in Argentina of imported raw materials, so that the protectionist consequences of the war were offset by the shortage of industrial imports. In Canada and main branches of industrial production were precisely those for which Canada herself had abundant raw materials, in demand also abroad: wood, pulp, and non-ferrous metals. These same branches became the most dynamic elements in Canada's exports during the 1920s. While traditional exports (directed mainly at Britain and Continental Europe) were falling, Canada's new staples, forestry and mining, were both processed domestically and sold abroad, mainly to the United States.

III INDUSTRIAL PRODUCTION IN CANADA AND ARGENTINA

If the sources of raw materials are taken into account, the industries that grew above average (1923–9), in order of importance, were non-ferrous metals, non-metallic minerals, iron, wood and paper, at a rate of 90 per cent, 67 per cent, 58 per cent and 53 per cent respectively. Of these, wood/paper and non-ferrous metals were sectors the production of which was destined mainly for export.[6]

With the exception of wheat, in fact, these were precisely the products which formed the major part of Canada's exports in the 1920s. Paper production especially was focused on the United States, and an enormous increase was registered in exports between 1910 and 1930. John Stovel, quoting the Royal Commission, explains that:

> The exports of pulp and paper and non-ferrous metals rose to 30 per cent of total exports in 1929, compared with 19 per cent in 1920. . . . The large fixed equipment represented by central electric stations, pulp and paper factories, smelters and metal refineries was the major factor in the exploitation of these resources.[7]

The Commission adds that the two new export areas became Central Canada and British Columbia: 'Their exports of forest products and non-ferrous minerals found their chief markets in the United States, in contrast to the Prairie export of wheat, which found its way to overseas markets in Britain and Europe.'[8]

Argentina's evolution took a different course. Even though industrialization was important, Argentina's industrial exports did not find their way into international markets to any significant extent, and the structure of exports remained broadly the same as in the pre-war period.

IV THE CANADIAN AND ARGENTINE TARIFFS

Stovel points out that 'for what it is worth the Canadian tariff level of 1925 was computed by the World Economic Conference of 1927 to be 23 per cent as compared with 37, 29 and 27 per cent for the United States, Argentina and Australia respectively'.[9] Even though Canada's tariff during the twenties declined,[10] more important to Canadian industry was the reduction of the US tariff on Canadian imports.

Easterbrook and Aitken explain that for newsprint, virtually unknown in 1900, Canada by 1913 was already the world's leading exporter (and by 1923 had tripled production):

> In many respects the pulp-and-paper industry exemplifies Canada's role in the world economy of the mid-twentieth century. On the one hand, the availability of cheap hydroelectric power, supplemented by vigorous government intervention in the control of raw material exports, has made possible the establishment in Canada of a new and powerful industry. . . . On the other hand, the prosperity of this industry hinges upon exports and therefore upon tariff policies and fluctuations in demand in foreign countries, particularly in the United States but also in Europe.[11]

For Argentina, Solberg (like many others) emphasizes that the principal obstacle to major industrial development was the lack of a protective tariff.[12] He argues that this policy derived from the great political influence of the landowners. The argument is based on what is seen as the relatively lower tariff (nominal) and, up to 1923, on the failure to adjust *aforo* values. But as Carlos Díaz points out, although the tariff itself may, on average, have been lower for 1922–7 than before, the higher exchange rate for the Argentine peso may actually have increased protection and further induced import substitution.[13] If the combined effects of the average tariff and the real devaluation of the pound are taken into account, the index of protection, which had fallen during the war years, rose during the 1920s, and was above the 1914 average (=100) from 1922 to 1928 (reaching 140 against the United States in 1928, and 136 against Britain).[14]

As to the influence of the Argentine landowner, it should be said that if a policy of devaluation can be more protectionist in its effects than the ostensible tariff, then an argument founded on a conflict of interest between landowners and industrialists is inconsistent. For while it is true that an undervalued peso was advantageous to the landowner (who, as an exporter, was paid in foreign currency while he met his local debts in pesos), it also helped the domestic entrepreneur because it made competing imports more expensive.

Clearly, any study which is based on the nominal tariff is incomplete. An analysis of effective protection in Argentina must pay attention to the rate of exchange, to international and domestic prices and, finally, to the difference between the *aforo* values and market prices.

V FOREIGN INVESTMENT

The importance of foreign investment in the economic evolution of both countries before the war is well-known. On the eve of the First World War, foreign capital in Canada may have amounted to a total of $US 3.8 billion, and in Argentina to $US 3.1 billion. In Canada, British investment accounted for 58 per cent of all foreign investment, and in Argentina for 71 per cent. It was in this area (foreign investment) that the two economies began to evolve in significantly different directions.

Foreign investment in Canada grew by 71 per cent between 1914 and 1931; in Argentina it rose by only 15 per cent. Besides, in Canada the growth was due mainly to the United States which contributed 63 per cent of all foreign investment, while in Argentina it accounted for only 19 per cent. Whereas before the war the inflow of huge quantities of foreign capital was a crucial factor in the development of both countries, and remained so for Canada during the 1920s, the same was no longer the case for Argentina.[15]

This is, indeed, something which needs to be taken into account, as it made a substantial difference to the subsequent evolution of both countries, more particularly because the development of Canada's manufacturing industry was so closely related to the incorporation of US capital.

VI TWO MODELS OF INDUSTRIAL DEVELOPMENT: EXPORT-ORIENTED VERSUS IMPORT-SUBSTITUTING

Even though the process of industrialization in Canada was intended also to supply the domestic market, some important branches of industry began to find major outlets in external markets (newsprint in particular, in the United States). In Argentina, by contrast, the market was almost exclusively domestic. Consequently, the two economies experienced very different opportunities; Argentine industry was far more restricted, in size of market, in access to technology, and in its relationship with the international capital market.

Furthermore, the export-oriented industries of Canada were accustomed necessarily to more competition than Argentina's, which looked rather to political protection to offset the more competitive prices of imports. In fact, even foreign investors in those industries which were directed at Argentina's domestic market sought political protection. It can also be argued that US investment in Argentine industry was due to the failure of British industry to remain competitive in international markets as a consequence of the over-valuation of the pound sterling.

Differences in the direction taken by Canadian and Argentine economic policy naturally had their repercussions on efficiency and prices. While Argentina preferred a policy of import-substituting industrialization (with a strong bias against exports), Canada remained more open to international markets. The lack of a protective tariff was not an issue for Argentina.

VII MONEY AND PRICES

The war took the United Kingdom off the gold standard. Canada and Argentina immediately followed suit. The consequence was a floating rather than fixed exchange rate; money issues had no longer to be related to gold reserves. On the other hand, the US dollar remained on the gold standard.

It seems that Argentina followed a stricter monetary policy than Canada when it came to determining the ratio of money issues to gold reserves. The need to finance war expenses could be the reason, and the Canadian government may have printed money as a means of offsetting its fiscal deficit. Canada's money supply grew 8 per cent a year between 1910 and 1920, by contrast with 6 per cent in Argentina. Canada's gold reserves fell to a minimum of 31 per cent, when the

TABLE 9.3 *Prices, Argentina and Canada, indices for 1913—30*

Year	*Argentina*		*Canada*	
	Cost of living index	*Wholesale price index*	*Cost of living index*	*Wholesale price index*
1913	100	100	100	100
1920	186	179.6	190	243.5
1921	166	149.3	161	171.8
1925	135	146.9	160	160.3
1929	133 (1926)	130.4 (1927)	160	149.3
1930			151	135.3

SOURCES for Argentina: *Revista de Economía Argentina* (June, 1931).
for Canada: *Canada Yearbook 1933* (Ottawa: Bureau of Statistics).

lowest level reached in Argentina was 80 per cent. Because of the war, there was in fact a significant outflow of gold from Canada at a time when Argentina was receiving new inflows. Canadian prices shot up by 144 per cent between 1913 and 1920; they rose 80 per cent in Argentina (Table 9.3). Inflation, however, was lower than the expansion of the money supply (90 per cent in Canada and 86 per cent in Argentina).[16]

VIII WAGES

Between 1913 and 1920 nominal wages increased more in Canada than in Argentina (98 per cent as against 62 per cent), although over the next five years the trend was reversed – the result of a deflationary policy, reflected in an increase in the interest rate. However, the nominal fall was not real. Because of the drop in prices, especially of food, real wages in Canada in reality rose until 1920. In Argentina over the same period, the increase in nominal wages (62 per cent) did not compensate for the steep rise in prices, so that real wages declined. Nominal wages rose again from 1918, and real wages from 1919 to 1925 (95 per cent in real terms over seven years): (Table 9.4). The fall

TABLE 9.4 *Nominal and real wages, Argentina and Canada, 1913–30*

Year	Argentina Nominal	Argentina Real	Canada Nominal	Canada Real
1913	100	100	100	100
1920	162	87	197.8	104
1921	179	107	191.2	118.7
1925	180	133	179.7	112.3
1929	194	145	192.7	120.4
1930	178	178	194.4	128.7

SOURCES for Argentina: Guido di Tella and Manuel Zymelman, *Las etapas del desarrollo económico argentino* (Buenos Aires: Editorial Paidos, 1973).
for Canada: *Canada Yearbook*.

in nominal wages in Canada between 1920 and 1925 (minus 2 per cent per year) corresponded with the fall in monetary issues (0.3 per cent per year in currency and minus 0.4 per cent per year in demand deposits).

By 1930 Canada had almost returned to the situation which had prevailed before war inflation. In Argentina, by contrast, there was not only a nil reduction in money issues between 1920 and 1930, but even a slight increase. This does not imply an issue above reserves; the ratio of reserves to new issues was still very high, and remained so because of the inflow of gold from abroad (reflected in an increase in the foreign debt).[17]

Argentina's high level of wages was one of the reasons why the index of wholesale prices fell less than it did in Canada.

IX FINAL COMMENTS

Evidence exists of a slowdown in the expansion of traditional staples and the emergence of a new generation, principally forestry and mining in Canada and cotton in Argentina. There is evidence also of the rise of new industries which employed such raw materials. But the amount of resources available, and their use in industrial activity, was far more important in Canada than it was in Argentina. Many of Canada's new industries were targeted at foreign markets, while in Argentina new industries dealt almost exclusively with the domestic market. This difference was to have important consequences for the post-war development of the two countries' industries, in terms of economies of scale, efficiency, capital investment, availability of technology, etc. As a result, it seems that successful industrialisation in Canada was a result not of strongly protectionist policies but of the availability of an outlet for the new staples abroad.

As for the role of the tariff, effective protection in Argentina in the 1920s depended not so much on the tariff itself as on the current rate of exchange and the evolution of puchasing parity in international markets. Besides, if effective protection were guaranteed largely by the undervaluation of the Argentine peso, there could have been no genuine clash of interest between local landowners and industrial entrepreneurs.

In both Canada and Argentina, the decline of British influence was accompanied by the rise of US influence. Although significant in both countries, the level of US investment was far higher in Canada. The flow of foreign capital into Canada became the most significant element in industrial development and in the growth of the economy in the twenties. Capital imports were of less importance for Argentina, nor even was the previous level maintained.

Finally, war inflation took a heavier toll in Canada than it did in Argentina, but from 1920 to 1925 the deflationary policies implemented by Canada produced a greater drop in prices and wages. It can be argued that this helped Canada's newly-developing industries in their exports to Britain and the British Empire.

The simple explanation, then, of the different development of the two countries is, first, Canada's proximity to the US market, second, Canada's access to Commonwealth markets, and finally, the existence in Canada, but not (on the same scale) in Argentina, of new staple industries and access to hydroelectricity. Differences in policy towards Protection may, after all, have had slight effect.

NOTES

1. This research was carried out with the assistance, gratefully acknowledged, of the Fundación Torcuato di Tella (Buenos Aires). A preliminary version of the paper was presented by the author at a seminar in the Department of History at the University of Texas at Austin, and at the Center for Latin American Studies of the University of California at Berkeley. The author is deeply grateful for the comments and suggestions of Richard Graham and Stanley Ross at Texas, and Tulio Halperín Donghi at Berkeley, as well as for those that he received from other participants in these seminars.
2. The figures on which this argument is based are drawn principally from the Instituto Alejandro Bunge's *Revista de Economía Argentina* (annual), the *Canada Yearbook*, CEPAL's *El Desarrollo Económico en la Argentina*, vol. 5 (1958), and the Dominion Bureau of Statistics, *Canada's International Investment Problems, 1926–54* (Ottawa, 1956).
3. Douglass C. North, 'Location Theory and Regional Economic Growth', in John Friedman and William Alonso (eds), *Regional Development and Planning* (Cambridge, Mass.: MIT Press, 1964) p. 240ff.
4. *Report of the Royal Commission on Banking and Currency in Canada* (Patenaude, Ottawa, 1933) ch. IV, p. 48.
5. Carl E. Solberg, 'Argentina y Canada; Una Perspectiva Comparada sobre su Desarrollo Económico, 1919–39', *Desarrollo Económico*, 21 (1981) 191ff.
6. The full range is described in the *Canada Yearbook*.
7. John A. Stovel, *Canada in the World Economy* (Cambridge, Mass. 1959) p. 222.
8. Ibid., p. 223.
9. Ibid., p. 225.
10. Orville John MacDiarmid, *Commercial Policy in the Canadian Economy* (Cambridge, Mass.: Harvard University Press, 1946) pp. 260, 264.
11. W. T. Easterbrook and H. G. C. Aitken, *Canadian Economic History* (Toronto: Macmillan, 1961) p. 545.

12. Carlos Díaz Alejandro, in this context, quotes W. M. Beveraggi-Allende and Félix Weil: *Essays on the Economic History of the Argentine Republic* (New Haven, Conn.: Yale University Press, 1970).
13. Ibid., pp. 277–8.
14. Ibid., pp. 297–8.
15. The figures are available in the publications recorded in note 2 above.
16. Ibid.
17. Ibid.

10 Public Finance and the Economy in Argentina, Australia and Canada During the Depression of the 1930s

PETER ALHADEFF

I

This paper deals with the repercussions of the Depression of the 1930s on government finance in Argentina, Australia, and Canada, three countries that depended for their international solvency and living standards on their export trade of primary products. It would not be unreasonable to expect the problems and the reactions of the national policy-maker to be similar, and indeed Argentina, Australia, and Canada stand out in the 1930s as examples of developing nations that tried to combat the Depression while adhering to the principles of classical finance. The conservative behaviour of the Argentine authorities, for example, has on occasion been explained by the powerful influence of an inherited body of economic thought, and it is true that throughout the Depression and during the rest of the 1930s the public sector was inclined to pursue a cautious management of the economy by balancing the budget, by keeping a good credit name in the Republic and abroad, and, as far as was possible in the 1930s, by preventing the currency from depreciating sharply.[1] In Australia, much emphasis has been given by the literature to the paramountcy of the Commonwealth Bank in the shaping of economic policy in the 1930s, and the adherence of the Bank to the canons of sound finance has been well illustrated;[2] the Premiers' Plan of 1931, 'a plan along strongly deflationary lines for restoring the Commonwealth's and the States' finances',[3] was, for that matter, the basis of Australia's response to the Depression. A representative view of the policies of the Canadian Government during the 1930s is that of the Royal Commission on Dominion-Provincial Relations:

> [Federal action was careful] to avoid risky and unorthodox monetary measures and to endeavour to maintain income in the sheltered and protected sector of the economy by drastic reductions against imports, by following 'sound' financial policies which would maintain confidence, preserve the public credit both internally and abroad, and thus facilitate the operation of the natural forces of recovery . . .[4]

The common concern with the practice of policies of sound finance was a result, above all, of the disarray left by the Depression in national government accounts. In Argentina, the Provisional Government took office at a time when the total receipts collected by the state could not pay for the expenses of its own administration.[5] Between January 1929 and September 1930 all principal items of Argentine revenue had fallen and, in the absence of a revival in world trade, the slump in import dues, the chief contributor to national revenue, was expected to continue. In fact, by 1932 import dues were 30 per cent below what they had been in 1929, and their contribution to national revenue sank from 47 per cent in 1930 to 32 per cent in 1934. Australian and Canadian public finance suffered much the same fate. Customs receipts were also the most important source of revenue of the Commonwealth and the Dominion governments and they declined as the Depression progressed, dropping as a proportion of total revenue between 1928/9 and 1933/4 from 37 per cent to 23 per cent in Australia, and from 41 per cent to 24 per cent in Canada.[6]

II

Thus, the initial impact of the Depression on government finance was not very different in either Argentina, Australia, or Canada. Each of these countries was forced to rely less on the proceeds of the external trading sector of the economy to raise public funds, and more on the domestic economy to pay for the services of the state and the expansion of its activities. Future increases of expenditure would have to be met now by additional internal taxation, and, with foreign borrowing, by floating bond or other issues in the local financial markets. In this context, it was sensible to advocate a policy of sound finance that laid stress on the judicious use of public money, the reduction of unnecessary state expenditure, and the good standing of national credit.

It was easier, though, for Australia and Canada to raise public finance by falling back on their own economies. Traditionally, the Argentine revenue system had relied on customs duties and other indirect taxes; in order to procure funds within the domestic economy and to give flexibility to Government finance it was necessary to pave the way for switching over from indirect to direct methods of collecting tax receipts. Much of the effort of the Argentine authorities in the early 1930s was therefore directed towards the establishment of an appropriate machinery to raise receipts domestically at short notice. Argentina's first income tax was announced early in 1931, and introduced in 1932. A new tax on business transactions was put into effect in 1934 and, a year after, petrol was taxed for the first time. These and other revenue charges were a first step towards severing Government revenue from the hazards of the import trade, and they compensated in time for the fall in customs revenue. President Justo, for instance, reported that without the new levies on business transactions, petrol, and income, it would not have been possible to arrive at a financial equilibrium between 1931 and 1934:[7] the income tax almost counterbalanced the fall in customs dues in 1934, and between 1932 and 1936 the combined receipts of the sales and petrol taxes made up for the fall in customs revenue.[8]

New taxes were raised also in Australia and Canada during the Depression to compensate for the fall in customs receipts, but they did not herald a new era of administrative finance for the public sector as in Argentina. The system of taxation operating in Australia and Canada was already quite complex in the 1920s: methods of direct taxation were firmly established before the Depression, with the income tax alone contributing an average of 11.5 per cent of total revenue in Australia and 14 per cent in Canada from 1928 to 1930. As a result, the Commonwealth and Dominion Governments were better prepared to tap the resources of their economy during the early 1930s. In Canada, for example, income tax receipts rose from 13 per cent of total revenue in 1928/29 to 22.5 per cent in 1930/31, while in Australia they increased from 12 per cent to 15 per cent in the same period.[9] Argentina, on the other hand, did not begin properly to collect income receipts until the worst of the Depression was over; the Republic had never been cross-examined as to its means before, and the setting up of a suitable administrative machinery took time.

The shift towards the development of alternative sources of internal revenue was more marked in Argentina than in Australia or Canada, and the transit from indirect to direct methods of taxation produced conflict. Late in 1932, when the budget of 1933 was about to be debated in Congress, the powerful Rural Society launched an anti-taxation campaign which argued for cuts in Government expenditure before new levies were raised.[10] Threatened with nationwide tax strikes, and flooded with protests from practically every industrial and commercial organization in the country, Congress refused to approve new tax projects submitted by the Minister of Finance in December 1932.[11] Wildcat tax strikes by retail shops in Buenos Aires and the Provinces against the incomes and sales taxes were commonplace in 1933 and 1934. There does not appear to be as much evidence of unrest over tax payments in Australia or Canada, even though, like Argentina, the trend was for total state receipts from taxation to increase as a proportion of national income or production, particularly in the early 1930s. In Australia, for example, taxes rose from 13 per cent of national production in 1928/9 to 18 per cent in 1932/3, while in Canada their share in national income grew from 8 per cent to 10 per cent. A comparable estimate for Argentina suggests a rise of 10 to 14 per cent, or alternatively, from 15 to 17 per cent during the same period.[12]

Taxation receipts took a bigger portion of material production in the 1930s, thus pointing to a more inward-looking evolution in the management of public finance during the decade. In future, fiscal policy could afford to be less reliant on the fortunes of foreign trade in each of the three countries. Particularly in Argentina, the overhaul of an old revenue system that was arguably long overdue grafted public finance firmly on to the domestic economy. But though this was achieved at more effort than Australia or Canada, in another sense the Argentine Government found itself better positioned to weather the storm of the Depression than either.

The scale of unemployment in Argentina was altogether different from that of Australia or Canada, and the financial burden of relief expenditure for the unemployed was much lighter for the Republic. In June 1932 the Argentine National Department of Labour estimated the number of unemployed at 334 000; after correcting for temporary and seasonal unemployment, the number was put at 263 000. This meant that only 5.6 per cent of the economically active were out of work, and this at the depth of the Depression itself.[13] At a total of 826 000, as much as a quarter of Canada's labour force was unemployed in 1933,[14] while in Australia, 420 000 men or women were out of work or searching for a job in 1931, or nearly a quarter of its unionized labour force.[15]

Even allowing for errors in the collection of Argentine statistics, unemployment was actually mild in the Republic during the Depression and not taken as seriously as elsewhere. The *Review of the River Plate* reckoned that where the evil of unemployment was concerned, Argentina was one of the least – if not the least – hard hit countries to be found anywhere in the world.[16] The well known economist Alejandro Bunge, a staunch promoter of industry as a means of diversifying Argentina's productive base and of supplying an engine of employment for the economy, told London's Argentine Club (September 1932) that the proportion of unemployed in Argentina as compared with active population was one of the lowest in the world; this was one of the ten points (*verdades*) on which Bunge chose to focus.[17] Furthermore, there was remarkably little debate in Congress on the issue of unemployment. While in Canada various Unemployment Relief Acts were sanctioned from 1930/3,[18] and in Australia, a three-year special unemployment relief plan was agreed in 1932,[19] in Argentina the bill proposing the creation of the National Board to Combat Unemployment was passed by ministerial decree as late as December 1933; Congress had not studied the draft version that was expected to become law, and action was taken by the Executive before waiting for its approval.[20] A plan to debate unemployment had already been defeated in August, when neither of the two prestige dailies, *La Nación* and *La Prensa*, felt the need to remonstrate in editorials. Parliamentarians gave it no high priority, and as such reflected to some extent the state of public opinion. This was less indicative of a lack of sympathy for the jobless than of the fact that the problem was less important.

Compared to Canada, and for geographical reasons, Argentina was relatively immune to the severe Depression in the United States. As a result, output fell less heavily in the Republic and unemployment was not as significant. The production of pulp and paper was Canada's most important manufacturing industry as measured by value of manufactured products or by distribution of salaries and wages, and as 85 per cent of the market for newsprint (one of Canada's leading exports) was in the United States, it bore heavy losses in the early

1930s.[21] Canada had also a more developed and sophisticated industrial base, which was likely to shed employment more easily. The proportion of industrials traded in the Toronto and the Montreal stock exchanges, for instance, was much greater than in the Buenos Aires *bourse*,[22] and Canadian manufacture was more sensitive to the movement of its capital markets; it was affected more immediately and deeply by the crash of October 1929 in New York. Canada's troubles were aggravated by the plight of her rural sector.[23]

In Australia, the high unemployment level of the early 1930s was partly the product of a domestic slump that started around the middle of 1927, and on which the Depression was grafted later.[24] As well as external factors, unemployment therefore recognized internal causes that were to give it an unusual dimension. By contrast, Argentina had enjoyed an era of prosperity before the Depression (referred to in the literature as the 'golden twenties'), and its unemployment problems were due exclusively to the world crisis. Argentina's employment record was also bound to be better than Australia's because more of her economically active population worked in agriculture (one-third against Australia's one-fifth),[25] and her agricultural output was very satisfactory in volume throughout the Depression (production of wheat and linseed was actually higher in every single harvest between 1930/1 and 1933/4 than in 1929/30, and on average so was maize.[26]

Much less government action was thus needed to assist the unemployed in Argentina than in Australia or Canada. Estimates of Government expenditure on unemployment relief in Australia suggest that, when outlays under different headings in the Commonwealth's Revenue Fund are pooled together, about £A55.9 million (£46.68 million)[27] was spent between 1930/1 and 1934/5. In direct unemployment relief alone, the Canadian Government disbursed during the same period $167.30 million (£33.46 million). These sums weighed heavily on the budgets of the Australian and Canadian Governments, consuming, respectively, 11 and 8 per cent of annual expenditure on their Consolidated Revenue account. The only contribution made by the Argentine Government to the National Board to Combat Unemployment was 2 million pesos (£130 000) in 1934, an insignificant 0.1 per cent of the annual outlay of the Government in that year.[28] The funds, however, were not used to create jobs but to transport workers to the harvest, to build up schools for workers, to conduct inquiries into unemployment, and to start a National Register of Unemployment.

Another advantage enjoyed by Argentina over Canada and Australia was that the use of public money to pay for railway losses during the Depression was minimal, as railway lines in the Republic were for the most part privately owned and in the hands of foreigners. In Canada, nearly half the Dominion's budgetary deficit between 1932/3 and 1934/5, and about 13 per cent of the expenditure of the Consolidated Revenue Fund, was taken up in financing the deficit of the government-owned railway network: since 1929, Canadian National Railways operated at a net loss, and both the Treasury (prior to 1932/3) and the Consolidated Revenue Fund (after 1932/3) footed the bill. Railway expenditure by the Commonwealth Government in Australia was very small by comparison, since most of the lines were owned and operated by the States (which were responsible also for their cash flow). However, internal finance was just as hard hit; railway losses explained at least part of the increase of one-third in payments of the Commonwealth Government to the States between 1929/30 and 1934/5 and the simultaneous rise from 11 to 16 per cent of those subsidies in the total outlays of the Consolidated Revenue Fund.[29]

Moreover, both Australia and Canada assisted their wheat producers directly, and public finance was again under greater strain than in the Republic. As part of the 'Grow More Wheat' campaign in Australia, a wheat bounty of £A3.3 million (£2.6 million) was paid to farmers in 1931/2 by drawings from the Loan Fund (which comprised, as a rule, proceeds of loans raised by the Commonwealth Government and the States) for nearly one-tenth of its receipts.[30] In 1932 the bounty system was abandoned; instead, £A2.3 million (£1.8 million) was paid out of ordinary receipts to be distributed directly by the States to farmers in need. Then, to boost its assistance policy to wheat producers, the Commonwealth Government imposed a flour tax which yielded only £A760 000 (£608 000) by 1934/5, so that additional funds had to be found from revenue.[31] Relief to the wheat-producing areas of Alberta, Saskatchewan and Manitoba in Canada was given in the form of a wheat bonus financed out of Dominion revenue in 1931 and 1932, and the total expenditure effected on that account amounted to $12.7 million (£2.54 million); by 1935/6 the special expenditure of the Canadian Government in connection with its wheat policy of the early 1930s (for bonuses and price stabilization) totalled $22.5 million (£4.5 million).[32]

These disbursements of the Commonwealth and the Dominion Governments were of limited help to producers; wheat growing was still the one major industry in Australia that did not participate in the recovery of 1932/5,[33] and government assistance in Canada could not redress the impact of the Depression in areas such as rural Saskatchewan, where as much as 80 per cent of farm receipts came from wheat. And, of course, wheat payments took their toll from public funds in Australia and Canada. On the other hand, little was done for the wheat farmer in Argentina until the end of 1933, when a minimum price guarantee for purchases of wheat, maize, and linseed was put into effect whenever the international quotations for those staples fell below a stipulated minimum.[34] The finance to pay for cereal purchases, however, was supplied not from ordinary or budgetary revenues but by modifying the system of exchange control (which Australia and Canada did not have) to yield a profit, and the gain was derived from the difference between the rate at which the State bought foreign exchange (i.e. cheap from exporters) and the rate at which it sold (i.e. dear to importers).[35]

III

It appears, therefore, that Argentina had less budgetary problems than Canada or Australia. The financing of unemployment and railway deficits was perforce much smaller, and government assistance to wheat producers came later and was then managed by adapting the system of exchange control to supply the necessary cash. In addition, the lack of direct forms of taxation in the early 1930s meant that expenditure cuts had to be practised with more zeal, and whereas between 1928/9 and 1933/4 real expenditure increased by 66 per cent in Canada and by 46 per cent in Australia, in Argentina the rise was only 10 per cent.[36] In the event, the Argentine Government was much better able to balance its budget during the 1930s.

Premier Bennett in Canada kept hoping for a budgetary equilibrium in the early 1930s, but deficits continued even under Mackenzie King after 1935, oscillating between 3 and 5 per cent of national income. All of Australia's most prominent economists and the Commonwealth Bank advocated a balanced budget during the Depression, but it was not to be. Although surpluses appeared in the Consolidated Revenue Fund after 1930/1, it is clear from the Treasury's balance sheet that it made sizeable advances to meet the accumulated deficit of the Loan Fund; the value of these advances, which remained virtually unpaid until the late 1930s, was the true measure of the Commonwealth's deficit (which hovered around 5 per cent of production value at least until 1934/5[37]). In sharp contrast, the budgetary losses of Argentina were reduced from 7 to 8 per cent of production value in 1930 to only 1 per cent in 1932 and 1933; by 1934 the Government's deficit was insignificant, and between 1935 and 1938 it was in surplus.[38]

This good budgetary record suggests that Argentina accommodated well to the difficulty of servicing her public obligations during the Depression. In part this was true, and an important reason was that the Republic was not overburdened by its liabilities. For the decade as a whole, Argentina had a lower ratio of debt service to export value than Australia or Canada; between 1930 and 1933, for instance, the figures were, respectively, 17 per cent, 22 per cent, and 23 per cent. Argentina's ratio of debt service to budgetary expenditure, though slightly higher than Australia's, was much lower than Canada's,[39] and in per capita terms Argentina's debt was by far the smallest: in 1932 it stood at 167 pesos a head (£12), compared with 863 pesos in Australia (£63) and 224 pesos in Canada (£16).[40]

Argentina, however, had more of a problem in obtaining exchange cover to pay for her foreign debt than either Canada or Australia. In October 1931 she had to set up exchange controls to check the increase in the cost of the external debt service brought about by the outflow of foreign exchange. In Canada, banks kept part of their exchange holdings abroad to an extent which they would never have done in Argentina, and this gave stability to the Canadian exchange market and served to protect the balance of payments.[41] In Australia, the Bank of New South Wales and a number of Melbourne banks reached agreement in 1930 to supply £3 million from their receipts in London to the Commonwealth Government, which paid for the sum in Australia at the current rate of exchange.[42] This avoided a government-run system of exchange control which would have detracted from the financial independence of the banks. Yet it is interesting that the system of exchange control in Argentina was not opposed by the local banks: they felt that it was better to prevent a potential loss of exchange, with the consequent depreciation of the currency, than to strive for independence from the Government, and in practice surrendered their holdings of foreign exchange without much demur.

Argentina's debt payment record thereafter was excellent. She was described in 1934 as being the only South American borrower to meet 100 per cent of her external debt service throughout the Depression, promptly, unquestioningly, and with good grace.[43] Actually, with smaller exchange problems, Australia appears to have had more trouble in servicing her debts. Relative to Argentina, Australia had over-borrowed in the 1920s,[44] forcing the creation of a Loan Council to co-ordinate the credit policies bill of the States and of the Commonwealth Government towards the turn of the decade. But even with a body that allowed Australia to be better prepared for the Depresssion than Argentina, the Government of New South Wales defaulted in July 1931, precipitating the collapse of the Government Savings Bank, the largest of its kind in the Commonwealth.[45] There was less of a problem with the service of the debt in Canada, as the Dominion Government had no history of overborrowing in the 1920s: in fact, the net debt of the Dominion was reduced on an annual basis between 1922 and 1930.[46] The Dominion record of no default since Confederation in respect of interest or repayment due upon Dominion or Provincial loans, either direct or guaranteed, was nevertheless broken in 1936 by the Province of Alberta.[47]

But on the whole, default was exceptional in Argentina, Australia, and Canada. In each of these countries public opinion was weighted against any arbitrary suspension of payments. In Australia, for example, the action of the Government of New South Wales confirmed the fear that little good could come from a unilaterally declared moratorium, and Premier Lang, who was responsible for taking the decision to default, resigned soon after – which pleased the Commonwealth Government. At the time, the mood in Argentina, Australia, and Canada was that, even at a sacrifice, the preservation of credit was vital to national livelihood. In the long and medium run, it was contended in all three countries that the maintenance of a good credit name guaranteed future access to sources of finance, creating also an atmosphere conducive to a continued flow of foreign capital for development purposes. In the short term (as was observed for Canada) that policy 'facilitat[ed] the operation of the natural forces of recovery' by avoiding any financial disruption that added to the monetary disturbance of the early 1930s.

Monetary action itself was predictably designed partly to bring about a 'return-to-normal' situation. In Argentina, since the closure of the Conversion Office (which guaranteed the automatic exchange of paper pesos for gold) the likelihood of a fall in the external purchasing power of the peso was a permanent worry for the authorities, and their resolve to prevent the currency from depreciating was firm and definite throughout the 1930s.[48] When the Loan Council invited Professors Copland, Gibblin, Melville and Shann to prepare recommendations for the Premiers' Conference in 1931, they were brought around unanimously to the view that a further devaluation of the Australian pound would have a depressing psychological impact and precipitate a flight from the currency,[49] and J. M. Keynes shared this opinion.[50] In Canada, it is clear that the Dominion Government desired to keep the depreciation at a minimum in terms of American funds; just as, in Argentina or Australia, proposals that the currency should be depreciated in the interests of primary producers were rejected as dangerous and unsound.[51]

Internal monetary policy also was conservative in the three countries: none was willing to use the money supply as a tool for reflation because it was felt that this would contribute to the instability of the money market. Typical is the outlook of the Bank of Canada that 'in the absence of structural changes which lessen dependence on export trade, no amount of internal monetary stimulus could fully offset the effect of a low level of foreign demand for goods and services'.[52] In a deflationary environment, inflation of the means of payment was regarded as nothing more than tampering artificially with the price level. In fact, the view of the monetary authorities in Argentina, Australia, and Canada appears to have been that it was better not to do than to do and do badly, and in each case there is consensus in the literature that monetary policy contributed little to recovery.[53]

An important clue to the monetary history of the early 1930s in Argentina, Australia and Canada was the course of interest rates. In Argentina and Canada (the two countries without a Central Bank), interest rates followed roughly the same course. In May 1933 'the first general movement of short-term interest rates in Canadian history' took place; deposit rates fell from 3 to $2\frac{1}{2}$ per cent.[54] In Argentina, banks began reducing the interest rate on discount and advances at about the same time. But it was only after the final terms of the Roca Funding Loan at 4 per cent were agreed in October 1933 (the loan was a result of the Anglo-Argentine negotiations conducted in London early in 1933) that the authorities managed to get concerted action from private banks to lower their interest charges.[55] Unlike Canada, Argentine banks required that the Government balance its accounts before they endorsed reductions across the board, and, for all practical purposes, the Argentine Government had achieved this towards the second half of 1933. Australia had the distinction of an early reduction of interest on its public debt when it implemented the Premiers' Plan of 1931 – though banking interest rates were to fall at about the same time as in Argentina and Canada. The strong presence of the Commonwealth Bank in the Australian money market and its commitment to sound monetary management, was in all probability the fundamental reason that allowed the Australian Government to convert its obligations at a lower interest rate with the agreement of the bondholders.[56] The Australian record in this respect was quite remarkable: Argentina had to wait until 1934 to effect savings in the service of the public debt, while in Canada, where no organized effort was made to reduce voluntarily or compulsorily the cost of Government borrowing either at home or abroad, interest payments began to decline only in 1934 and 1935.[57]

IV

It does not seem, then, that the Argentine, Australian and Canadian authorities reacted differently to the economic problems of the early 1930s. They shared a bias towards a conservative monetary management, a desire for a healthy budget in the face of adversity, and, finally, the will to maintain a good credit name at a time when most primary producing countries were being forced to default. Although these might not have been a bold set of measures to combat the Depression, at least they were expedient, they avoided making matters worse for the currency, and because the policies were traditional in character, they could be understood and relied upon by the general public.

Also, good financial housekeeping could pay. Argentina's outstanding credit reputation allowed her to obtain a 4 per cent loan in London as part of the Roca-Runciman Treaty of 1933. The issue was floated at par, and the attractive interest rate (which was one to one-and-a-half percentage points lower than the average rate carried by Argentina's external obligations) reflected in no small part the trust the City placed in the credit-worthiness of the Republic. The 4 per cent rate of the Roca Loan was in the event to hasten a fall in domestic interest rates and to have a clear reflationary impact on production.[58] Yet it was in the domain of public sector borrowing where the advantages of a sound financial management could be most readily appreciated. During the 1930s, and especially in the second half of the decade, Argentina, Australia, and Canada made use of their domestic capital market to an extent that they had never done before, making public finance more autonomous than ever from the foreign financier.

Towards the end of 1933, Argentina began to convert her internal debt at lower interest rates. Her good credit name was a major factor in getting the co-operation of the local bondholder, who had to trust the Government if he were to exchange his old interest-bearing denominations for new lower-interest paying issues of a longer duration; if interest rates were to be reduced properly all around, nothing could be gained by forcing the holder to exchange his old paper for new. Argentina converted her internal debt successfully between 1933 and 1934, and quite apart from their effect in precipitating and confirming the trend for lower interest rates and cheaper money, these operations saved considerable sums in Government expenditure by reducing the annual outlay on debt service.[59]

The conversion of the internal public debt was the prelude in Argentina to the conversion of the bulk of the external debt at lower interest rates, and then the repatriation of much of that debt by exploiting the resources of the local capital market. The success of the internal conversion operations, and the favourable trade position of the Argentine economy towards the mid 1930s, made the foreign bondholder receptive to the requests for lower interest charges by the Government. After all, what he was being asked for was to forfeit a temporary gain in the expectation of payments over an extended period of time, which, in the light of the Argentine Government's past record as a borrower, was an attractive proposition. The Republic first converted its debt in London, and in time proceeded to do the same with the smaller debt in Swiss francs and later the debt in US dollars. About 30 per cent of Argentina's foreign debt was repatriated by floating issues internally in the 1930s, so that by 1937 three-quarters of the funded debt was held within the country, by contrast with about half in 1928,[60] and less than one-fifth in 1914.[61] Argentina's position as an international debtor was in fact better than it had ever been.

It would not be difficult, therefore, to make a case for the punctual payment of the public debt as serving national aspirations in Argentina during the 1930s. To a lesser extent, the same could be said for Australia, where the importance of the domestic market as a source of funds for the Commonwealth Government and the States increased throughout the 1930s; in 1931/2, for instance, 48 per cent of the total debt matured in Australia, whereas by 1936/7 53 per cent was being redeemed there. In Canada, the relation between the external and internal debt was stable in the 1930s, though domestic finance had always been a more important source of funding for the Dominion Government.[62]

Nevertheless, even in Canada there were interesting developments in the management of public finance which suggest a better utilization of local savings. Since 1934 Treasury bills began to be issued to the public as well as to the chartered banks,[63] thus extending the market for Government short-term accommodation outside the banking sector proper, and permitting Canadian authorities more flexibility in raising finance. The same happened in Argentina after 1938,[64] while in Australia, and particularly after 1931, Treasury bills partly replaced London funds among the liquid assets of banks.[65]

All of this was a reflection of the ascendancy of the domestic economy as a supplier of public funds, as well as a new, inward-looking approach in the control of Government finance. The emergence of central banking in Argentina and in Canada, and the extended functions conferred on the Commonwealth Bank in Australia after 1929, contributed further to the internalization and relative autonomy of national finance in the three countries.

Here, and by way of conclusion, it should be stressed that the Depression would probably have run a different course without the prosperity of the 1920s. It has been said of Australia that 'the high levels of savings among people, and their prudent investment by institutions . . . made for financial stability, even in the worst phases of the crisis'.[66] This seems also largely to have been true for Argentina and Canada. In Argentina, it was demonstrated most convincingly in 1932; small private savings, the bulk of which was almost certainly produced in the 1920s, provided immediate solvency for the public sector after the flotation of the *Patriotic Loan*. It is difficult to exaggerate the importance of this event at the time, or its significance for future economic and financial developments during the 1930s.

NOTES

1. See P. Alhadeff, 'The Economic Formulae of the 1930s: a Reassessment', in G. di Tella and D. C. M. Platt (eds), 'The Political Economy of Argentina, 1880–1946', forthcoming.
2. See C. B. Schedvin, *Australia and the Great Depression: Economic Development and Policy in the 1920s and the 1930s* (Sydney, 1970).
3. League of Nations, *Public Finance 1928–37*, vol LXI (Geneva, 1938) p. 11.
3. Royal Commission on Dominion-Provincial Relations, *Report: Canada, 1867–1939*, vol. I (Ottawa, 1940) p. 151.
5. S. G. Irving, 'Economic Conditions in the Argentine Republic', report to the UK Dept. of Overseas Trade, 31 January 1931 (HM Stationery Office) p. 19.
6. Comité Nacional de Geografía, *Anuario Geográfico 1941* (Buenos Aires, 1942) pp. 404–6; League of Nations, *Public Finance 1928–37*, vol. LXI (Geneva, 1938) pp. 7–8; and League of Nations, *Public Finance 1928–37*, vol. XXXIII (Geneva, 1938) p. 6.

7. 'Acción Impositiva', in República Argentina, *Poder Ejecutivo Nacional 1932–38*, vol. I (Buenos Aires, 1938) n.p.
8. República Argentina, *Memoria del Departmento de Hacienda 1934*, vol. I (Buenos Aires, 1935) p. 70.
9. For Argentina see Comité Nacional de Geografía, *Anuario Geográfico 1941* (Buenos Aires) pp. 404–6, and Fundación Banco de Boston, *Argentina: Evolución Economica 1915–1976* (Buenos Aires, 1978) p. 15; for Australia see *Public Finance 1928–37*, LXI, pp. 7–8 (value of production from 'Economic Conditions in Australia' UK Department of Overseas Trade, Annual Reports, 1928–38); for Canada see *Public Finance* 1928–37, XXXIII, 6 (National income from A. E. Safarian, *The Canadian Economy in the Great Depression* (Toronto, 1959), Appendix A, Table 50).
10. *New York Times*, 29 November 1932, p. 32.
11. *New York Times*, 22 December 1932, p. 13.
12. See note 9 above.
13. The figures of the NDL, the result of an unemployment census conducted in 1932, were the standard quantitative reference of the press and Congress. For the NDL's classification of the unemployed by province, trade, nationality, and sex, see The Bank of London and South America, *Monthly Review of Business and Trade Conditions in South America and Portugal*, XV, December 1932, p. 6, and XV, 178, September 1933, p. 267. The proportion of unemployment to total population has been obtained from the same source (XV, 180, November 1933, p. 326), and the number of the economically active from C. F. Díaz Alejandro, *Essays on the Economic History of the Argentine Republic* (Yale, 1970), Appendix, Table V.
14. D. G. Creighton, *Canada's First Century* (London, 1970) p. 205.
15. C. B. Schedvin, *Australia and the Great Depression*, p. 211–12, and R. J. Cooksey (ed.), *The Great Depression in Australia* (Sydney, 1970) pp. 3–4.
16. *The Review of the River Plate*, LXVII, 12 April 1935, p. 13.
17. *The Times*, 29 September 1932, p. 12.
18. League of Nations, *Public Finance 1928–37*, LXI, p. 14.
19. D. B. Copland, *Australia and the World Crisis, 1929–33* (Cambridge, 1934) p. 5.
20. *La Prensa*, 20 December 1933, p. 12.
21. Royal Commission on Dominion-Provincial Relations, *Report: Canada 1867–1939*, I, p. 163.
22. Unlike the European or American Stock Exchange markets, the Buenos Aires Stock Exchange traded an insignificant proportion of industrials. In 1930 shares of limited liability companies accounted for 5 per cent of the turnover of the stock exchange, but by 1933, and due to a strong demand for Government bonds, their proportion was further reduced to 3 per cent: see *The Economist: Argentine Supplement*, 8 February 1936, p. 16. Trade in industrial and mining shares was instead a prominent feature of the movement of five of the six stock exchanges in Canada (the exception was Calgary, which dealt mainly in oil shares); about one-fifth of the mining issues listed in Canada was also traded on American markets, and two-fifths of all mining shares were American holdings: see A. F. W.

Plumtre, *Central Banking in the British Dominions* (Toronto, 1940) p. 140.
23. See, for example, G. E. Britnell, 'The Depression in Rural Saskatchewan' in H. A. Innis (ed.), *The Canadian Economy and its Problems* (Toronto, 1934) pp 97–110.
24. For a discussion about the dating of the downturn in Australia, see E. A. Boehm, 'Australia's Economic Depression in the 1930s' (review article of C. B. Schedvin's, *Australia and the Great Depression*), in *Economic Record*, vol. 49 (178) pp. 606–23, 614–5.
25. For Argentina see C. F. Díaz Alejandro, *Essays*, Appendix, Table V, and for Australia E. A. Boehm, 'El Desarrollo Económico Australiano a Partir de 1930', in J. Fogarty, E. Gallo and H. Diéguez, *Argentina y Australia* (Buenos Aires, 1979) p. 120.
26. Comité Nacional de Geografía, *Anuario Geográfico 1941*, pp. 207, 210, and 212.
27. Throughout this paper, the sterling expression of the Argentine peso, the Australian pound, and the Canadian dollar has been obtained from 'Table for Rough Conversion of Currencies According to Annual Exchange Rates', in League of Nations, *The International Statistical Yearbook* (Geneva), issues from 1929 to 1939.
28. For unemployment relief in Argentina see League of Nations, *Public Finance 1928–37*, vol. xxxv, (Geneva, 1938) p. 16; expenditure is given in the *Anuario Geográfico 1941*, p. 406. For expenditure on unemployment relief in Australia from The Consolidated Revenue Fund (which does not include loans to local authorities, the bulk of which was for unemployment relief and accounted for in the Loan Fund), see Schedvin, *Australia and the Great Depression*, p. 340; CRF total expenditure is from League of Nations, *Public Finance 1928–37*, LXI, pp. 10–11. For unemployment relief in Canada and expenditure of the Consolidated Revenue Fund see League of Nations, *Public Finance 1928–37*, XXXIII, pp. 10–11.
29. See the same sources as in note 28 above.
30. League of Nations, *Public Finance 1928–37*, LXI, pp. 7 and 11.
31. Schedvin, *Australia and the Great Depression*, p. 342.
32. See the same sources as in note 28 above.
33. Schedvin, *Australia and the Great Depression*, p. 340.
34. Unlike earlier steps taken in Australia and Canada to help the farmer, this measure afforded widespread relief to the cereal producer, and it is generally recognized that the real economic recovery of the Republic can be dated from its implementation.
35. For a more detailed discussion of the scheme to finance cereal producers, see V. Salera, *Exchange Control and the Argentine Market* (New York, 1941) and P. Alhadeff, 'Dependency, Historiography, and Objections to the Roca Treaty', in C. Abel and C. Lewis (eds), 'Latin America and Economic Imperialism', forthcoming.
36. See the same sources as in note 28 above.
37. This reading of Australian accounts runs counter to Schedvin's observation that 'by 1934/35 budget "equilibrium" had for all intent and purposes been achieved'; Schedvin, *Australia and the Great Depression*, p. 327.

38. For Argentina, see *Anuario Geográfico 1941*, pp. 369 and 406; for Australia, see *Public Finance 1928–37*, LXI, pp. 2–3; and for Canada see *Public Finance 1928–37*, XXXIII, p. 2. Production value in Argentina and Australia, and national income in Canada, are as quoted earlier.
39. For Argentina, see Ministerio de Hacienda, *El Ajuste de los Resultados Financieros 1928–36*, p. 146, and *Anuario Geográfico 1941*, pp. 404–6, and 434–5; for Australia, see *Public Finance 1928–37*, LXI, 13, and League of Nations, *International Statistical Yearbook 1939–40* (Geneva, 1941) pp. 182–7; for Canada, see *Public Finance 1928–37*, XXXIII, p. 11, and League of Nations, *International Yearbook 1939–40* (Geneva, 1941), pp. 182–7.
40. Argentina's per capita debt was also much smaller than Great Britain's (at 930 pesos a head or £68), France's (at 381 pesos or £28), Italy's (at 204 pesos or £15), and the United States' (at 189 pesos or £14): figures quoted from A. Bunge, 'La Independencia Económica Argentina', *Revista de Economía Argentina*, XXVIII, May 1932, 331. In the downswing of the Depression, Bunge described Argentina as one of the least indebted nations in the world, and claimed that the Federal and Provincial Governments retained intact their capacity for credit: see *The South America Journal*, 15 August 1931.
41. A. F. W. Plumptre, 'The Evidence Presented to the Canadian Macmillan Commission', *Canadian Journal of Economics and Political Science*, 2 (1936), p. 63.
42. D. B. Copland and G. A. Weller, *The Australian Economy: Simple Economic Studies* (Sydney, 1933) pp. 83–4.
43. *The Economist*, 28 April 1934, 933. In the early 1930s a handful of Provinces and Municipalities suspended payment either of interest or sinking fund, but the Argentine Government continued to meet its foreign debt obligations in full: see Public Record Office (London), F0371/15799 and 16543, *Argentine Report 1932*, p. 20.
44. See Copland, *Australia and the World Crisis*, Schedvin, *Australia and the Great Depression*, and W. R. MacLaurin, *Economic Planning in Australia, 1929–36* (Cambridge, 1937).
45. Schedvin, *Australia and the Great Depression*, pp. 234–6.
46. F. W. Field, 'Economic Conditions in Canada', report to the UK Dept. of Overseas Trade (HMSO, 1930) p. 16.
47. F. W. Field, 'Economic and Commercial Conditions in Canada', report to the UK Dept. of Overseas Trade (HMSO, 1935–6) p. 25.
48. See Alhadeff, 'The Economic Formulae of the 1930s: a Reassessment'.
49. Schedvin, *Australia and the Great Depression*, p. 244.
50. 'J. M. Keynes and the Depression in Australia', in L. J. Lovis and I. Turner (eds), *The Depression of the 1930s in Australia* (Melbourne, 1968) pp. 220–1.
51. A. F. W. Plumptre, 'Canadian Monetary Policy', in H. A. Innis (ed.), *The Canadian Economy and its Problems*, pp. 160–1.
52. Bank of Canada, *Annual Report to the Minister of Finance and Statement of Accounts*, 10 February 1940, pp. 13–14.
53. See A. F. W. Plumptre, 'Canadian Monetary Policy', p. 165; C. B. Schedvin, *Australia and the Great Depression*, p. 301; and in this

collection of essays, M. J. Twomey's 'Economic Fluctuations in Argentina, Australia and Canada during the Depression of the 1930s.'

54. A. F. W. Plumptre, 'Canadian Monetary Policy', p. 163.
55. P. Alhadeff, 'Dependency, Historiography, and Objections to the Roca Treaty'.
56. Under the terms of the Premiers' Plan an agreement was signed on 21 July 1931 by the Commonwealth and the States for debt conversion. Within the next few months, the existing Government securities (Commonwealth and States) were exchanged by bondholders into new long-term securities maturing in from seven to thirty years, with an average reduction of 22.5 per cent in the previous rates of interest. These conversion operations reduced the average annual rate of interest from £A5.6s. 10d. per cent to £A3.18s. 9d. per cent, representing an annual saving of about £A7.53 million: League of Nations, *Public Finance 1928–37*, LXI, p. 17.
57. Australian scholars like Schedvin, who have criticised the conservatism of the Commonwealth Bank throughout the Depression, might find some comfort in this fact and temper their assessment of the policies it adopted in the early 1930s.
58. See P. Alhadeff, 'Dependency, Historiography, and Objections to the Roca Treaty'.
59. Three billion pesos worth of bonds (£200 million) were converted from a 6 to a 5 per cent interest basis, saving the Government 30.8 million pesos annually (£2 million) between 1934 and 1938, or about 15 per cent of its yearly debt service and 3 per cent of its total expenditure, 'La Conversión de la Deuda Pública', in República Argentina, *Poder Ejecutivo Nacional 1932–38*, I, n.p.
60. For Argentina, see *Anuario Geográfico 1941*, p. 409; for Australia, 1929/30–1935/6: League of Nations, *Public Finance 1928–37*, LXI, pp. 16–17, and 1936/7–1938/9: 'Economic Conditions in Australia', UK Dept. of Overseas Trade, *annual reports*, 1936–9; for Canada, 1929/30–1935/6: League of Nations, *Public Finance 1928–37*, XXXIII,. pp. 16–17, 1936/7–1937/8, Dominion Bureau of Statistics, *The Canada Year Book* (Ottawa, 1936–9).
61. V. L. Phelps, *The International Economic Position of Argentina* (Philadelphia, 1938) p. 119.
62. See the same sources as in note 60 above.
63. League of Nations, *Public Finance 1928–37*, XXXIII, p. 17.
64. Banco Central de la República Argentina, *La Creación del Banco Central y la Experiencia Monetaria Argentina entre los Años 1935–1943*, vol. I (Buenos Aires,, 1972) pp. 581–2.
65. Plumptre, *Central Banking in the British Dominions*, p. 85.
66. Copland, *Australia and the World Crisis, 1929–33*, p. 27.

11 Economic Fluctuations in Argentina, Australia and Canada During the Depression of the 1930s

MICHAEL J. TWOMEY

I INTRODUCTION

Can three countries separated by vast distances and with such divergent histories be compared during a period as tumultuous as the Depression of the 1930s? Contemporaries did make these comparisons, and these three 'countries of recent settlement' have been the focus of a growing number of studies since then. With regard to economic structure, a number of similarities suggest the value of such a study.

Since the turn of the century, all three countries had grown appreciably in terms both of total and per capita output, with manufacturing growing faster than rural activities.[1] By 1929, industrial value-added as a percentage of total GDP was similar: 22 per cent in Canada, 17 per cent in Australia, and 20 per cent in Argentina, although Canada had a more 'developed' industrial plant. Exports as a percentage of GDP were about 19 per cent in Canada, 18 per cent in Australia and 22 per cent in Argentina. Argentina's per capita GDP was half of Canada's, while that of Australia fell nearly midway between the other two. Each country was involved in triangular trade with the US and the UK, and all three received large capital inflows. In the 1920s, net immigration accounted for 30 per cent of the population increase in Argentina and Australia, but less than 10 per cent in Canada. About one-third of Australians and Argentines lived in rural areas before 1929; the percentage was somewhat higher in Canada.

During the 1920s each government spent heavily on the expansion of the domestic network of railroads.[2] The growth of wheat production and exports depended on those expanding rail facilities, particularly in Canada. Both Canada and Australia made use of tariffs for industrial development before the Depression, more so than Argentina, for which they were intended more as a source of tax revenue.

In addition, there were strong similarities in their reactions to the Depression. Increased tariffs and devaluations meant effective flight from the gold standard. Tax structures were changed, which lessened reliance on tariffs while introducing or increasing income taxes. Declining immigration reduced pressure on employment. Wheat farming was subsidized. The importance of monetary policy was recognized, and central banking functions centralized and/or strengthened. Although the rationale for countercyclical policies now referred to as Keynesian was known to small groups of academics or others, no country experienced a strong intellectual movement supportive of it, and none implemented such policies.

Let us round up this background discussion by indicating some important political occurrences. In Australia, a coalition of the Nationalist and Country parties, referred to as the Bruce-Page regime, which was rather less protectionist than its predecessors or successor, was in power from 1923–9. Economic stagnation, reaching back to 1925, eventually led to manufacturing interests backing Scullin's Labour Party, whose election victory just before the Wall Street crash began a move away from the orthodox measures defended by the Commonwealth Bank (the central bank). In the ensuing policy clash, the latter group's position dominated, and the 'Premiers' Plan' of 1931 signalled the defeat of non-orthodox monetary and fiscal strategies. Scullin was soon defeated by another coalition led by 'Honest Abe' Lyons (previously a Labour leader), which held office until 1939. In the interim, however, the three crucial policy initiatives of devaluation, increased tariffs and market intervention, in the form of the 'Grow More Wheat' campaign and various unemployment policies, had been carried out.

Canadian political developments in the first half of the twentieth century were dominated by Mackenzie King of the Liberal Party, who, however, lost in the summer of 1930 a badly-timed and poorly-campaigned election to the Conservatives. The new premier, Bennett, did not have a clear policy to counteract the Depression, and although he moved belatedly towards a New Deal type programme, King was returned to office in late 1935, eventually passing it on to his hand-chosen successor in 1948, two years before his death. The conservative government under Bennett did raise tariffs (against the opposition of the Liberals), and, as in Australia, did participate in the system of Empire preference, but Canada's exchange rate was allowed to change only after the devaluation of the British pound, and by a smaller percentage.

Argentine political developments present important similarities. The 14-year rule of the Radical party, led by the now-aged Yrigoyen, was ended by a coup in late 1930. The subsequent regimes of the 1930s represented the more traditional economic interests, sometimes not too coherently. The 'infamous decade' was a major 'Prologue to Perón';[3] policies took their inspiration more from the nationalist corporativism of Continental Europe than from the tradition of British interventionism. In terms also of specific economic policies, Argentina's devaluation preceded Britain's and was of the same order of magnitude as Australia's. Tariffs were levied, and one might speculate that the gap between practice and a 'selective' tariff which would aid those industries potentially 'economic' and 'efficient'[4] was no greater in Argentina than in the other two countries. Argentina was the only one of the three countries to impose exchange controls, but, in contrast to a number of her South American neighbours, she did not enter into default on the national debt.[5] Argentina's efforts at mutual tariff reductions with the US were unsuccessful, while the Roca-Runciman trade treaty with England created considerable controversy at home. The resulting commercial isolation was quite influential in moulding Argentina's position of neutrality at the outbreak of the Second World War.

Let us proceed, then, to look at the different economic performances of the three countries. Australia, which had been stagnating for some years, experienced a post-1929 decline that was the smallest in magnitude – 9 per cent. The decline in Argentine output was about 14 per cent, while that of Canadian income was 30 per cent. By the end of the decade, only Australia had surpassed her 1929 level of per capita income, while recovery was slowest in Canada.[6]

The major purpose of this chapter is to explain the differences in the time paths of output over the decade, paying special attention to the decline in output. Our framework of analysis is a simple model, utilizing aggregate supply and demand curves. Differences in the behaviour of supply are noted first, and a lengthier discussion of demand follows. These lead to a few evaluative comments comparing government policy, as well as to some other concluding observations.

II AGGREGATE SUPPLY AND DEMAND

It has recently been noted that the study of the economic performances of different countries during the Depression must include considerations of aggregate supply,[7] in addition to the more traditional discussion of demand. Of course, a considerable amount of theoretical work in macroeconomic analysis has recently been devoted to supply side considerations. Using a two-stage, least squares procedure, I have calculated that the slope of the aggregate supply curve for goods in Canada (0.43) was much lower than that of Argentina (1.22) or Australia (1.77).[8] In this case bigger is indeed better, for it implies that a given decline in demand leads to a smaller fall in output and, presumably, employment. As comparable unemployment data for these countries are not available, we will restrict our attention to total production.

A related indicator of labour's well-being is the level of real wages. There are clear indications that during the 1920s they rose most in Argentina: after 1929 they continued to rise in Australia and especially in Canada, while oscillating around a stable level in Argentina. In each of the countries under review there was labour unrest during the 1930s, as well as government intervention in the labour market. These factors should have affected aggregate supply, and it would be of interest to see if the differences in the evolution of real wages affected output performance, by, for example, linking the higher growth of real wages in Canada with that country's flatter supply curve and lower output in the late 1930s. Unfortunately, the econometric tests attempted so far have not given any consistent information in this respect.

Turning now to the demand side, we will compare nominal values of its three proximate determinants – exports, investments, and government expenditures –for 1929 (the 'peak year'), and for the year of lowest aggregate output (referred to as the 'trough year'), using 1938 as an end-of-period reference point. In all these countries investments dropped more than exports or government expenditure, although the difference between the decline of investments and exports in Australia was minimal. While exports and investments did recover somewhat, the autonomous variable which provided the largest net stimulus in each country over the decade was government expenditure. The most drastic fall was experienced by Canadian investments,[9] amounting to 15 per cent of 1929 GNP. The fall of Canadian exports, Argentine investments and exports were each about 10 per cent of GDP, while

Australia's corresponding total were about half that level. The peak-to-trough declines in the aggregate sum of exports, investments and government expenditures were 26 per cent of total 1929 nominal income in Canada, 22 per cent in Argentina, and 11 per cent in Australia, which is also the ranking of the decline in real output. Proponents of Keynesian-type counter-cyclical policy should note that the decline in the amount of investments in Canada and Argentina, and of exports in Argentina, were each approximately equal to the total 1929 level of government expenditures. The situation was somewhat less drastic in Australia, but one must doubt the historical plausibility of appreciably mitigating the Depression via countercyclical fiscal policy. By the end of the decade, nominal values of exports and investments still had not recovered their 1929 levels in Canada and Argentina, in spite of devaluations and other inflationary policies.

For further analysis we turn to consider the current account and the government deficit totals. While the value of total current account credits declined in Canada by somewhat more than commodity exports, the current account balance was improved to the extent of over 5 per cent of 1929 GNP between 1929 and 1933. The fiscal deficit increased, due to an increase in transfer payments. The same pattern with regard to the current account and the government deficit appears in Australia, where the deficits were basically created at the state level – principally New South Wales.[10] After the economies turned around, both countries tried to re-balance their budgets. In Argentina, the current account was again able to improve by a small amount, in spite of the drastic fall of exports. However, the government's deficit was decreased by about 1 per cent of 1929 GDP between 1929 and 1932,[11] increasing again subsequently.

References are made to current account and fiscal deficits to suggest the importance of other macroeconomic variables, besides investments and exports, in determining the evolution of demand. For example, if in spite of a severe drop in exports the current account remains relatively balanced, then obviously imports have changed, and the presumption is that this signifies a shift of the import function, in addition to movements along that curve induced by income changes. My econometric work suggested that these shifts were one to four per cent of 1929 GNP. These shifts would be due to tariffs and devaluations, and – in Argentina – to exchange controls. Contrary to what is often supposed, the overall import content of investments was not high, so that the decline in investments did not by any means pass entirely into imports.[12]

Tax revenues will decline when output and prices drop; modern multiplier analysis suggests that if government expenditure is lowered in an attempt to balance the budget, the decline in income is accentuated. Evidence suggests that this was what happened in Argentina. In Canada and Australia the widening deficits also reflect both the downward sluggishness of government expenditures and 'shifts' of the tax function, but the 'full employment deficit' did not increase sufficiently to attribute to fiscal policy any positive role in lessening the decline in demand.

III EXPORTS

The relative performance of exports parallels the story of aggregate output. Whether viewed in real or nominal terms, Australia's exports performed best (or least poorly), while Canada's fared worst. Two explanatory factors stand out; the composition of exports, and the degree of devaluation.

Wheat exports in Argentina and Canada followed the contraction of the world market.[13] Australia went against this trend, especially during the early 1930s when the 'Grow More Wheat' campaign coincided with good weather to increase production and exports. Argentina's wheat exports experienced large variations during the 1930s, as did her exports to the UK. Australia's exports to the UK had a decidedly upward trend, while it is noteworthy that Canada's maintained their level in spite of the decline in her total wheat production and exports. Other non-empire, wheat exporting countries lost ground, both absolutely and relatively.

Argentina and Australia had two other major products in common, meat and wool. In the face of declining real (internal) prices, Australian wool exports held up well; with this product accounting for 40 per cent of total exports, a favourable overall performance for the country was assured. Argentina's wool exports were also strong, but accounted for only a small fraction of her total trade.

The world demand for imported meat, as proxied by the UK import totals, also seemed relatively stable during the Depression. The same is true for Argentina's total meat exports. However, Argentina lost about a quarter of her meat export market in Britain to Australia and New Zealand, especially the latter. Now, meat had accounted for 15 per cent of Argentina's 1929 commodity exports, and the loss of one-quarter of that amount is not overly significant, especially when it was apparently regained in other markets. Unfortunately, it is difficult to ascertain with our data if Argentina suffered a price loss in the meat market because of the diversion of her trade. Of course, these are relevant issues for an evaluation of the Roca-Runciman treaty; Argentine meat exporters did not hold their own, much less advance, in the British market.[14]

How might devaluations have affected exports? To the extent that each country was a price taker, changing the exchange rate would have raised the internal price of the traded goods relative to other prices (and wages), leading to at least a short run increase in supply and more foreign exchange.

Together with New Zealand, these three countries dominated world exports of wheat, meat and wool. Some have suggested that the devaluations by Argentina and Australia lowered wheat prices in 1930 and 1931. Because prices and real and nominal incomes were already falling in the rest of the world, this position is difficult to demonstrate empirically, but we suspect that the devaluation was less important in that regard than other events.

Let us turn instead to two issues, the ability of devaluation to change internal relative prices, and what appeared to be the supply effects of successfully doing so. Econometric results suggest that about 70 per cent of the devaluations were translated into changed relative prices, the rest being lost in the resulting general increase of prices. However, the regression of real exports on relative internal prices in these countries gave negative coefficients for five out of seven products. This implies that whatever real expansionary effects the devaluation-induced price change might have had, during this period they were overshadowed by other factors, ranging from a fixed market-share, purchasing and imperial preference, to Depression-induced credit constraints, and the general aversion to trade that characterised the period.

A final aspect of the devaluation question would be its potentially negative effect via interest payments. Taking round numbers characteristic of these countries, if foreign interest payments are 15 per cent of total government expenditures, then a 20 per cent devaluation would by itself force up government outlays by 3 per cent. It would be a very rigid tax system that could not generate the necessary incremental tax revenue, due to inflation, if no real output increases. It is curious that foreign interest payments were proportionately smallest in Canada, the country most reluctant to devalue.

Declining terms of trade are a well-known complaint of Latin

American countries, and this characterised Canada and Australia as well as Argentina. The movement against Australia's prices was almost as prejudicial as that affecting Argentina, although Canada's relative foreign prices dropped significantly less. Although this may be explained by the difference in base years of the price indexes, it may also be related to the stronger ties between Canada and the US, and the larger fall in Canadian imports of manufactured goods.

IV CAPITAL FLOWS

Commodity trade was not the only mechanism by which the contraction originating in the US and Europe reached peripheral countries. Fleisig has recently made some attempts at quantifying the impact of the capital account on the economies of groups of LDCs,[15] and we shall look at that question for the countries under consideration. At issue is the magnitude of the decline in foreign direct investment and other capital flows, as compared with total investment. Although the balance of payments statistics for this period are not good, some tentative conclusions emerge.

Most of the capital entering Australia was borrowed by the central and state governments for investment in infrastructure. That the total government deficit increased while external financing decreased, suggests that domestic banks were put under some pressure; perhaps some 'crowding out' of private investment may even have occurred. Another aspect of the Australian situation is the fact that capital inflows had been declining previously, and could also have contributed to the post-1929 decline in investment via lagged, accelerator-type effects. Schedvin[16] devotes considerable attention to the capital market, emphasising the contemporary criticism of the governments with regard to the magnitude of their borrowings (and the uses to which they were put), and to the negative effects of the drying-up of both British and American funds due to the competition of the speculative boom on Wall Street of 1927–9. The Australian case definitely supports Fleisig's argument for the importance of the decline in capital flows.

In the 1920s British lending to Canada had been completely eclipsed by the US, and Canada was the largest single recipient of US long-term capital flows after Germany. About 60 per cent of the capital flows went to the private sector, as portfolio rather than direct investment (as had been the case earlier in the century). However, the data suggest that Canada was a net exporter of capital (mainly to the US) just before 1929, and a net importer during 1929–32. Overall, changes in capital account flows, however measured, were not a major, direct factor determining the collapse of Canadian aggregate demand. Thus Fleisig's analysis does not appear to be valid for Canada.

As in Australia, foreign investment in Argentina had started to decline before 1929, although total *private* investment in that country continued to rise until 1929. Foreign direct investment (as estimated by ECLA) was only about 15 per cent of total private investment in 1929; total foreign capital flows were an even smaller fraction of the sum of private investment and government expenditures, and we conclude here too that the drying-up of the international capital market was not a significant, proximate cause of the decline in aggregate demand in Argentina.

V MONETARY FACTORS

In recognition of the recent monetarist revolution in macroeconomics, and the importance which Friedman and Schwartz attribute to monetary factors in the Depression in the US,[17] a detailed analysis of this variable seems appropriate. Rather than analyse the effects of monetary factors in a fully elaborated IS–LM setting, we shall follow the Friedman–Schwartz methodology of sketching the evolution of the important monetary aggregates, in an attempt to suggest the relative share of their impact on the overall economic performance.[18]

Before the creation of Argentina's central bank in 1935, monetary control was split between entities; the Caja de Conversión (which received gold and issued notes), and the Banco de la Nación, an 'official commercial bank with close ties to the government' which was also responsible for rediscounting. In Australia, the Commonwealth Bank was evolving into the position of a central bank,[19] and we will review below criticisms of its inactivity. The Canadian situation was strongly influenced by the provision of the Finance Act of 1914, under which the supply of Dominion Notes to the chartered banks via rediscounting was essentially unlimited, suggesting that the quantity of money was demand determined.

The quantity of money did not drop as much as did income, leading to declines in velocity of 11 per cent in Australia, 21 per cent in Canada, and 22 per cent in Argentina. As discussed in the longer version of this paper, the more broadly defined monetary aggregates did not decline as much as M1, implying an even larger fall in their respective velocities.[20] Nowhere were there widespread bank failures as in the US.

We shall now proceed to analyse the determinants of the money stock, with the goal of evaluating the effects of gold movements and government policy on the money supply.

For reasons that differ in each country, the domestic money supply was relatively insulated from gold flows, and we are fortunate that studies are available providing some detail of these processes.[21] In the Friedman–Schwartz framework, the intermediate stage between gold (and foreign exchange) and the quantity of money is high-powered money: the sum of coin and government notes in the hands of the public or the banks, plus bank reserves deposited in the central bank or reserve office. Thus, there are two steps joining gold flows to the money supply. The first link is broken if the central bank increases its lending to the banks, via discounting, or the government prints money to finance a deficit. The second link will be broken if banks run down their reserves, or the public significantly alters its wealth allocation between cash and bank deposits.

Argentina made the strongest efforts to maintain its money supply. The collapse of exports led to significant gold losses in 1929 and 1931, minimized in 1930 by capital inflows. The gold window of the Caja de Conversión was closed in 1929, and by the end of 1931 a Committee of Exchange Control was operating. In 1931 the Banco de la Nación was permitted to increase its discounts to the banks, while those of the Caja de Conversión to the Banco de la Nación were also augmented. Thus gold flows dominated changes in high-powered money only up to 1930, and during 1929 and 1930 the banks reduced their reserves to maintain the level of lending. In the Friedman–Schwartz terminology, a change in the reserve ratio counteracted changes in the monetary base caused by gold flows.

The Australian situation parallels that of Argentina, in that bankers allowed their reserves to fall (in the face of a gold outflow), so that changes in high-powered money were again offset by changes in the reserve ratio.[22] However, the one country with an institution approximating a central bank found it very reluctant to engage in significant rediscounting, although it did increase high-powered money by helping to finance the government's deficit. Schedvin is especially critical of the overall lack of expansionary monetary policy in this respect.[23]

The difficulties experienced by Canada due to the operation of the

Finance Act were eventually remedied by the establishment of the Bank of Canada in 1935, but as demonstrated by Courchene, the commercial banks had too much incentive to increase their reserves before the crash, while subsequently the same regulations effectively discouraged rediscounting when it might have been most helpful. A specific effort on the part of the government in 1932 to increase reserves was neutralized by the banks. In the light of what appears to have been the bankers' unwillingness to lend, it does not seem that the government can be solely faulted for the decline in the money supply.[24] On the other hand, we noted above that the overall Canadian balance of payments caused an outflow of gold before the crash, and an inflow thereafter, so that that variable tended to counteract the drop of the money supply during the Depression.

VI CONCLUSIONS

The above analysis suggests a two-part, comparative evaluation of the Depression experience: the factors causing the fall and subsequent recovery of output, and the role played by the governments in influencing output and employment. The fall in aggregate demand was dominated by the collapse of exports and private sector investment. This is discussed in detail in the text, as well as the relative importance of monetary factors and foreign investment.

A number of factors contributed to the differential speed of recovery. Increased government deficits in 1930 and thereafter helped counteract part of the drop in demand. Tariff increases and exchange rate devaluations did seem to stimulate the economies, both by redirecting expenditure internally, and perhaps by stimulating export activities. The decline in imports was particularly important in Argentina. The behaviour of world prices and exports was very product-specific, with Australia suffering least, although Canadian import prices dropped more than those of the other countries. The data presented here suggest that the effect of the Roca-Runciman treaty on the economic performance of Argentina and Australia should be downvalued.

The fact that none of these countries engaged in significant, countercyclical monetary or fiscal policy before their own economies had at least begun to recover, is not a new discovery, although it may deserve to be repeated. This makes evaluation of government policy even more perilous, because the deficits did increase contrary to stated government intentions. The same situation existed for exchange rate changes; the larger devaluations by Argentina and Australia responded to greater balance of payments pressure rather than more 'enlightened' attitudes.

Rather than attempt an overall, quantitative comparison of government policy, then, I will highlight those factors which subjectively seem to be the most important. The greater strength in Canada of *laissez-faire* attitudes amongst a broad spectrum of policy makers contrasts with Scullin, Land and others in Australia who believed in intervention. Argentine economic policy-making appears to have been the most active of the three; the longer-run efficiency and political costs of exchange control and price intervention combined with other political developments in making the overall effect of the decade of the thirties a negative one. To the extent that a threshold was passed in the early 1930s, therefore, it was not so much in the adoption of Keynesian-type policies, but the forced realization that earlier strategies were not adequate to guarantee sufficient well-being; monetary and fiscal structures were subsequently adopted which eventually permitted greater domestic control and less reliance on external factors.

Some final observations relate to various puzzles, or 'contradictions', that arise from this analysis, and which can be grouped into three areas:

1. Ideologies: the traditional, political party stereotypes of pro-business, pro-labour or pro-agriculture do not give a reliable indication of which government would adopt what kind of policy, normally for all three countries.
2. Argentina does not assume the rôle of a free-spending, politically-incoherent country. Perhaps unfortunately, she was the most successful of the three in achieving the commonly-held goal of balancing the budget. Moreover, regional conflict in Australia frustrated the central government's policy much more than it did in Argentina, while it could also be argued that provincialism similarly incapacitated strong central leadership in Canada.
3. Policy: for those who grant that the traditional Keynesian policy would have been more effective than the gold standard orthodoxy, at least three conflicts appear. First, neither fiscal nor (had the institutions been developed) monetary countercyclical policy could have completely counteracted the initial demand

shocks. Secondly, in emphasizing tariffs and devaluations we are effectively encouraging the 'beggar thy neighbour' policies that have been so criticized in analyses of other countries during this period. Thirdly, the decline in domestically generated investment was very important in each country. In part, this was due to cyclical and other accelerator type phenomena which countercyclical action might have reduced. However, it is true also that this decline was worsened because of the investors' perceptions about the near-term future of their economies. To the extent that orthodox policies would have reduced those fears, and bearing in mind the magnitude of the necessary countercyclical policies that would have been necessary, does it not seem that orthodox policies might have been preferable after all? The greater stability of Australian investment would suggest this to be the case, while the Argentine experience might arguably be dismissed by appeal to political uncertainty.

In summary, Keynesian countercyclical policy probably would have been inadequate to the task. It is not clear that the neo-orthodox policies being attempted today in disturbingly similar situations are any more successful. Given the vacillation nowadays amongst those economists who confront these issues, to whom might a policy-maker have listened during the 1930s? If investment cannot be resuscitated by the economics of Keynesians, of orthodoxy, or of voodoo, what is needed?

NOTES

1. Under pressure of space, tables of statistics and econometric results in the longer version of this paper read at the symposium have had to be omitted. However, they are available on request from the author.
2. Private railways were relatively unimportant in Australia, while the bulk of the Argentine lines were in (private) British hands.
3. The title of an interesting book edited by M. Falcoff and R. H. Dolkart (Berkeley, 1970).
4. The terms are from the report of Australia's Vernon Committee: E. A. Boehm, *Twentieth Century Economic Development in Australia* (Camberwell, 1971) p. 149.
5. The other two countries did, however, make an effort to discourage an outflow of gold. Incidentally, all three countries experienced brief periods of foreign loan default on the part of local government agencies.
6. In compensation for the terms of trade effect, the drop in Canadian output

was about 26 per cent. It is important to note that Argentina's relative decline in terms of growth of per capita output was much more a post-1940 phenomenon than pre-1940.

7. R. J. Gordon and J. A. Wilcox, 'Monetarist Interpretations: an Evaluation and Critique', in K. Brunner (ed.), *The Great Depression Revisited* (The Hague, 1980).
8. Using as exogenous, predetermined variables the values of exports, investments, and government expenditures. In a companion piece to this paper (M. Twomey, 'The Depression in Latin America: a Macro Approach', forthcoming in *Explorations in Economic History*), it is argued that Canada's flatter supply curve is related to her higher per capita income level and more sophisticated industrial structure.
9. It might also be noted that the Canadian financial market in Montreal and Toronto experienced the same boom and bust cycle as Wall Street. This factor, which has so dominated discussion of the decline in investments in the United States, has hardly been mentioned in the Canadian literature. A. E. Safarian's discussion of investments attributes much importance to accelerator and other cyclical effects, as well as declining profit expectations and the 'deterioration of the international situation'. See his *The Canadian Economy in the Great Depression* (Toronto, 1970). We might also note that the decline in railway expansion accounts for less than one-fifth of the decline in Canadian investments.
10. New South Wales accounted for approximately half of total government deficits in 1930 and 1931.
11. Taking account only of the central government (although it is known that the post-Yrigoyen governments forced consolidation and orthodoxy on the provincial and local governments). This contrasts with neighbouring Brazil which generated considerable increases in fiscal deficits in the early 1930s.
12. The marginal propensity to import out of investment was only about one-fourth. This breaks down into a relatively uniform 0.1 for construction; for machinery it varies from 0.4 in Canada to 0.7 in Argentina. Construction accounted for over half of total investments.
13. Due fundamentally to the import substitution campaigns of the continent, although partially offset by the reduction in US exports, due to climatic factors.
14. British negotiations with these countries are well described by I. Drummond, *British Economic Policy and the Empire, 1929–39* (London, 1972).
15. H. Fleisig, *Long-term Capital Flows and the Great Depression: The Role of the United States* (New York, 1975).
16. C. B. Schedvin, *Australia and the Great Depression* (Sydney, 1970).
17. M. Friedman and A. J. Schwartz, *A Monetary History of the United States, 1867–1960* (Princeton, 1963).
18. In at least Argentina and Australia, debates of the Friedman-Meiselman/Modigliani type have occurred. See C. L. Barber, 'The Quantity Theory and the Income Expenditure Theory in an Open Economy, 1926–58: A Comment', *Canadian Journal of Economics*, 32, pp. 375–9, and B. F. Reece, 'The Demand for Money in Australia

between the Wars: A Comment', *Australian Economic History Review*, 12, pp. 174–8.

19. In 1929 the Chairman of the Commonwealth Bank observed that 'the establishment of the central reserve banking system in Australia still remains an open question': quoted by A. F. W. Plumptre, *Central Banking in the British Dominions* (Toronto, 1940) p. 91.
20. For comparison, the velocity of M1 and M2 in the United States dropped 24 per cent and 27 per cent respectively between 1929 and 1932: Friedman and Schwartz, *Monetary History of the United States*, p. 774.
21. Each country also took steps in 1929 to prevent outflows of gold. Argentina and Australia forbad them to certain groups, while Canada arranged an informal embargo: T. J. Courchene, 'An Analysis of the Canadian Money Supply: 1925–34', *Journal of Political Economy*, 77, pp. 363–91; R. A. Schearer and C. Clark, 'Canada and the Inter-War Gold Standard, 1920–35: Monetary Policy without a Central Bank', unpublished ms.; R. A. Halperín, 'The Behaviour of the Argentine Monetary Sector: an Econometric Analysis' (unpublished Ph.D. dissertation, Colombia University, 1968); Schedvin, *Australia and the Great Depression.*
22. Changes in the currency were minimal in each country. To the author's knowledge, this important element of the Friedman–Schwartz analysis of the United States does not seem to be significant in any country on the periphery.
23. Schedvin, *Australia and the Great Depression*, ch. 8, especially pp. 207–10. Further discussion of these matters appears in the articles by Schedvin and Guiney in the *Australian Economic History Review*, 11, pp. 147–78.
24. These issues are discussed also in R. C. McIvor, *Canadian Monetary, Banking and Fiscal Development* (Toronto, 1958).

12 Marketing Boards in the White Dominions, with Special Reference to Australia and Canada

IAN M. DRUMMOND

I

The original 'Dominions' of the British Commonwealth – Canada, Australia, New Zealand, South Africa – are examples of what W. W. Rostow has taught us to call 'countries of New Settlement'. So are some Latin American states, such as Argentina, Chile, Uruguay, and perhaps Brazil. Although differing in many important respects, all such states – especially perhaps the former 'white dominions' – share certain characteristics, one of which is a reticence about their domestic institutional arrangements. This reticence is easy to understand. Because the domestic, political and intellectual establishments are usually quite small, inward looking, and in part expatriate, every interested person at home thinks he knows all he needs to know about the local institutions, and believes that no one abroad could possibly care about them. In the circumstances why write about them? This reticence is troublesome to those of us who want to trace common patterns or explore divergences, but it is a fact of scholarly life.

The purpose of this chapter is three-fold: to explore some remarkable parallels in the institutional development of the several British Empire economies between 1919 and 1939, to point to some of the implications for the working of the international economy, and to ask why these developments were so widespread within the Empire and so uncommon elsewhere. These two decades saw a remarkable exfoliation of institutions which were always called 'marketing boards' – 'quangos' set up with government blessing, often although not always confided to the management and control of the farmers themselves. So far as I can discover, these institutions were not found to any extent outside the British Empire, yet by 1939 they were to be discovered almost everywhere within it. In other countries – even quite closely related ones, such as the United States – the same or similar problems produced very different institutional solutions. Where 'boards' were set up, they appear to have been part of the government apparatus. To aid non-Empire farmers, other institutional devices were generally used. The economic historian asks himself why this should have been so. What was different about the Empire?

Some confusion can occur because the label, 'marketing board', was applied to organizations which possessed very different kinds, and degrees, of power. Some could promote; some could market; some could control. Some boards undertook one of these three functions; some undertook two or even three.

In a few instances a marketing board was simply a promotional agency which attempted through advertising to create or expand markets. Money might come from producers, governments, or both. During our period the most important example of this sort was the Empire Marketing Board, which the United Kingdom government created in 1924–5. Its funds came entirely from the United Kingdom Exchequer, and the money was spent partly on advertising and partly on research which was intended to increase the vent for Empire foodstuffs in the United Kingdom. One beneficiary was Australia, whose government hoped to export high-value chilled beef, instead of low-value frozen beef, to the British market. When the Board was first established, the technology of refrigeration was insufficiently developed to allow this; but thanks to research which the Board financed, on the dissolution of the Board in 1933 a suitable method had been devised – to the discomfiture of Argentina, whose beef exports were bound to suffer from the resultant competition. As for the advertising efforts of the EMB, these were meant to create a 'non-tariff preference' for Empire goods, expecially meat, fruit, wine, and dairy products. Insofar as their efforts succeeded, they would naturally induce more sales or higher prices for Empire suppliers, chiefly at the expense of non-Empire suppliers in South America, the United States, and Europe.

When the Ottawa Agreements of 1932 produced much more

substantial and forceful measures of discrimination against non-Empire suppliers, there was no logical reason for the United Kingdom to spend any more money on the EMB which was therefore wound up the following year. However, by then a much more effective network of marketing boards, producer-dominated and based both in Britain and in several of the Dominions, was already well established. With encouragement from the several governments, and supported not only by money but by the compulsive force of law, these producer boards, some of which dated from the mid-1920s, rapidly increased in number and power. In general, these boards were both 'controllers' and 'marketers'.

Producer marketing boards needed government help in several respects. Laws were needed to compel producers to join the boards, to market through them, and sometimes to accept limitations on their production – limits which the boards would devise. During the 1920s and 1930s it does not appear that producer marketing boards in the Dominions made much effort to control production, although some certainly did regulate exportation, and in Britain itself the boards quickly became the main agency through which the National Government attempted to plan the revival of British agriculture after 1931. Further government action was needed to separate domestic markets from world developments. Without such measures – tariffs, import quotas or prohibitions, sometimes levies on domestic production or sales for the subsidization of exports – boards would have market power only in exceptional circumstances where isolation and high transport costs provided effective protection in domestic markets. The boards themselves did not receive government subsidy, nor were they usually agencies for the distribution of state funds to farmers; on the other hand, they can be seen as a means by which governments tried to help farmers – or to help farmers help themselves – at no direct cost to the exchequer.

These controlling and marketing boards can also be seen as a substitute for producer cooperatives, which played so large a role in the regulation and promotion of Danish food exports, but which developed more slowly in Britain, and rather patchily in the Dominions. Neither the Australian nor the New Zealand arrangements originated in cooperative marketing. In South Africa, as in Canada, origins and patterns were more mixed.

Some boards aimed at domestic markets, while others treated the management of the domestic market as a necessary ancillary to the improvement of farmers' returns from foreign markets. The patterns were infinitely various. In the southern Dominions marketing arrangements seldom restrained production by administrative means before the 1930s, while insofar as they raised farmers' net returns they tended to increase output at a rate which exceeded the rate at which domestic markets were growing. A regulated price would be imposed on the domestic market, or a regulated differential maintained between domestic and world prices; insofar as production was not controlled and was sometimes subsidized, the arrangement tended to generate an unregulated and uncontrolled surplus which had to be dumped abroad – almost entirely in the British market, the only one which was reasonably open. In the period 1932–9, as the United Kingdom authorities accepted the idea of producer regulation themselves, unregulated dumping was, in some trades such as the meat trade, superseded by regulation and quota systems, while for some other products, such as butter and cheese, the dumping continued and even increased.

In and after 1932 the United Kingdom authorities saw the Dominions' marketing boards chiefly as devices through which the flow of product to the United Kingdom could be regulated, so as to raise prices for all British producers – at 'home' and in the Empire – at the expense of non-Empire suppliers. In due course this concern would give rise to such international bodies for supply regulation as the Empire Meat Producers' Conference and the Empire Fruit Council. But these arrangements were unstable because, in the Dominions, producers tended to think that they had a God-given right to sell as much as they could supply to the British market.

II

There was a general realization among Dominion politicians that where a group of farmers exported most of its output, and where at the same time that output was a significant part of national income but not a dominating proportion of world production, there was relatively little that could be done to help producers. International terms of trade could not be moved in their favour; international bargaining about tariffs, preferences, and quotas would of course be important, but their effect was uncertain; two-price systems with higher domestic prices would have relatively little effect on farm income because so much was exported, while governments could not afford to subsidize producer-groups that were in some sense large relative to the nation as a whole.

Thus it was only in 1936 that the New Zealand government began to provide price supports for dairy products; thus the Australian government never made any serious effort to manipulate the wheat or wool markets; thus, for prairie wheat, the Canadian authorities were prepared to provide 'orderly marketing' and at first not much more, although by 1940 the Canadian Wheat Board had become, more or less accidentally, a means of subsidising prairie farmers.

Australian governments concentrated their attention on those agricultural products which were the products of 'closer settlement' – butter, dried and other fruits – and on sugar, a crop for which the 'white Australia policy' created specially high costs. None of these products was of special interest to the Argentine. In New Zealand, concern centred on lamb, butter, and cheese; wool remained unregulated. By 1932 both Australians and New Zealanders were obsessed by the possibilities of substitution between their meat exports and those of Argentina; the Australians, however, were adamantly opposed to the regulation of export volumes, while the New Zealanders agreed reluctantly, and only temporarily, in 1933–4.

While pleading with the British Government for help through preferences, the Australasian Dominions were equally willing to help themselves. This self-help took three forms – cost-reduction, quality-control, and the manipulation of markets. With respect to the first two techniques, nothing much need be said. The techniques are familiar, and the payoffs obvious. We need only remark that quality-control was linked to that elusive goal – the establishing of a 'non-tariff preference' after 1926. The Empire Marketing Board laboured in the same vineyard: if British housewives could be taught to know and like Empire goods of standard and predictable high quality they would buy them, tariff or no. But the Dominion Governments were no more inclined than their English allies to leave such developments to chance. And they were very concerned to raise the numbers and the incomes – total and average – of their primary producers. Hence their interest in marketing boards.

In New Zealand, export controls followed fast upon the dismantling of the wartime, bulk-purchase arrangements. In Australia, too, the Commonwealth and State Governments moved quickly to replace such arrangements with other manipulations of the several markets. It is tempting to see some link between the new Australasian control schemes of the 1920s and the disappointments of 1923–4 with respect to new preferences in the United Kingdom market. But given the affected products, it is more plausible to argue that the various boards were established to seize the opportunities which the limited successes of 1925–6 (with respect to preferences) had opened. After all, it was canned fruit, dried fruit, and wine which benefited from new tariff preferences in the United Kingdom and Canada. And it was these products where the Australian marketing arrangements were most ingenious.

In North America, too, the 1920s saw many experiments with 'pools' and cooperatives, and much talk of 'organized marketing'. But it was apparently wartime experience, not overseas models, which provided the inspiration for the new market manipulations of the Australians and New Zealanders. From 1916 to 1920–1, New Zealand and Australian agriculture sold most of its products under 'bulk purchase' agreements, by which the Imperial Government paid cash at stable prices for the entire exportable supply. Meat, wool, butter, and cheese were all treated in this way, and bulk purchase schemes were wound up at an awkward time. They survived the postwar boom, thus depriving farmers of the very high prices of 1918–20, and were wound up just in time to deposit producers in the arms of the postwar slump of 1920–2. And this slump, in turn, must have made 'properly managed markets' attractive. Thus governments were eager to 'manage' markets so as to raise the short-run returns of their farmers and herdsmen. But they were increasingly interested in the longer-run advantages of such higher incomes: only if agricultural incomes could be permanently raised and stabilized would it be possible to settle more families on the land.

Britons seem to have been as uninterested in these devices as Australasians were obsessed by them. So long as Britain did not tax foodstuffs, this unconcern was justified, because it did Britain no harm. Indeed, though New Zealand commodity management policies were very likely to raise British import prices, Australian devices might well lower them both in any given year – when supplies were already fixed by past events – and (in the long run) when the price-fixing policies of the canned fruit industry would tend, by restricting supplies, to raise prices in Britain.

Though the mechanics varied, the Australian schemes all tried to maximise the producers' income by restricting the supply on the domestic market and unloading the remaining output on the British market. Since all production costs had already been incurred in each crop year, growers' profits would be maximized if total receipts were maximized. And the boards could control only one thing – the quantity of output placed on the domestic market. Their policies would necessarily create a two-price system, in which the domestic price would exceed the export price. Without 'control', the domestic price would be lower, and more of each year's output would be absorbed domestically. So *less* would then have been dumped in Britain – and British prices would have been higher than in fact they were.

III

In the 1920s, there were few products for which Australasia could thus meet British and Dominion demand. Admittedly, Australia and New Zealand sold more wool than Britain and the Dominions could buy. But nobody was manipulating the wool market, and nobody proposed an imperial preference on wool. In butter, meat, dried fruit, wine and canned goods, exportable surpluses were small relative to British purchases from Europe, Argentina, Greece, the Iberian peninsula and the USA. But in all these products, outputs were expected to rise. Indeed, increases were planned. Soldier settlements, immigration settlements, land reclamation, railway extension, closer cultivation, better methods – all were already being adopted, all were planned to continue, and all were expected to have dramatic effects on Australia's exportable surpluses. In New Zealand, in spite of verbal gesturing, immigration was not encouraged. But agricultural extension and transport improvement certainly were. Thus in the longer-run, more and more products would require market-control if the preferences were to be of benefit. And given the preferences and the controls, the benefits would grow steadily because the beneficiary industries were expected to grow. This growth, in turn, was expected to be, to some extent, autonomous. Population would automatically increase. Better methods would be applied. Trees, vines, cows, sheep and persons, already 'planted' on the land, but not yet 'bearing', would come into production. But to some extent this was to be induced – by the market management and by the preferences themselves.

Following the Ottawa Conference of 1932 the United Kingdom's desire to restrain meat imports produced further controls both in Australia and in New Zealand, which were obliged to regulate production as well as exportation. In Australia it was necessary to set up a Meat Board, which would present requests for market shares to the International Beef Conference. Australian politicians and officials feared that the result of export controls, given the impossibility of effective controls on production, would be an unsaleable glut of meat in Australia. New Zealand had been equally reluctant to accept limitation of vent in the United Kingdom, but before the Australians acquiesced, New Zealand did so too. The already-established, New Zealand Meat Producers Board had no real difficulty in allocating production quotas, a task which the Australians found impossible with respect to meat – although not for various fruits and related products. According to W. B. Sutch, in New Zealand the Board made the necessary internal adjustments, although with difficulty; quarterly quotas produced special difficulties for a supplier as distant as New Zealand. Preference was given, he tells us, to 'the types of meat which would secure higher prices in the United Kingdom'. New Zealanders believed that Australians congratulated themselves that in general they had obtained the allowables they wanted; the sufferers, obviously, were the Argentines, and to a very limited extent the Canadians and the Americans.

IV

Parallel developments in Canada were rather slower. Indeed, although there were some earlier experiments, it was only in 1934–5 that 'controller' and 'marketer' boards can really be said to have become established in the senior Dominion.

As so often in Canada, there were constitutional problems. With some over-simplification one may say that, in Canada's federal system, the provinces control most aspects of property and civil rights, while they cannot control interprovincial or international trade, nor can they act on the international stage. If marketing boards were to have any powers of coercion – if they were to be 'controllers' – they would necessarily concern themselves with property and civil rights, and so would have to be established and administered under provincial jurisdiction, or in some framework to which the several provinces had given their assent. But if the boards were to have effective power in the domestic market, many would need powers to control interregional trade – powers which they could not constitutionally be given by either level of government acting on its own.

During the early 1930s this constitutional situation was trying for Canada's national government, which was obliged to negotiate the international sharing of markets while believing that it had no constitutional power to regulate production or marketing. It tried all the same on behalf of those provinces such as British Columbia which wished to give power to cooperative marketing boards; but not only could the boards not receive powers to control inflows of produce, the courts created some doubt as to whether they could control *outflows* (and even suggested that provincial marketing boards were illegal under the national Combines Investigation Act). However, two court decisions regarding radio and aeronautics, handed down in 1932, suggested to the national government that it might have the power to create a nation-wide framework for producer marketing boards, and early in 1934 it proceeded to do so. The measure, the Natural Products Marketing Act, was struck down as *ultra vires* of the Dominion in January 1937. However, in 1936 the province of British Columbia introduced its own Natural Products Marketing Act, which proved to be *intra vires* of the province, and which other provinces copied sooner or later. In due course, also, the national government exempted the provincial boards from the operation of its own combines law, and arranged to delegate it powers regarding interprovincial and export trade to appropriate provincial boards. These arrangements for producer-controlled marketing boards generally required a majority vote of the relevant producers, a regulation of the provincial authorities establishing the administrative framework, and total producer control, through the board membership, of all aspects of production, pricing, and marketing. Producers might or might not be told how much to produce, how many acres to plant, or how many livestock to own, but in general they were certainly obliged to market their produce through the relevant board.

At first sight, Canada's wheat marketing arrangements during the 1930s look rather similar to these producer-controlled boards, which by 1940 managed apples, pork, tobacco, grapes, and many other products. The Canadian Wheat Board, which was set up in 1935, had a similar origin in that it sprang from farmers' demands, obsessions, and suspicions. However, it was created not as a cooperative but as an arm of government, whose purpose was to dispose of wheat stocks which, in turn, had been accumulated by the cooperative prairie 'wheat pool' just before the onset of the Depression. In the price-declines of the early 1930s the cooperative pools were unable to continue in business; the Dominion took over the realization of their holdings, and for five years it managed the market so as to sustain price; eventually the Prime Minister decided that it was pointless to pretend that the national government was not in charge of wheat marketing, and proceeded to establish a Board. Unlike the other marketing boards, however, Canada's Wheat Board had no power to market newly-produced wheat, except insofar as the farmers voluntarily consigned their new crops to it. Thus, although the Wheat Board was far more grandiose than the small-scale, provincial marketing boards, for some years its effective powers of intervention and coercion were much more limited. Nor can it be blamed for the difficulties which Argentina and other wheat-exporting countries were having after 1929. Indeed, Canadian politicians and officials believed that it was Argentine wheat-marketing practices, in and after 1930, which created the wheat crisis to which Canadian government intervention was the response.

V

Why should the Congress of Americanists care about these arcane 'Imperial' bodies? First and most obviously, in some important respects the marketing boards made life more difficult for some South American primary producers. The Australian and New Zealand arrangements certainly stimulated the production and export of meat, butter, sugar, fresh and tinned fruits, wine, and indirectly, perhaps, the marketing of hides, skins and wool. South African arrangements, which we have not surveyed here, had similar effects with respect to wine and fruit. When Britain herself came, in 1932 and thereafter, to imitate the marketing board system, the framework of 'compulsory producer cooperation' was a natural one to employ for the governing and guiding of Empire trade in foodstuffs. International trade was then shaped and shared by administrative measures, which were operated through like-minded officials and agencies in the several countries. Where for ideological reasons a country would not take part, or for constitutional reasons it could not, such a country may well have found itself at a disadvantage in bargaining for a share of the British market.

The Dominion politicians who invented manipulated marketing in the 1920s had no such ends in mind, if only because at that time no one in Britain would have contemplated such an organization of the trade in temperate-zone foodstuffs. But by 1930 much of Britain's Labour Party was only too anxious to consider it, and in 1931/2 the British Conservative Party was converted to the same faith. But if the Dominions, or some of them, had not already been accustomed to 'organize' much of their external trade in foodstuffs, the task of Britain's National Government would have been far more difficult, and the fates of non-Empire suppliers might have been less unpleasant than they proved to be. Perhaps, also, Canada's Conservative government would have been less inclined to execute so dramatic an ideological *volte-face*, deciding in 1934–5 for marketing boards as a solution to the nation's agricultural problems.

Second and more perplexing is the contrast between the framework of agricultural manipulation which evolved in Britain and the Empire, and the very different frameworks in such apparently similar states as Argentina. Why, in the Empire, was there so much of what one observer called 'compulsory cooperation'? And why was there so much producer self-government, rather than organization through government departments?

Certainly there was some idea that producer self-government was an extension of democracy, even if government had to help by compelling minority interests to join, or by providing a framework of law, subsidy, and compulsion within which marketing boards could work. In Australia the national government had taken a much more active role in the formative years than governments in other British dominions; marketing boards were, in effect, government's way of escaping from the subsidy trap, while allowing producers to appear to be governing themselves. In New Zealand the original idea was to let farmers help themselves through the collective regulation and management of marketing. In Canada, for constitutional reasons, most 'controller' boards were confined to the provincial level of operation, a fact which prevented them from playing the sort of international role which the Australian and New Zealand boards could perform. When nation-wide marketing of Prairie wheat was finally introduced, there was no guaranteed price, production control, or anything more than control over delivery, storage, and exportation. The provincial marketing boards could be, and were, seen as examples of producer self-government; the national government might bargain about tariff arrangements with the United Kingdom, and some provincial boards could and did take part in intra-Imperial bodies such as the Empire Fruit Council. But since production and domestic markets are usually highly regionalised it is possible in principle to confide many agrarian matters to the producers themselves. Where producers could not be trusted to run their own affairs, as in the dependencies of British Africa, the terminology of marketing boards might be used because Empire officials were familiar with it, yet the boards were government departments in everything but name.

Besides providing a form of producer self-government, the boards could given an impression – generally more than a façade – of separation between 'politics' and decisions about production and pricing. All the Dominions were intensely politicized societies, and in all of them there was a good deal of confusion about the proper role of government. Certainly the State dispensed and obtained favours. Indeed, that was perhaps the principal reason for its existence. 'Protection for everyone', as the leader of the Australian Country Party proclaimed in 1923. But protection, if possible, at no voter's expense. Or if expense could be detected, God forbid that any one might blame the government for causing it. Hence the attraction of 'quangos' such as marketing boards, where the production and pricing decisions would be taken neither by politicians nor by civil servants, and the double attraction of 'producer self-government', by which governments could escape both the budgetary burden of agricultural subsidy and the blame for burdensome regulation and for the exploitation of non-agricultural voters. With luck, these voters might think that the losers were all foreigners – Californian fruit packers, Greek currant driers, Danish dairy farmers, French vintners, Argentine graziers. No one cared about *them*. Not only did the obnoxious foreigner buy almost nothing from the Dominions; he did not vote in their elections. For the United Kingdom, which did sell goods to the relevant foreign countries, it was necessary in the 1930s to be more circumspect.

Producer self-government makes no sense unless it is reasonable to believe that the producers are capable of self-government and interested in exercising it. Here various things may be relevant, and may in some degree explain agricultural marketing. The first is scale. It is more reasonable to suppose that the tobacco growers of Southern Ontario can organise their own affairs than to suppose that the tobacco growers of the southern USA can do so. Second is experience, both in local government and, to some extent, in producer co-operation. Third is education, and fourth is wealth, or at least an initial position of relative prosperity.

Finally, we should observe that the exfoliation of marketing boards testifies to the fact that the British Empire was to some extent a unit so far as the spread of new, institutional gadgetry was concerned. People within one Empire country generally knew something about developments elsewhere, especially within a single industry. 'Outsiders', neither knowing nor caring, would not always know what was happening 'inside' even if they were looking for models to imitate. But on the 'inside' – 'within the family', as politicians sometimes said during the 1930s – nothing could be more natural than imitation.

Sometimes there were attempts at imitation from 'outside', but the results were usually quite different from the apparent model. The Argentine authorities took great interest in the Canadian Wheat Board, and when they established their own they claimed to be imitating the Canadian model. But the Argentine Board really functioned as a department of the central government apparatus. Further, because in Argentina there were few facilities for storage, Argentine arrangements for the mobilization and distribution of the wheat crop were not seriously comparable with Canadian. Nevertheless, the 'organization' of grain marketing, whether or not the Canadian institutional model was followed in all respects, provided an international framework within which barter and bulk purchase could reappear during the Second World War.

REFERENCES

This paper draws upon a variety of archival and published material. Among the relevant sources are the following:

New Zealand, Parliamentary Debates, vol. 203, p. 283, vol. 193, pp. 123, 175, 317; Commonwealth of Australia, *Parliamentary Debates*, vol. C, pp. 1698ff; vol. CII, p. 82; Australia, Conference of Commonwealth and State Ministers, Melbourne, October and November 1921, *Report*; Commonwealth Archives Office, Canberra, CP 2 90/4/1: telegram Bruce to Page, 16 November 1923, CP 317/9; telegrams, Page to Bruce, 10 October and 15 October 1923; CP 103/3/8: memorandum of Departments of Markets and Migration, 13 August 1928; H. T. Easterly, *The Queensland Sugar Industry* (Brisbane: Government Printer, 1936), chs III, IX; J. B. Brigden, 'Control in the Queensland Sugar Industry' in W. Holland (ed.), *Commodity Control in the Pacific Area* (London: Allen & Unwin, 1935); D. A. Macgibbon, *The Canadian Grain Trade* (Toronto: Macmillan, 1932); D. A. Macgibbon, *The Canadian Grain Trade, 1931–1951* (Toronto University Press, 1952); C. F. Wilson, *A Century of Canadian Grain: Government Policy to 1951* (Saskatoon: Western Producer Prairie Books, 1978); J. Castell Hopkins *et al.*, *The Canadian Annual Review* (Toronto: Annual Review Publishing Co.).; *The Canada Year Book*.

A longer version of the chapter, including more historical detail and comprehensive references to the sources, is available from the author.

13 The State and the Provision of Electricity in Canada and Australia, 1880–1965

CHRISTOPHER ARMSTRONG
AND H. V. NELLES

I

Both Canada and Australia are vast, transcontinental nations, with much of their territory empty and inhospitable to settlement. Like Argentina, New Zealand and the United States, they are 'regions of recent settlement', similar in natural resources and the roles they play as exporters of primary products.[1] Populated almost entirely by Europeans, mainly of British stock, the two former British colonies share political traditions and governmental forms which underlie their federal and parliamentary systems. Thus it is only natural to expect that there should be certain, marked institutional similarities between the two countries.

In this chapter we have chosen to examine the shifting balance between public and private ownership in the electricity supply industry to analyse the similarities and the interesting differences which the two nations reveal. Electricity supply began only a century ago. At the outset it was entirely in private hands, while nowadays the industry has been almost completely nationalized in Canada and in Australia. State ownership of electricity involves a significant shift of authority from the private to the public sector, but it is not one which has been mirrored in the other energy industries nor in the industrial sector. Did ideological conviction, technological determinism or social change persuade Australians and Canadians of the need for public ownership? Why did the changeover occur earlier in some places than in others? What institutional forms have been adopted through which state control has been exercised? These questions this chapter seeks to answer.

Public enterprise now plays an important role in the economic life of most countries.[2] Yet significant differences remain in the balance struck between the private and public sectors. Industries nationalized in one country remain in private hands elsewhere; within federal states, striking variations can occur between different jurisdictions. Moreover, while state enterprise has greatly expanded during the past century this expansion has been neither steady nor continuous. Bursts of nationalization have sometimes been followed by years of quiescence or even periods of retreat.

In Canada by the mid-1970s about 70 per cent of electricity was supplied by public agencies, while in Australia the proportion was well over 90 per cent.[3] From the beginnings of the industry in the 1880s, its passage from private control has occurred in three distinct phases, roughly contemporaneous in both countries. The first lasted up to about 1905, during which small, arc-lighting plants were established in the major cities and incandescent lighting developed. By the turn of the century there were already a few experiments with municipal trading, notably in Australia's two largest cities, Melbourne and Sydney, although private firms still coexisted.[4] In Canada, the first major city to undertake this experiment was Winnipeg (in 1906), but municipal plants were mainly confined to smaller centres like Saskatoon and Regina in Saskatchewan and Edmonton in Alberta. But most people received their power from privately-owned utilities, like the London-based, British Columbia Electric Railway which supplied the province's two major cities, Vancouver and Victoria.[5]

The creation of the Hydro-Electric Power Commission by the province of Ontario in 1906, with the intention of tapping the potential of Niagara Falls, was the first state enterprise to extend beyond the bounds of a single city. Under the aggressive leadership of Sir Adam Beck, the utility soon began to acquire and build generating capacity, purchasing a major plant at Niagara in 1917 and beginning construction of the largest hydroelectric station in the world (opened in 1922). By 1930, Ontario Hydro controlled the production and distribution of 75 per cent of the province's electrical energy.[6] In Australia, the state Electricity Commission of Victoria was formed in 1919 to produce thermal power on the brown coalfields of the Latrobe valley about 100 miles from Melbourne. Under the adept management of Sir John Monash, the SEC built its plant and acquired its major private rival in 1930.[7] During the same period Tasmania and Western Australia also founded state-run enterprises, hoping to use power to promote economic growth.[8] But the campaign for public ownership by no means carried all before it. Even a strong Labour government in the state of Queensland failed to move against the private utility which served Brisbane.[9] In the province of Quebec an agitation against the 'electricity trust', culminating in the early 1930s, failed.[10] The effort to create a Saskatchewan Power Commission modelled on Ontario Hydro languished during the 1930s, while the whole principle of public ownership fell under a cloud in New South Wales owing to well-documented charges of corruption within the Sydney Electricity Department.[11] The ultimate balance to be struck between public and private ownership remained much in doubt.

After the Second World War, however, the process of nationalization gained momentum rapidly in both Canada and Australia; almost all the major, private power producers were taken over. Not only did sweeping nationalisation occur in Queensland, Quebec, South Australia and British Columbia, but, in jurisdictions with substantial municipal enterprises like Manitoba and New South Wales, these were folded also into state-wide or province-wide public systems. Only in Alberta and the small power markets of the Maritimes, did strong private utilities remain in operation.[12] Everywhere else by the mid-1960s the trend was unmistakable: what had once been private property had passed almost entirely into the public domain.

The comparison of Canada and Australia, two countries with so many similarities, should help to reveal the causes of that shift. This chapter will argue that an important motive for nationalization was not socialist ideology but the conviction that public ownership would ensure cheap electricity to fuel economic growth. State enterprise also reflected a technological dynamic as electrical utilities were extended beyond the boundaries of a single municipality and became state- or province-wide. What altered the pace at which public ownership spread in different jurisdictions was the availability of power for development, and the nature of local political arrangements such as the relationship between the various levels of government.

II

Much has been written about 'colonial socialism' in Australia, that is, the broad scope of the public sector in the late nineteenth and early twentieth centuries. N. G. Butlin has estimated that by 1900 public capital formation had attained a level almost equal to private, a proportion far in excess of other countries.[13] Was the takeover of electricity supply in the Commonwealth, then, simply a part of this process? And was this trend reinforced by the appearance in Australia of a powerful Labour party with a commitment to public enterprise? If so, what of Canada, which seems to have had neither tradition of colonial socialism nor a significant left-wing party?

Colonial socialism, so-called, did give birth to Australian public enterprises as diverse as savings banks and irrigation works. All of these, however, seem to have had one overriding goal: to increase the rate of economic growth. In the nineteenth century, Australian colonial governments borrowed abroad and invested in transportation and communication, not with the aim of replacing capitalism but of making it work better. Electricity supply was not then of sufficient importance, nor did its technology require management on a state-wide basis, so it was largely left in private hands (with the exception of the few experiments in municipal trading). However, once the Labour party began to win power, it did expand the public sector. In Queensland, for instance, between 1915 and 1925 the Ryan and Theodore governments bought or established the following: a chain of butcher shops, a fishing trawler, a hotel, a cannery, a produce agency, an ore crushing and treating plant, a sugar mill and railway, a plant nursery, a state insurance office, sawmills, cattle stations, cold stores, and coal, arsenic and gem mines. But as T. J. Ryan's manifesto for the 1918 election made clear, the intention was *not* by wholesale nationalization to lay the foundations of a socialist state:

> The object has not been to secure monopoly or to squeeze out of business legitimate private traders, but to protect the public by competing with the latter on fair and efficient lines. Present indications point to competition from the State providing a more efficient method of keeping down prices and ensuring good service than any amount of direct regulation could do.[14]

Ryan made it plain that he did not favour the nationalization of entire industries but aimed only to prevent the formation of trusts and monopolies. Rather than overthrowing capitalism this would make 'the capitalist system work in the interests of the many and not of the few'.[15] Although Labour's platform called for the municipal ownership of utilities, Ryan permitted the private electrical company in the capital to extend its franchised territory to cover South Brisbane in 1916.

The Labour government in Queensland seems, in fact, to have been following a tradition of state paternalism which predated the rise of Labour.[16] That Queensland was not unique is clear from R. S. Parker's study of New South Wales, where Labour also won power in 1910.[17] By then the railways, the trams of Sydney, a savings bank and several smaller undertakings were already in public hands, while the city had its own electrical utility. Between 1910 and 1917, 21 additional businesses were set up, but, as in the state to the north, these were intended to reduce the cost of essential goods and services to consumers and to government, and not to undermine capitalism. R. L. Wettenhall contends that,

> The striking extent to which the 'public sector' has advanced without ideological support in the context of a party system formally characterised by division into socialist and anti-socialist camps on the British pattern is one of the distinctive features of Australia's public enterprise system. The basis for the growth of the system has been throughout pragmatic . . . if Australia's public enterprise has an ideological foundation it is because pragmatism has been erected into an ideology in its own right.[18]

Canada lacked both the tradition of colonial socialism and a strong left-wing political party throughout most of this period. Indeed, one of her major experiments in public enterprise convinced many citizens that such activities by the state were unwise. The Confederation agreement of 1867 included a commitment to construct a railway linking the eastern provinces to central Canada, and the new federal government decided to entrust this Intercolonial Railway to a commission to build and operate. The Intercolonial became a byword for inefficiency: the route was selected through parliamentary logrolling, and its employees were chosen through political patronage. As a result, when the time came to build another line westward to the Pacific, most Canadians agreed that it would be best to encourage a private syndicate to undertake the task (through a combination of land grants and direct subsidies) to ensure efficient management.

Thus there existed in Canada a definite bias against public ownership. In 1892 one Ontario official drew an explicit contrast between the Canadian and Australian experience. He warned wryly against too much dependence by businessmen upon government, which brought to his mind the caricature of an Australian: 'Whenever he stands he leans upon a post.'[19] Direct subsidies to private entrepreneurs became the favoured means of ensuring construction of undertakings considered essential in Canada, a method which was never used to any great extent in Australia. Many other railway projects received this kind of backing, including two additional transcontinentals, although over-building ultimately led to their financial collapse and the incorporation of both lines, with the Intercolonial, into the state-owned Canadian National Railways betwen 1917 and 1923. Though the means adopted were different in the two countries, the aims were identical – the promotion of economic development through the use of state credit.[20]

What legitimized public ownership of electricity supplies for Australians and Canadians if it was not socialist ideology? Electricity quickly demonstrated its technical superiority as a source of lighting. Like water, transit and telephone services, urban-dwellers came to consider it more and more of a necessity (ironically, because of this superiority, gas companies in both countries were left in private hands). If private enterprise could not or would not supply at an economic rate, then citizens became increasingly ready to countenance state action.

At first this meant not public ownership but regulation through franchising. Services like electricity, water and telephones were 'natural monopolies' rendered inefficient by the duplication of transmission facilities. Without the discipline of competition there was an obvious risk of poor service or high rates. A franchise granting a local monopoly to one entrepreneur for a fixed term provided the assurance he needed to undertake his investment, yet offered a means to exercise some control. Experience with franchises soon left many municipal leaders disillusioned. Friction between gas companies and city councils was a common experience. In Canada the courts interpreted franchise agreements in unanticipated ways, resulting in costly lawsuits which had to be fought all the way to the Judicial Committee of the Privy Council.[21] By the late nineteenth century some local politicians were convinced that municipal trading was the only way to guarantee effective control over utilities, whether tramways, telephones or electricity supply.

In 1891 the Australian Gas Light Company petitioned the legislature of New South Wales for a charter which would have extended its street-lighting monopoly in Sydney to include electricity. There was an immediate outcry. The council hastily applied for the right to build its own municipal electricity plant. Some citizens were so aroused that they even criticized this application because it would have permitted the council to franchise a private company raher than undertaking the task itself. When the enabling legislation was finally passed in 1896 it had been shorn of this offending provision, and the city's Electricity Department finally went into production in 1904.[22] Melbourne also decided to construct its own streetlighting plant in 1891, which began operations in 1894. Nonetheless, at about the same time, ratepayers in Toronto were asked to approve a municipal system (but declined to do so), while the voters in Adelaide approved a private system.[23]

Technological change in the electrical industry tended to reinforce the trend towards public ownership. A single plant came to serve an ever-increasing area and, as large hydroelectric stations were constructed in Canada and steam-powered turbines installed in Australia, costs fell rapidly. Electric motors improved their efficiency so that demands for traction and industrial power outstripped lighting needs, in Australia's case by about 1910.[24] System managers learned that the key to low costs was a high load factor and a diversity of consumers to spread the peaks so that equipment could be fully utilized. Large stations connected together by high-voltage transmission lines enabled plants to be brought into service as required. While none of these changes required public ownership, they all pointed towards organizations which had state-wide responsibilities and possessed the ability to raise large sums of capital at low cost. Public authorities often seemed best equipped for that.

Popular demand for cheap power, and dissatisfaction with franchise agreements, underlay much of the pressure for municipalities to enter electricity supply. In Canada there lingered a positive distrust of public enterprise based upon the experience of the Intercolonial Railway, and this may explain in part why Australian cities like Melbourne and Sydney began municipal trading at an earlier date. Certainly in Canada there was also a feeling that competition between public and private enterprises was improper because the state could call upon its unlimited credit, although this did occur in Winnipeg and in Saint John (New Brunswick). In Ontario, municipalities were even required by law to purchase existing companies before they could set up in competition.[25] Nevertheless, it was the province of Ontario which embarked upon an important experiment in public ownership with the creation of the Hydro-Electric Power Commission in 1906.

III

The genesis of Ontario Hydro reveals that the desire to promote economic growth through cheap electricity was one of the most potent arguments which proponents of nationalization could put forward. In Canada and in Australia fears of a shortage of power legitimized state intervention. By the same token, as comparative abundance of electricity provided arguments against public ownership since electricity rates tended to be lower (particularly if there was any competition between suppliers).[26] The increasing size and cost of central stations, and the concomitant need for large borrowing, might also mandate state enterprise if a project seemed too big or risky for private entrepreneurs. Then government might have to act, or run the risk that lack of power would restrict growth. Moreover, public enterprises were able to make investments in non-economic goals, which yielded no easily quantifiable gain and which private investors would ignore.

By the 1890s technology had been developed which made possible the generation and transmission of hydroelectricity over long distances at a cost lower than for most thermal power. The province of Ontario depended for its energy upon imported anthracite, which gave the exploitation of the 'white coal' of Niagara Falls an obvious attraction. A miners' strike in Pennsylvania in 1902 sent prices soaring. At the same time Ontarians realized that two of the power-plants under construction on the Canadian side of the Falls were American-owned and intended to export electricity to New York State. Belatedly, a group of entrepreneurs from Toronto procured the right to build a third plant at Niagara, but this syndicate already controlled the streetlighting and traction franchises in Toronto and had earned a reputation for bad service and high rates. Moreover, citizens of the smaller cities and towns of the western Ontario peninsula were concerned that the state capital might monopolize these power resources and leave them at a disadvantage. From this mixture of unfulfilled ambition and inter-city rivalry there emerged a 'public power' movement during the first few years of the century, headed by the businessmen of southern Ontario's towns and cities. In 1906 one of these men, Adam Beck, was chosen by the new Conservative government as the first chairman of the Ontario Hydro-Electric Power

Commission which was set up to buy current from the private producers at Niagara and to transmit it along its own lines to municipal utilities. Under Becks's leadership Ontario Hydro rapidly expanded into power production during the First World War, and its (carefully-nurtured) reputation for supplying cheap power spread throughout the English-speaking world.[27]

The importance of scarcity of power in the Ontario case may be seen by a comparison with neighbouring Quebec (where the public power movement made little headway). The St Lawrence River and its main tributaries flowed near all the major centres of population and provided numerous sites suitable for hydroelectric development. For instance, Boston capital founded the Shawinigan Water and Power Company to operate in the St Maurice valley near Trois-Rivières, while Montreal interests installed plants at Lachine and Chambly near the city. The latter were amalgamated into the Montreal Light, Heat and Power in 1903, then interlocked by a series of investments and joint undertakings with the Shawinigan interests which also came to control Quebec City. While these companies charged high rates to domestic consumers and earned large profits, industrial power remained relatively cheap. Crucial backing from the business community for public ownership was lacking, compared to Ontario. In the 1930s an agitation against the 'electricity trust' failed. Although a Royal Commission was appointed in 1934, it merely recommended stricter regulation. Only in 1944 was Montreal Light, Heat and Power taken over by the province despite objections from leading businessmen, and the majority of the industry remained in private hands until 1963.[28]

The very costliness and complexity of some power projects seemed to demand action by state agencies, as was the case with Victoria's plan to develop its brown coalfields and to free itself from dependence on black coal imported from New South Wales. A miners' strike in 1916 emphasized Melbourne's vulnerability, and the idea of a thermal, generating station located on the coalfields gained popularity. In 1919 a Nationalist government created the State Electricity Commission. The technical difficulties of using lignite with a high moisture content were such that without public credit the original plant could never have been finished in the 1920s. The size and risk of the scheme required public ownership.[29]

Nationalization could also be used in pursuit of non-economic objectives, a fact demonstrated by the Quebec electricity industry. In 1944, Montreal Light, Heat and Power was transformed into Hydro-

Quebec in an attempt by the Liberal government to win votes in the city, but the victory of the conservative Union Nationale in that year brought a halt to further expansion of the public sector. During the 1950s there developed a strong feeling of French Canadian nationalism which found expression in criticism of the anglophone-dominated, business establishment of the province, including the thirteen remaining private power companies. When the Liberals returned to power at long last in 1960, Natural Resources Minister René Lévesque set out to convince his colleagues of the need to complete the takeover for nationalistic reasons.

A single, interconnected utility might be more efficient, and Hydro-Quebec's management shared the natural ambitions of bureaucracy, but more important was the fact that Lévesque could point out that the provincial utility had 190 francophones among its 243 engineers, while the private Shawinigan company had just 20 francophones among its 175. Asked if the state enterprise could run a system for the entire province, Lévesque replied acerbically,

> For eighteen years, French Canadians have been running Hydro-Québec and they are doing just as well today as anyone else . . . *aussi bien aujourd'hui que tous les 'gentlemen' des compagnies.* This is the only important sector of our economy where we have trained people who are capable of taking over the whole thing.

Lévesque finally convinced his colleagues to fight a general election in 1962 on the issue of becoming *maître chez nous* by taking over the remaining companies, and the voters approved.[30]

The decision by the provincial government to spend $300 000 000 on nationalization represented an investment in nationalism.[31] The aim was avowedly to open technical and managerial positions to francophones – to members of the Quebec middle class who formed an important segment of the new nationalist movement. Unskilled and semi-skilled jobs had never been closed to francophones (although they might have to use English as the language of work), so they could expect to benefit relatively little from the takeover. But that did not prevent them from supporting it. Such nationalist feelings were not confined to Quebec. In Ontario, too, the public power movement drew upon anti-American feelings for fear that cheap power, siphoned away to the United States, could place the province at a permanent disadvantage in the competition for economic development. Sir Adam Beck played frequently upon such feelings in his campaign against the private utilities, and it became an article of faith that Ontario should never export power to the Americans. Public enterprise was thus a means of achieving social goals broader than merely reducing the cost, or improving the availability, of energy supplies.

Without nationalization, proponents argued that certain desirable objectives might prove impossible to achieve. Some power projects would not be undertaken at all by private enterprise because of the cost or the risk; the state had to step in. Sometimes, too, non-economic considerations proved significant: the desire for security of supply, or the achievement of nationalist aims, regardless of the costs borne by power consumers. The ideology which underlay the movement for public ownership was thus not the ideology of socialism. Rather it combined the desire to promote economic development with differing views of how the benefits of that growth were to be allocated among different groups within society. In some places this created a public power movement at an early date, while in others nothing of this kind occurred until the mid-twentieth century.

IV

Political factors helped also to govern the progress of nationalization, in particular the relations between governments and private entrepreneurs and between different levels of government. Some metropolitan areas, for instance, had a multitude of local authorities, others a single municipal administration. Entrepreneurs were quick to recognize the value of franchises which conveyed local monopolies, and soon began to court the councillors who dispensed them. The larger the territory covered, the more valuable the franchise, and at the same time the greater the number of local councils, the more numerous the opportunities to enter the field. Moreover, in both Canada and Australia municipalities were the creatures of the higher levels of government, and much depended upon what authority the state or province was willing to grant them. To what extent did parliaments impose their will on civic politicians? Did they accede readily to local wishes? These concerns, whose connection with the issue of electricity supply was sometimes tangential, could affect profoundly the ultimate balance between the public and private sectors.

Metropolitan areas, containing large numbers of local authorities on the British model, were more common in Australia than in Canada. Sydney was the most striking example, with over 60 separate councils at the turn of the century. When the city of Sydney began supplying electricity in 1904 there was a municipal system in suburban Redfern as well as a private company in Balmain. But the City Electricity Department was given the right to supply current outside the city proper. The Redfern system was soon acquired, but the other private company was left to serve Balmain and four adjoining municipalities until the 1950s.[32]

In Melbourne and Brisbane also, public and private enterprises coexisted. The Melbourne municipal streetlighting system began to supply private consumers in 1895, and by 1898 was selling power to other suburbs. Meanwhile, a number of private companies were amalgamated into a single strong firm, Melbourne Electric Supply Company, which sold bulk power to some councils and handled direct retailing elsewhere, a situation which persisted until it was acquired by the State Electricity Commission in 1930.[33] In Queensland's capital, the City Electric Light Company had a franchise to serve the central city well into the 1950s, and even procured an extension of its territory to South Brisbane in 1916 from a Labour government. When the council of the newly-created Greater Brisbane sought to take over part of the company's plant in the later 1920s, it was discouraged from doing so by the cost. Instead, a municipal service was started to serve the tramway and those suburbs which were not under contract to the company.[34] Thus the existence of a multiplicity of local councils in Australia's major metropolises made it possible for companies to acquire and retain a foothold from which they were difficult to dislodge, despite growing enthusiasm for public ownership.

In Canada the problem of divided municipal jurisdiction was less acute, except in Montreal where there was a score of municipalities on the island of Montreal. As elsewhere, entrepreneurs quickly learned that a streetlighting contract was one key to profitability, since it provided all-important cash flow and a basic transmission system from which service to private customers could branch out. A number of small companies sprang up during the 1890s, but eventually all were amalgamated into Montreal Light, Heat and Power by the adept Herbert Holt. He exploited the division of municipal authority by erecting a thicket of franchises surrounding the city of Montreal, varied in length and conditions. Though local newspapers and politicians might inveigh against the 'trustards', there was little they could actually do. When rate reductions were demanded, Holt, who had the advantage of rapidly falling costs from returns to scale on hydroelectricity, would respond by asking for long extensions of the franchises. Faced with adhering to high rates, most Montreal area councils settled for modest concessions. Even the city itself could not seriously contemplate a takeover, because Holt rapidly increased the book value of the company (mainly through stock-watering), so that its acquisition as a 'going concern', including goodwill and franchises, was beyond the means of the municipality. Holt astutely anticipated the potential returns to scale, and took steps to capture them. He eventually succeeded in eliminating all his serious rivals in the city. Public ownership campaigns bore little fruit in Montreal.[35]

Toronto was different. There the city included almost the entire built-up area because it steadily annexed its suburbs as they developed prior to the First World War. Thus utility entrepreneurs were compelled to deal with the city council if they wanted access to important markets. Friction with utilities was also a major cause of an important change in the structure of civic government during the 1890s. As the number of wards grew through annexations, the council reached an unwieldy size; not only was executive leadership difficult but opportunities for corruption flourished. Revelations about bribery in the letting of the streetlighting contract in 1894 produced a reform movement which led to the creation of an executive Board of Control to handle sensitive matters such as awarding franchises. Thus the city administration was better able to deal with utility companies, and could exercise its enthusiasm for the public power movement. In 1909 Toronto created a municipal system, drawing its power from Ontario Hydro, to compete with the existing private company. Unlike Montreal (which did not undergo similar reforms until 1910), shrewd entrepreneurs were unable to work out favourable deals with suburban councils or use divided jurisdiction and large councils to protect themselves against angry customers.

The development of public enterprise was also greatly affected by the relations between the municipalities and higher levels of government. Both councils and companies derived their charter powers from parliament, which could generate intense controversy. In Ontario, for instance, some operators tried to obtain the right to string wires on public streets without municipal permission. When the provincial assembly refused to permit this after protests from local councils, some of the more enterprising promoters even sought to obtain acts of incorporation from the federal parliament. Claiming that their undertakings were 'for the general advantage of Canada', they hoped to free themselves from both provincial and municipal regulation and gain immunity from takeovers. Particularly during the first decade of the century, the Private Bills Committee in Ottawa became a cockpit for several such fights.[36] In Quebec, Montrealers complained that Montreal Light, Heat and Power was accorded an unusually respectful hearing in the provincial capital, especially by the appointed Legislative Council. To ensure such treatment, Herbert Holt was careful to secure as directors such political luminaries as Sir Lomer Gouin, the former premier. On the west coast the managers of the British Columbia Electric Railway devoted great care and attention to maintaining good relations with the government of the day.[37]

V

City-state relations were important also in Australia. Antagonism between urban and rural interests was particularly strong in Queensland, and the Brisbane council was originally refused the right to enter the electricity business by the state government, despite the fact that a private firm was already operating without legal authority. In 1899 the municipality finally got the necessary powers, but the government fixed the terms so as to compel the city to take over the company's plant. When the council balked, its right to compete was revoked in 1903 and the company's territory extended. Even the advent of a Labour government supposedly committed to nationalization, in 1915, did not improve the situation, nor did the creation of Greater Brisbane in 1925. Eventually the city started its own powerplant in competition with the company (which persisted until after the Second World War).[38] In New South Wales the government stepped in when serious corruption was revealed in the Sydney Electricity Department in the late 1920s, and actually suspended the city council altogether between 1928 and 1930, ruling through an appointed commission. In 1935 it was decided to establish a 'Sydney County Council' responsible solely for electricity supply, but when war broke out there still remained four power producers in greater Sydney, the SCC, the private Balmain company, and the New South Wales Departments of Railways and Public Works. Only in 1950 did the state take the decision to amalgamate all of these into a State Electricity Commission, over the strong protests of the Sydney city council.[39]

The experience of Queensland and New South Wales pointed out the fact that the establishment of a state-wide utility required the active intervention of the government. Similarly in Canada the public sector grew because the provinces provided support at critical moments. In

Ontario, the Toronto municipal system required legislation before it could set up in competition with the Toronto Electric Light Company. When ratepayers tried to block the Hydro-Electric Power Commission's plans by claiming that its contracts with the municipalities were unlawful, Adam Beck forced through last-minute legislation validating the contracts and immunizing them from challenges in the courts. Time and again when Ontario Hydro needed wider authority Sir Adam was able to persuade the cabinet to grant this. Likewise, in the state of Victoria, Melbourne politicians were critical of the centralizing tendencies of the State Electricity Commission in the 1920s, but Sir John Monash was able to carry the government with him. The drive for a province-wide utility in Saskatchewan faltered in the 1930s when the government refused to coerce municipalities into joining the Saskatchewan Power Commission, but it revived in the 1940s when a party with a different philosophy took power.[40]

If the public sector expanded more in one jurisdiction than another, political factors were often of critical importance. Was municipal authority fragmented amongst a number of small and relatively weak councils? Could local authorities count upon cooperation and support when they asked for jurisdiction to deal with private utilities or to create municipal undertakings? Lacking central support, local politicians often found themselves without the legal powers or the financial resources necessary to deal with canny entrepreneurs.

VI

While the public sector grew in both Canada and Australia, the legal forms adopted at first for such enterprises were quite diverse (although they became more and more alike as time passed). In Australia, experience with state control of railways through the regular departmental structure seemed to demonstrate that efficient management required independent experts operating without 'political' interference. The 'statutory corporation' was created to prevent parliamentarians meddling in day-to-day management, and this form was used for functions as diverse as savings banks and water supplies.[41] At the time of the First World War the Labour party began to argue that, if these bodies were to serve the public, then elected representatives ought to have real opportunities to shape their policies. Adherents of the older view replied that this would simply open the door to the twin evils of patronage and inefficiency. Although Labour's case gained some adherents during the 1920s, this notion was largely ignored thereafter, and efforts were resumed to make statutory corporations as independent as possible. The state-wide electricity commissions were all granted fairly wide autonomy, although major investments had still to be approved by the governments guaranteeing their debts.[42]

Such a debate did not develop to the same extent in Canada as it had in Australia. True, the Intercolonial Railway was notorious for political interference in its affairs. Many people simply concluded from the Intercolonial that all public enterprise was best avoided, but this view lost its hold as some public services, like electricity, came to be deemed essential. Yet Canadians did not respond by seeking to free 'crown corporations' from political influence,[43] as was evident from the fact that the chairman of Ontario Hydro was a member of the provincial cabinet in the first critical years after 1906, and that subsequently a number of other ministers sat on the commission. Adam Beck set a pattern by his willingness to remind his colleagues that their political popularity was dependent upon a supply of cheap power; he did not hesitate to call out the pressure groups of the public power movement to emphasize the message. Indeed, lack of independence from the government of the day has been something of a hallmark for provincial utilities in Canada. In 1964 David Cass-Beggs was dismissed by the new Liberal government of Saskatchewan, which disliked the policies he had followed under the previous administration. He later remarked that

> a publicly-owned utility is an extremely important part of most provincial economies . . . so its chairman must have close links with the government as well as a willingness to interpret and defend government's economic policies.[44]

In Australia, local and municipal interests have received somewhat more recognition in the management of electrial utilities, perhaps because these often originated as municipal undertakings. Nonetheless, in the 1920s Melbourne councillors protested unsuccessfully against the expansion of the State Electricity Commission of Victoria. In 1935, when the Sydney County Council took over the city's Electricity Department, the local council denounced this as 'robbery' and condemned it by a vote of 17 to 2. Similar protests were heard in 1950 when the government created the State Electricity Commission. Ironically, the chairman of the SCC declared that 'this proposal is purely socialistic and can't possibly benefit the community'. An SCC resolution denounced the creation of 'another socialist body, bureaucratically controlled and appointed'. Two hundred local councils registered protests through the Local Government Association.[45] What is notable is that the agitations in Sydney and Melbourne were ignored.

While Ontario Hydro was formally a municipal cooperative, its central administration played a key role from the outset. Later (sometimes much later) the other provinces followed suit, most notably Quebec which eliminated even small, private cooperative producers in short order after 1963, and took control of the entire electricity supply industry from dam-site to electricity meter, making it a highly centralized organization and one of Canada's largest industrial undertakings.[46] Thus despite the formal recognition of the role of municipalities in Australia, their responsibility, as in Canada, has largely been confined to distributing power at retail when prices are fixed by the wholesaler. Bureaucratic centralization and the technology of the industry have concentrated authority in the hands of the provincial and state commissions in both countries.

VII

Comparisons between the electricity supply industry in Canada and Australia indicate close similarities; private companies were gradually replaced and public enterprise predominated by the 1960s. At first, local authorities undertook electricity supply themselves rather than rely on entrepreneurs: Melbourne's service began in 1894, Sydney's in 1904, Winnipeg's in 1906, along with plants in many smaller places. Before long, however, state-wide bodies began to appear, first Ontario Hydro in 1906, then Victoria's State Electricity Commission in 1919. Nonetheless, public ownership did not win universal acceptance, and by the Second World War much of the industry remained privately-controlled. From that time onward the pace of change quickened, so that state/province-wide commissions had become the norm almost everywhere by the 1960s.

Socialist ideology played no important role in this process for either country. The success of the Labour Party in Australia was not the key to the spread of public enterprise. Indeed, important advances like the creation of the State Electricity Commission in Victoria were undertaken by non-socialist parties, while a Labour government in Queensland after 1915 failed to take over the industry. Labour governments in both Western Australia and Tasmania did establish their own utilities, but they seem to have been influenced mainly by the desire to promote growth rather than socialist principles. In Canada, left-of-centre parties were much weaker. Only in Saskatchewan did the election of the Co-operative Commonwealth Federation government in 1944 bring about an ideological shift which led to the rapid growth of the languishing Saskatchewan Power Commission. Most Canadians displayed little enthusiasm for public enterprise around the turn of the century, which may have retarded the spread of municipal trading compared to Australia. Yet early in the century the public power movement began to command broad public support in places such as Ontario and Manitoba.

The degree to which support for public electricity supply crossed party lines is evident in the cases of South Australia and British Columbia. When nationalization occurred, both were governed by parties strongly committed to free enterprise. A Royal Commission recommended the takeover of the Adelaide Electric Supply Company in the mid-1940s (a recommendation concurred in even by the company nominee on the commission), and Premier Playford's government determined to act. Not even a revolt among some of its parliamentary supporters was sufficient to prevent the creation of the Electricity Trust of South Australia.[47] W. A. C. Bennett came to office in British Columbia at the head of a right-wing coalition in the 1950s, and spent much time flaying his 'socialist' opponents. Yet that was insufficient to deter him from taking over the largest private utility in the country (B. C. Electric) in 1961, without a word of advance warning. Although the ostensible reason was unfair federal taxation of private utilities, in reality Bennett wanted to establish a firm grip over provincial energy policy as part of negotiations with Ottawa on future hydroelectric projects. To secure this he did not hesitate to move against the company.[48]

Ideologically significant to the public power movement was the conviction that it was the key to rapid economic growth. From the days of colonial socialism in Australia, the state has been supposed to provide conditions in which capitalism might flourish. An abundance of cheap electricity became recognized as a key factor, a recognition shared as much by Social Crediters in British Columbia and the recent Liberal–Country coalition in South Australia as by Conservatives in Ontario, the Nationalists in Victoria, and the Labourites in Western Australia and Tasmania at the time of the First World War. Where public enterprise made least headway was precisely where power was abundant, as in Quebec. There, the successful drive for nationalization had to wait until public ownership became identified with the non-economic objectives of French-Canadian nationalism. The lesson was the same in each case; what private enterprise would not or could not do, the public sector must undertake.

The organizational shape of these nationalized undertakings in Canada and Australia developed close similarities. In part this stemmed from the technological evolution of the industry. When generating plants were small, and current could be transmitted only short distances, there were numerous private companies franchised by local authorities. When public ownership developed, it was municipalities which constructed plants. Problems arose when plants grew in size, and transmission lines extended across local boundaries. Particularly in the hydroelectric industry, it was often necessary to transmit power from a distant source to market. Civic politicians discovered that they lacked the authority to control companies whose operations spread beyond municipal boundaries. Only the higher levels of government seemed to possess both the jurisdiction and the financial resources required to undertake such activities. States and provinces began to appoint regional or state-wide bodies which could draw upon the public credit, although where the government failed to act, as in Queensland, Alberta or Quebec, the cause of public ownership temporarily stalled.

Until recent times there have been strong technological and economic arguments for continued expansion of these utilities; the marginal cost of supplying additional power was usually below average costs. Ever-larger generating stations must be constructed to produce cheaper power. State enterprises required lower rates of return on their investment and could borrow large sums comparatively cheaply, which made it possible for them to build bigger and bigger projects.[49] This may explain why, for instance, the electricity supply industry's history has run counter to the 'decline of colonial socialism' in Australia after 1930,[50] as virtually all private firms have been eliminated since 1945. Once appointed, bureaucrats in charge of public undertakings in both Canada and Australia naturally wished as far as possible to centralize control. Organizational uniformity was thus the child of both technology and bureaucracy.

Despite the steady shift from private to public enterprise in electricity supply over the past century, the process did not occur at the same pace in both countries, nor even in all parts of Canada (Alberta, the province where significant private electric companies survived, did, interestingly enough, take a firm grip upon a rival energy source, natural gas production, during the 1950s[51]). A complex mixture of forces thus came into play in determining the timing of nationalization. Most important was the role public power was believed to play in promoting economic growth. At the same time, technology appeared to point in the direction of central control of supply over a wider and wider area. While that did not require public ownership, experience made nationalization seem the most effective means of reconciling conflicting private and public interests. Public ownership became the preferred means of regulation for this particular industry. No one of these factors made the shift from private to public control inevitable, although taken together they did bring about nationalization almost everywhere by the mid-1960s.

NOTES

1. J. W. McCarty, 'Australian Capital Cities in the Nineteenth Century', in McCarty and C. B. Schedvin (eds), *Urbanization in Australia* (Sydney University Press, 1974) p. 11. The phrase 'regions of recent settlement' is Ragnar Nurkse's.
2. See *The Economist*, 3 March 1979, for a chart showing the extent of public ownership in the eighteen largest capitalist countries.
3. The contrast between the countries is even less than it might appear, because 15 per cent of all power in Canada is produced and consumed internally by private industrial users like forest and mining undertakings. See Marsha Gordon, *Government in Business* (Montreal: C. D. Howe Institute, 1981) p. 36; N. G. Butlin, A. Barnard, J. J. Pincus, *Government and Capitalism: Public and Private Choice in Twentieth-Century Australia* (Sydney: Allen & Unwin, 1982) p. 243.
4. Michael Cannon, *Life in the Cities: Australia in the Victorian Age*, vol. III (Melbourne: Nelson, 1975) pp. 111–13; Gordon F. Anderson, *Fifty Years of Electricity Supply* (Sydney County Council, 1955) pp. 10–28.
5. Alan F. J. Artibise, *Winnipeg, A Social History of Urban Growth 1874–1914* (Montreal: McGill-Queen's University Press, 1975) pp. 88–101; Clinton P. White, *Power for a Province: a History of Saskatchewan Power* (Regina: Canadian Plains Research Center, 1976) pp. 5–13; Patricia E. Roy, 'Direct Management from Abroad: the Formative Years of the British Columbia Electric Railway', in Glenn Porter and Robert D. Cuff (eds), *Enterprise and National Development, Essays in Canadian Business and Economic History* (Toronto: Hakkert, 1973) pp. 101–21.
6. H. V. Nelles, *The Politics of Development, Forests, Mines and Hydro-Electric Power in Ontario, 1849–1941* (Toronto: Macmillan, 1974) pp. 215–306, 362–75, 399–426; W. R. Plewman, *Adam Beck and the Ontario Hydro* (Toronto: Ryerson, 1947) *passim.*

7. Cecil Edwards, *Brown Power: a Jubilee History of the State Electricity Commission of Victoria* (Melbourne: the Commission, 1969 pp. 1–120.
8. Wilfred Prest, 'The Electricity Supply Industry', in Alex Hunter (ed.), *Economics of Australian Industry: Studies in Environment and Structure* (Melbourne University Press, 1965) p. 130: J. R. Robertson, 'The Foundation of State Socialism in Western Australia, 1911–16', *Historical Studies: Australia and New Zealand*, v (1962) pp. 309–14.
9. Gordon Greenwood and J. R. Laverty, *Brisbane, 1859–1959: a History of Local Government* (Brisbane: Ziegler, 1959) pp. 433–5, 569–71.
10. Clarence Hogue, André Bolduc, Daniel Larouche, *Québec: un siècle d'electricité* (Montréal: Libre Expression, 1979) pp. 109–14; Patricia Dirks, 'The Public Power Movement in Québec City, 1929–34', *Urban History Review/Revue d'Histoire Urbaine* v (1981) 17–29.
11. White, *Power for a Province*, pp. 115–30; Anderson, *Electricity Supply*, pp. 36–111.
12. Newfoundland entered Confederation only in 1949 and so is not dealt with here. Nova Scotia completed the takeover of its private utilities only in the 1970s and Prince Edward Island remains in private hands.
13. W. K. Hancock, *Australia* (New York: Scribner's, 1931) pp. 129–33; N. G. Butlin, *Investment in Australian Economic Development, 1861—1900* (Cambridge University Press, 1964) p. 6.
14. N. G. Butlin, 'Colonial Socialism in Australia', in H. G. J. Aitken (ed.), *The State and Economic Growth* (New York: Social Science Research Council, 1959) pp. 35–42; D. J. Murphy, 'State Enterprises', in Murphy, R. B. Joyce, Colin A. Hughes (eds), *Labour in Power: the Labour Party and Governments in Queensland, 1915–57* (St. Lucia: University of Queensland Press, 1980) pp. 140–2.
15. D. J. Murphy, 'The Establishment of State Enterprises in Queensland, 1915–18', *Labour History*, 17 (1968) 13.
16. On this point see Glen Lewis, 'Queensland Nationalism and Australian Capitalism', in E. L. Wheelwright and Ken Buckley (eds), *Essays in the Political Economy of Australian Capitalism*, vol. II (Sydney: Australia and New Zealand Book Company, 1978) pp. 110–47.
17. 'Public Enterprise in New South Wales', *Australian Journal of Politics and History*, 4 (1958) 208–23. J. R. Robertson, 'State Socialism in Western Australia' places more emphasis on the socialist ideology of the Labour party in that state, but also notes the desire to promote economic growth by supplying services essential to private business.
18. 'Public Ownership in Australia', *Political Quarterly*, v (1965) 426.
19. Archibald Blue in Ontario Bureau of Mines, *Annual Report* (1892) pp. 29–30.
20. G. R. Stevens, *Canadian National Railways*, 2 vols (Toronto: Clark Irwin, 1960, 1962) *passim*.
21. Toronto, for instance, had a number of unsatisfactory lawsuits with its franchised utilities.
22. Anderson, *Electricity Supply*, pp. 10–28; H. E. Maiden, *History of Local Government in New South Wales* (Sydney: Angus & Robertson, 1966) pp. 208–10.
23. Under its 1897 charter the Adelaide Electric Supply Company was

required to secure the approval of the ratepayers in a referendum before extending service to any municipality; it always succeeded in obtaining this. See D. Wakelin, *Fifty Years of Progress* (Adelaide: Electric Supply Company, 1947) pp. 4–8.

24. E. A. Boehm, 'The Impact of Electricity', *Economic Record*, 31 (1955) 62.
25. The so-called 'Conmee clause' of the Ontario Municipal Act, named after its proposer, James Conmee, was passed in 1899: see *Statutes of Ontario*, 62 Vic., c. 26, s. 35, ss. 4. British Columbia imposed similar limitations.
26. This argument is developed at greater length in Christopher Armstrong and H. V. Nelles, 'Contrasting Development of the Hydroelectric Industry in the Montreal and Toronto Regions, 1900–1930', *Journal of Canadian Studies*, 18 (1983) 5–27.
27. Nelles, *Politics of Development*, pp. 215–306.
28. Hogue et al., *Québec, un siècle d'électricité*, pp. 11–169; J. H. Dales, *Hydroelectricity and Industrial Development: Québec, 1898–1940* (Cambridge, Mass.: Harvard University Press, 1957) pp. 50–100.
29. Edwards, *Brown Power*, pp. 15–87.
30. Paul Sauriol, *The Nationalization of Electric Power* (Montreal: Harvest House, 1962) pp. 75–6; Peter Desbarats, *René: A Canadian in Search of a Country* (Toronto: McClelland & Stewart, 1976) p. 34.
31. Albert Breton, 'The Economics of Nationalism', *Journal of Political Economy*, v (1964) 376–86.
32. Maiden, *Local Government in N.S.W.*, pp. 210–15; Anderson, *Electricity Supply*, pp. 48–9.
33. 'History of the Melbourne City Council Electric Supply Department, 1891–1955', (typescript) pp. 1–5.
34. Greenwood and Laverty, *Brisbane*, pp. 433–4, 569–71; J. R. Laverty, 'Greater Brisbane: a Response to Problems of Metropolitan Government', *Australian Journal of Politics and History*, v (1972) 34–51.
35. Hogue *et al.*, *Québec: un siècle d'électricité*, pp. 58–70.
36. S. 92, ss. 10 (c) of the British North America Act gives the federal government jurisdiction over 'such works as, although wholly situate within the Province, are before or after their execution declared by the Parliament of Canada to be for the general advantage of Canada or for the advantage of two or more of the Provinces.' A list of such declarations may be found in Andrée Lajoie, *Le Pouvoir Déclaratoire du Parlement, Augmentation Discrétionnaire de la Compétence Fédérale au Canada* (Presses de L'Universitité de Montreal, 1969), Annexe, and an account of the effort to use them in the electricity industry in Christopher Armstrong and H. V. Nelles, 'Private Property in Peril: Ontario Businessmen and the Federal System 1898–1911', in Porter and Cuff (eds), *Enterprise and National Developments*, pp. 25–31.
37. Patricia E. Roy, 'The Fine Arts of Lobbying and Persuading: the Case of the B.C. Electric Railway, 1897–1917', in David S. Macmillan (ed.), *Canadian Business History: Selected Studies, 1947–1971* (Toronto: McClelland & Stewart, 1972) pp. 239–54.
38. See note 34 above.
39. D. J. Nolan, 'Sydney County Council: its Organization and Administra-

tion', *Public Administration* (Australia), v (1939) 205–21; Anderson, *Electricity Supply*, pp. 134–229.

40. Nelles, *Politics of Development*, pp. 271–306, 362–75; Edwards, *Brown Power*, 69–87; A. D. Spaull, 'Sir John Monash and the State Electricity Commission of Victoria', *Public Administration*, 28 (1969) 233–4; White, *Power for a Province*, pp. 87–130.
41. R. L. Wettenhall, 'Savings Banks, Bureaucracy and the Public Corporation', *Australian Journal of Politics and History*, 10 (1964) 65; T. H. Kewley, 'Some General Features of the Statutory Corporation in Australia', *Public Administration* (Australia), 16 (1957) 3–38; Kenneth Wiltshire, 'Public Enterprise in Australia', in Andre Gélinas (ed.), *L'enterprise publique et l'interêt publique/Public Enterprise and the Public Interest* (Toronto: Institute of Public Administration of Canada, 1978) 75–6.
42. F. W. Eggleston's classic, *State Socialism in Victoria* (London: P. S. King, 1932), is imbued with the conviction that the 'failures' of statutory corporations arise from 'political' interference.
43. J. E. Hodgetts, 'Responsibility of the Government Corporation to the Governing Body', *Proceedings of the Institute of Public Administration of Canada* (1953) 389–99.
44. Cass-Beggs is quoted in White, *Power for a Province*, p. 315. He subsequently served as head of the provincially-owned electrical utilities in both Manitoba and British Columbia under CCF governments, and, not surprisingly given his views, was again dismissed when changes of government occurred.
45. Edwards, *Brown Paper*, 75–81; Anderson, *Electricity Supply*, pp. 138–42, 224–6.
46. On the role of Ontario Hydro and its resistance to control even by the legislature, see Nelles, *Politics of Development*, pp. 493–5. Hydro-Québec and its vast development schemes on James Bay and elsewhere are chronicled in Hogue et al., *Québec, un siècle d'électricité*, pp. 287–403.
47. D. Wakelin, *Fifty Years*, pp. 148–65; A. Campbell Garnett, *Freedom and Planning in Australia* (Lancaster, Penn.: University of Wisconsin Press, 1949) pp. 199–201, 214–15.
48. Martin Robin, *Pillars of Profit, The Company Province, 1934–1972* (Toronto: McClelland and Stewart, 1973) pp. 227–36. As one of Bennett's ministers, P. A. Gagliardi, quaintly put it in 1962 'We really believe in free enterprise, but we don't let anyone stand in our way' (quoted in ibid., p. 232).
49. Aidan R. Vining, 'Provincial Hydro Utilities', in Allan Tupper and G. Bruce Doern (eds), *Public Corporations and Public Policy in Canada* (Montreal: Institute for Research on Public Policy, 1981) pp. 157–9, makes the point that rising marginal costs have had much to do with criticism of the expansionary policies of utilities like Ontario Hydro during the 1970s, as existing customers are asked to bear the high costs of providing additional capacity.
50. Butlin *et al.*, *Government and Capitalism*, pp. 320–7, suggest that direct public participation in the economy has declined relatively, although

there has been rising allocative spending on social welfare. No such decline in direct participation occurred in electricity supply.

51. In a plebiscite in 1948 Albertans were almost equally divided on the issue of whether or not the government ought to take over the private power companies. Much of the opposition arose from fears that rural electrifications would entail very heavy costs. The formation of the Alberta Gas Trunk Line Company in 1954 is described in John Richards and Larry Pratt, *Prairie Capitalism: Power and Influence in the New West* (Toronto: McClelland & Stewart, 1979) pp. 67–8.

Index